MEANING AND KNOWLEDGE

SRI GARIB DASS ORIENTAL SERIES NO. 91

Meaning and Knowledge

An Interpretation of Indian and Contemporary Epistemological Concepts.

RACHAPPA I. INGALALLI

SRI SATGURU PUBLICATIONS
A Division of
INDIAN BOOKS CENTRE
DELHI—INDIA

Published by :

SRI SATGURU PUBLICATIONS

A Division of

INDIAN BOOKS CENTRE
Indological & Oriental Publishers
40/5, Shakti Nagar
Delhi—110007
(INDIA)

First Edition—Delhi 1989

ISBN 81-7030—205-6

Processed by M/s. ABF AGENCY, Delhi.

Printed at :
Sainion Printary
Delhi—110032.

Contents

	Acknowledgement	*vii*
	Introduction	1-14
I.	Definition	
1.	The Concept of Definition (Lakṣaṇa) in Nyāya and Advaita Systems	17-28
II.	Meaning	
2.	Word and Meaning in Pāṇini's System	31-36
3.	Advaita Theory of Meaning	37-45
4.	Sense and Reference in Navya-Nyāya	46-54
5.	The Concept of Viṣayatā in Navya-Nyāya	55-65
6.	Sambandha (Relation) in Navya-Nyāya	66-78
7.	The Concept of Lakṣaṇā in Navya-Nyāya and Advaita Vedānta	79-87
III.	Truth	
8.	Advaita Conception of Truth (Satyam)	91-98
9.	Navya-Nyāya Conception of Truth	99-118
IV.	Knowledge	
10.	Gaṅgeśa's Concept of Knowledge (Pramā)	121-129
11.	Gaṅgeśa's Definition of Perceptual Knowledge	130-136

12. Gaṅgeśa's Concept of Inferential Knowledge (Anumiti) 137-144

13. Gaṅgeśa's Parataḥ-Prāmāṇya-Vāda 145-152

14. Postulational Knowledge (Arthāpatti-Pramā) 153-163

15. Advaita Conception of Knowledge 164-173

16. The Advaita Doctrine of Mahāvākya 174-184

17. Role of Reason in Advaita System 185-191

18. Darśana as a Source of Knowledge 192-197

19. Structure of Scientific Knowlege 198-207

20. Structure of Apriori Knowledge and Gödel's Proof 208-222

Index 223-224

Acknowledgement

This book is an attempt at interpreting the traditional epistemological concepts of definition, meaning, truth and knowledge in terms of contemporary epistemological terms.

The book is the outcome of my research in epistemology. Some of the units incorporated in this book have already appeared in the following journals; I sincerely express my thanks to the publishers and editors of *The Adyar Libarary and Research Bulletin* (1984) Madras, *The Vedant Kesari* (October 1984 August 1987) Madras, *Prabuddha Bharata* (Feb. 1985) Calcutta, *Pathway to God*—The Journal of the Academy of Philosophy and Religion (April 1988), Belgaum, and *The Journal of Social Sciences* (1987) Karnatak University, Dharwad.

I am very grateful to Pandit Bhalachandra Sastriji, Pracharya Shri Shankaracharya Samskrit Pathashala Dharwad who kindly explained me certain portions of Gaṅgeśa's *Tattva-cintāmaṇi* and Visvanātha's *Kārikavalī* and *Muktāvali* along with Dinakara's *Dinakari*. My thanks are also due to Professors L. C. Mullatti, B. K. Matilal, Jitendranatha Mohanty, and Sivajivan Bhataccharya who kindly permitted me to discuss certain issues considered in this book.

I am thankful to Shri Naresh Gupta, Indian Books Centre, Delhi for his kind interest in the publication of this book.

RACHAPPA I. INGALALLI

Introduction

In Indian epistemology the concepts of definition, meaning and knowledge are interrelated. The concept of definition (lakṣaṇa) plays an important role in the tradition of Indian epistemology because whenever a person wants to acquire knowledge of facts through language he must understand the definitions of concepts and things through the meanings of the expressions in that language. Thus the present book in the sequel deals with the concepts of definition (lakṣaṇa), meaning (artha) and knowledge (pramā).

I. *Definition* : In the long traditions of Nyāya and Advaita systems the techniques of definition have played an important role to constitute the basic frame-works of these systems. According to Nyāya-bhāṣya the function of definition is to specify the notion of an object under consideration so that legitimate distinction among the objects is facilitated; certain ambiguity in the characterisation of lakṣaṇa is brought out in the process of analysis. Annaṃbhaṭṭa's formulation of the definition referring to 'asādhāraṇa·dharma (unique property) is also critially considered. Both Śivāditya and Udayanācārya formulate the structure of definition as an instance of kevala-vyatireki (exclusively negative inference) and it is critically understood through Professor Matilal's interpretation. Next, Advaita theory of definition is explicated. Of the two types of definition, svarūpalakṣaṇa (essential definition) reveals the essential nature of a thing under consideration-taṭastha and lakṣaṇa (accidental definition) points out only accidental but unique property of definition in order to demarcate the object of definition. Similarities and differences between Nyāya and Advaita theories of definition are pointed out. Futher some critical observations are also made with reference to western theories of definition.

II. *Meaning* : Pāṇini's darśana is a source of semantics. In the Mahābhāṣya a distinction is made between a word and meaning, and such a distinction seems to provide a criterion of demacration between a word and meaning. The two radical views of Vājapyāyana and Vyādi are considered. For Vājapyāyana meaning of an expression implies universal; however Vyādi's view identifies meaning of an expression as individual. Reconciliation of these theories has been attempted with reference to Nyāya semantics. An attempt has been made to understand Pāṇini's semantics interms of modern (western) referential theory of meaning.

Advita semantics implies that primary meaning of an expression as universal (jāti) is contrasted with individual (vyakti) theory of meaning. The relationship between the universal (jāti) and the particular (vyakti) is also contrasted with Plato's theory of Ideas. Plato's theory like Advaita theory of universal does not emphasise the invariable relation between universal and particular. If the primary meaning does not fit in a context then secondary meaing is to be fixed. Thus in Advita tradition two types of meaning are postulated: Primary (vācyārtha) and secondary meanings (lakṣyārtha). Secondary meaning is related to primary meaning. There are two types of classifications of metaphorical meaning (Cl and C2); C 1: pure implication and double implication. In pure implication there is direct relation to the primary meaning; but in double implication there is indirect relation to primary meaning. According to C 2 secondary meanings are of three types (i) jahallakṣaṇā (exclusive implication) (ii) ajahallakṣaṇā (inclusive implication) and (iii) jahadajallakṣaṇā These three varieties of C 2 may be subsumed under pure implication of C 1, for each one of them involves direct relation to primary meaning.

According to non-connotative view of western symantics proper names like Devadatta lack meanings for they do not have sense or connotation. But another modern theory of sense and denotation falsifies non-connotative theory. Consequently Advaita theory of meaning is compatible with latter semantics.

In Navya-nyāya semantics we find referential theory of meaning according to which meaning of an expression is due to its reference to certain object in the universe. One of the modern trends in understanding the concept of meaning in Navya-nyāya is interms of western theory of sense and reference. It has been argued that śakyatā and śakyatāvacchedaka donot coincide with reference and sense. However it is shown that in meaning, universal element (jāti) corresponds to Frege's sense and individual factor stands for denotation or reference. Further certain possible objections to sense-reference theory have been considered from the quarters of modal semantics. It is argued that for modal semantics about rigid designators the concept of sense is indispensable.

The concept of viṣayatā (content-ness) in Navya-nyāya implies the semantic structure of a cognition (jñāna). Every meaningful cognition has viṣayatā. A qualificative cognition consists of three elements namely, viśeṣyatā (qualificand-ness), prakāratā (qualfireness) and saṃṣargatā (relation-ness) holding between viśeṣyatā and prakāratā. And these three elements come under a common category of viṣayatā (contentness). Viṣayatā functions as a matrix of a cognition and truth value of a given cognition emerges from the configuration of viṣayatā of that cognition.

The concept of sambandha is a component of viṣayatā. The concept of sambandha (relation) in Navya-nyāya system is critically considered in terms of contemporary ideas in theory of relations. Modern theory of relations exhibits certain important aspects like the definition of relation as a set of ordered pairs, an ordered pair as class of classes, domain and range of relations and properties of relations. While sketching the cardinal features of relations, concept of ordered triple, quadurple, n-tuple are shown to be reducible to different ordered pairs. An ordered triple <x, y, z> is capable of being reduced either to

$\langle\langle x, y\rangle, z\rangle$ or $\langle x, \langle y, z\rangle\rangle$ which are logically different. Consequently corresponding relations are also different. Relation as set of ordered pairs is also understood as the Cartesian product :

$$X.\,Y=\{\langle x, y\rangle x\in X.\ y\in Y\}.$$

Next the Nyāya definition of sambandha is taken up. Relation is that which determines (conditions) adjuncthood and a subjuncthood.

In relation pratiyogi and anuyogi have a definite order. The direction or the order in the relation is always from pratiyogi to anuyogi. Even in converse relation the order is the same. Prof. Matilal's reductive account of diadic or nadic predicates to monadic predicates is considered and it is argued that relations are structurally different from properties and monadic predicates cannot accommodate diadic predicates within their matrices. Valid relational arguments turn out to be invalid if they are reduced to categorical forms. Nyāya definition of sambandha captures the sense of relation as a set of ordered pairs. Relation of contact (saṃyoga) relation of similarity (sādrṣyatva), causal relation (kāraṇtā) exhibit certain properties of relations like symmetry transitivity etc. There are also differences between two theories of relations. Modern theory of relations has no (explicit) ontic commitments; Nyāya theory of relations is developed within the realistic framework but tries to go beyond it.

Both Navya-Nyāya and Advaita systems postulate two types of meanings of expessions namely primary meaning (vācyārtha) and secondary or metophorical meaning (lakṣyārtha). Lakṣaṇā is the be arer of lakṣyārtha. Rendering of lakṣaṇā as 'metaphor' is justified by sorting out certain relevant similarities between the characterisations of lakṣaṇā and its western counterpart 'metaphor'. The specific problem is about the cognitive status of metaphorical statements. Given a statement such that its literal meaning does not fit in a given context; how are we to decide in what sense a metaphorical sentence is meaningful or true ? For fuller understanding of a metaphor, traditional classifications of a metaphorical statements are analysed. Although Nyāya thinkers differ from Advaitins in their view of primary meanings, an attempt has been made to reconcile the two apparently contending theories. On logical grounds 'jativāda' and 'jati-viśiṣtavyaktivāda' are reducible to each other and consequenty the corresponding theories of metaphor coalesce. It is argued that a metaphorical statement is meaningful if it is reducible to literal sentence. And consequently a metaphorical statement is to be acknowledged as true proposition if its literal paraphrase is confirmed by actual observation of the correspon ding state of affairs.

III. *Truth* (*Satyam*) : The concept to truth is a necessary component of knowledge (pramā) and hence the analysis of truth is prior to the explication of knowledge (pramā). In Advaita epistemology there is a distinction between satyam (truth) and jñānam (knowledge), for instance the ultimate reality is in the form of stayam-jñānam. The same distinction is also streched in the domain of practical affairs (vyavahārika-viṣaya). Both etymology and the usage of the word 'satyam' imply that 'satyam' designates the actual (exsisting) state of affair. According to Śaṅkara's interpretation, the scriptural imperative 'satyam vada' (speak the truth) implies that a speaker of truth must be reliable or trustworthy and must be capable of communicating the truth without twisting the information about the actual state of affairs. In the course of the analysis of truth several arguments far and against are considered. Further it is shown that according to Śaṅkara there is a distinction between the nature of truth and a criterion or test of truth. From logical point of view the nature of truth is prior to its test. The principle of non-contradiction (abādha) is considered to be the criterion of truth. The criterion of truth is to servé as a technique for sorting out the correct beliefs in truths from false beliefs in the contexts of human experience. It is argued that abādha as a criterion of truth implies the coherence aspect of truth. Logical technique involved in the criterion of abādha (non-contradiction) enables us to remove the obstructing veils to understand the nature of truth.

The theory of truth in Navya-nyāya as formulated by Gaṅgeśa also implies the distinction between pramā as knowledge and prāmāṇya as trnth. Truth is a necessary condition for knowledge and knowledge (pramā) is shown to be justified true belief. Gaṅgeśa's definition of truth as a property of a true cognition is analysed in terms of qualifier, qualificand and relation. Notions of qualifier and qualificand are clarified. And in the process of analysis comparison is made with Frege's concept of proposition. Next the definition of falsity (aprāmaṇya) is considered in order to contrast with the definition of truth. Consequently it is shown that the deflnition of truth and falsity have exclusive domains and there is no interaction between the two definitions.

Further the distinction is made between the structure of a true cognition and the structure of corresponding fact. For a given fact there may be more than two true cognitions which may differ in their viṣayatas (contentness). Since a true qualificative cognition is capable of being expressed in a declarative sentence, an attempt has been made to analyse the structure of a true sentence. Finally certain similarities and differences are sorted out in the course of understanding the Nyāya concept of truth with reference to western semantic conception of truth.

IV – *Knowledge* (*Pramā*) : Gaṅgeśa in the chapter on pramā-lakṣaṇa-pūrva-pakṣa considers various views about the notion of pramā, consequentaly he rejects opponent's views and formulates his own theory about pramā in the chapter 'pramā-lakṣaṇa-siddhānta. Pramātva (Knowledge-ness) is the generic characteristic (avacchedaka) of pramā (knowledge). Different definitions D1—D10 are considered and found to be unsatisfactory. Gaṅgeśa's defines pramā (knowledge) as: (D) An apprehension of qualifier (prakāra) belonging to its qualificand (viśeṣya) through appropriate relation (sambandha). An opponent's objection to D is replied by understanding *tadvati* as tat *sambandhavati*. It is shown that 'D' is not applicable to any instance of aprmā (false belief). Structure of pramā is made explicit with reference to the definition of knowledge as justified true belief. Consequently pramā is reinterpretated as justified true cognition. And the applicability of this characterisation of pramā to pratyakṣa-pramā, anumiti, upamiti and śābda is shown to be adequate.

In the Navya-Nyāya system of Gaṅgeśa pratyakṣa-pramā (perceptual knowledge) is formulated in relation to the pratyakṣa-pramāṇa (perception) so that pratyakṣa-pramā is justified by it.

Gaṅgeśa reviews several definitions of pratyakṣa-pramā in order to formulate more adequate definition:

D1 : "Perceptual knowledge is a true apprehension based on sense-object contact" and

D2 : "Perceptual knowledge is a true apprehension generated by the functions of sense organs" are too wide definitions because they are also applicable to inferential and memory knowledges where sense-organs duly function. Another Definition namely.

D3 : "Perceptual knowledge is direct apprenension" is also inadequate because direct apprehension (sāksāta-kāra) is not qualified by its relational abstract (sāksāta-kāritvam).

Gaṅgeśa formulates his definition (D) of pratyakṣa-pramā as: Perceptual knowledge is charcterised by immediacy of an apprehension (pratyakṣasya sākṣātkāritvam lakṣaṇam). This definition implies immediacy as universal (jāti) and sākṣātkaromi (I apprehend directly) as anuvyavasāya (after cognition). Further it is arguméd that d : jñānākaraṇakam jñānamiti tu vayam (perceptual knowledge is not brought about by the instrumentally of any antecedent knowledge) is also implied by D. Although perceptual errors involve an element of immediacy, they are not the species of pratyakṣa-pramā as they are the instances of apramā. Further pratyabhijñā (knowledge by recognition) is distinguished by perceptual knowledge as the former contains an element of memory knowledge. Perceptual knowledge is a species of justified true belief and perceptual justification is direct so that perceptual knowledge claims are self justified.

Gaṅgeśa's definition (D) of inferential knowledge is characterised as that knowledge which is generated by a prior knowledge of the nature of a minor term qualified by a pervasion (vyāpti-viśiṣṭa-pakṣadharmatā-jñāna-janyam jñānam anumitiḥ) 'D' contains an important concept of vyāpti (pervasion). Gaṅgeśa's definition of vyāpti from siddhānta lakṣana is explained critically. Another important concept in D is pakṣa (minor term) and pakṣa is a necessary condition for inferential knowledge. Anumiti (inferential knowledge) is understood as justified true cognition. Justification is mediate. And anumiti is the logical consequence of the premises of anumāna-pramāṇa.

Gaṅgeśa the founder of Navya-nyāya philosophy is an exponent of parataḥ-prāmānya-vāda (Theory of extrinisic validity of truth). In his epoch making work *Tattva-cintāmaṇi* Gaṅgeṣa deals with svataḥ and paratah pramāṇya vādas in utpattivāda and jñaptivāda sections. From epistemological point of view jñaptivāda (theory of justification) is important to understand the structure of parataḥ-prāmāṇya-vāda. In Indian Philosophical tradition the problem of prāmāṇya-vāda (theory of validity) has been formulated as : how are we to justify in any particular case, whether a given cognition (jñāna) is true (yathārtha) or false (ayathārtha) ? whether the factors which generate a true cognition also justify the validity of that cognition? Or some extrinsic (ab extra) conditions are required? Traditionally svataḥ-prāmāṇya-vāda (theory intrinsic-validity) and parataḥ-prāmāṇya-vāda (theory of extrinisic validity) have come forward to answer the above questions. Gaṅgeśa in jñaptivāda section first presents the a view of svataḥ-prāmāṇya-vāda as pūrva-pakṣa (opponent's view) and then in his siddhānta formulates arguments to refute opponents' view in order to establish his theory of extrinsic validity. Svatha-prāmānya-vāda implies that truth of congnition is apprehended by intrinsic factors (svataḥ) where svataḥ' means svāśrayagrāhaka niyatogrāhya. Accordingly Prabhākara's school svāśrayagrāhaka means the truth of a cognition C 1 is apprehended by the awareness of that cognition C 1 and not ab-extra. According to Miśras' school 'svāśrayagrāhaka' stands for the introspective apprehensionon (anuvyavasāya) by which the truth of C 1 isapprehended. However on svataḥ theory the apprehension of the truth of C 1 coincides with the possession of that C 1. The svataḥ-theory of Mīmāṃsakā opposes Nyāya theory by pointing a kind of infinite regress. If the truth of a cognition C 1 needs to be tested by another cognition C 2 then C 2 also needs confirmation by another cognition C 3 and so on ad infinitum. But Gaṅgeśa argues that if truth of cognition were aprehended intrinsically then in the case a cognition that arises in unfamiliar circumstances ought not be doubted. However there are doubtful cognitions and hence apprehension of truth is not intrinsic to a cognition. Gaṇgeśa formulates his answer to the Mīmāṃsakas objection of infinite regress. The cognition which apprehends the truth of another cognition may be one which does not require confirmation from another cognition. C 1 may be ascertained by C 2 and C 2 may not require C 3 for its confirmation. For instance where there is absence of doubt about a cognition say 'This is āmalaka under the palm', there the primary knowledge itself amounts to certainty about the object so that fruitful activity follows from that alone (yatrāprāmāṇyaśaṅkā nāsti karatalāmalākādi jñāne tatra vyavasāya evarthaniścaya iti tata eva pravrttirniṣkampā). This point is most significant contribution to epistemology. It has important bearings on the problems of modern philosophy of science or epistemology.

Next, postulational knowledge (arthāpatti-pramā), is considerad. Firstly three views on the nature of arthāpatti are considered and found inadequate as they stand. These are (1) Bhāṭṭas's view that postulation is a means of resolving a conflct; (2) Prabhākaras' view that postulation is characterised by an element of doubt and (3) Banerjee's interpretation of Advaitic view that postulation is a hypothesis. Although all these three views are inadequate as they stand the Bhāṭṭa's view seems to be most promising of the three; the stress is on this view to accept a modified version of it. Then this modified view is compared with Quine's conception of a veridical or truth telling paradox. Several points of similarty between the two are brought out with process. These are : (1) both are sources of true cognitions and (2) both are (deductively) valid inferences (3) an element of surprise is inherent in both veridical paradox and postulation. There are also significant points of difference between the two viz : (1) It is possible that true and false propositions give rise to true proposition in case of a paradox, whereas postulation yields true proposition from true propositions only. (2) Postulation is expressed in the from of disjunctive syllogism having disjunctive universal proposition but this is not so in case of veridical paradox, as it stands. Next the question whether postulation is an independent pramāṇa is considered. The traidtional reasons for independence are : (i) postulation has its own unique instrumental cause, namely, a disjunctive major premise (ii) postulation is reducible, if at all, to kevelavyatireki inference which is not inference at all according to Mīmāṃsakas and Advaitins. Of these reasons (ii) is pursued by considering a paradigm case (example) of kevalavyatireki inference and it is shown that postulation does not exhibit any characteristic of kevalavyatireki inference. Nevertheless, it ts argued that Naiyāyikaś view that arthāpatti is reducible to inference is of the anvaya-vyatireki type and this view is basically correct. Only the type of inference of which arthāpatti is reducible is anvaya-vyatireki, not kevelavyatireki.

A cardinal view of Advaita philosophy is that self knowledge is the knowledge par-excellence and summum-bonum of human life. Śaṅkara's definition of knowledge is analysed and its fuller implications are brought out in order to highlight logical and scientific spirit of the alleged definition. Universality, objectivity and impersonality are the chief characteristics of knowledge. From a logical point of view knowledge is justified true belief. Śaṅkara's definition satisfies the logical requirement of justification condition.

Usual misunderstanding of Śaṅkara's view regarding empirical knowledge has been rectified. To this effect it has been argued that realistic frame work of Śaṅkara's epistemology makes room for empirical perspective also. On Śaṅkara's own account logical status of empirical knowledge is not different from contemporary scientific approach of understanding empirical knowledge. Certain inadequacies of empirical knowledge are made explicit with reference to Swami Vivekananda's idea, namely while knowing a given fact of the external world say 'X' human mind projects its own element say 'Y' (so all that we claim to know is not that real 'X' in itself but 'X+Y'. And in such a context the possibilty for the postulation of self-knowledge arises. The seeker after self-knowledge should possess integral strength of body, mind and self; a weak person may not obtain self-knowledge (na ayamātmā bala hīnena labhyah). The role of reasoning in the path of self-knowledge is secondary. Even śruti is not the final authority. But only anubhūti or spiritual experience is final arbiter to justify self-knowledge.

The scriptural testimony (śruti) plays an important role in the form of unique source of self-knowledge. The four mahāvākāyas contained in the śruti function as means of self-knowledge or knowledge of Reality (brahman). The four mahāvākyas : Prajñānam brahma (consciousness is reality), tatvamasi (that thou art) aham brahmāsmi (I am reality) and ayamātāmā brahma (This self is Reality) are analysed. The inter relationship of the four mahāvākyas is worked out. The function of the mahāvākyas in human knowledge and culture is unique; they integrate man's subjective experience and objective knowledge into a whole thereby giving meaning to life and enabling man to function efficiently. Consequenty the pragmatic outlook implied in the doctrine of mahāvākya also becomes clearer when applied at the level of interpersonal affairs in order to understand the nature of true human relations.

Jijñāsā as spiritual inquiry implies rational technique of understanding the truth recorded in the scripture (śruti) originally intuited by the enlightened souls. Of the three important species of reasoning frequently used the first one is characterised as five membered syllagism used by Śaṅkara. The syllogistic reasoning is similar to Nyāya syllogism. By virtue of illustration (udāharaṇa), Indian syllogism differs from Aristotalean syllogism. Secondly, reasoning by comparison is a means to draw probable conclusions about spiritual facts. Most important type of reasoning is dialectic. Dialectic is a chain of simple arguments arranged into pros and cons.

Concluding part of dialectic stands for the proof of truth. Reason also functions as a criterion of purportful scripture; the criterion implies that statements of scriptures should be free from internal contradictions so that śruti is characterised as a coherent system. Although reason and scripture (Śruti) are autonomous, interaction between them is possible however interaction does not reduce them to each other. Reason ought to function in the domain of scriptural truths but controlled by the framework of scripture (śruti). Finally the focus of spiritural goal is on self knowledge (ātmānubhuti) through the steps of reason and scriptural authority.

In Indian tradition darśanas are treated as sources of higher knowledge i.e. systems of philosophical knowledge. Darśana indicates a system of thought acquired by intuitive experience and justified by logical argument. As a system of knowledge, darśana satisfies certain formal criteria such as internal consistency. A darśana as a system in order to explain the facts of the world usually involves certain models like physicalistic model of Nyāya-Vaiśeṣika or phenomenalistic model of Mādhyamika Buddhism. However the choice of one model rather than the other depends upon the conceptual scheme of the system. Darśana as a fullscale system deals with the areas of epistemology, semantics logic, metaphysics and ethics. Darśana as a system of philosophical knowledge functions mainly in two ways : Firstly a darśana reflects on the content of human experience in order to conceptualise it and secondly at the level of application, darśanas furnish necessary guidelines for enriching practical life.

Classical definition of knowledge implies belief, truth and justification as necessary and sufficient conditions so that scientific knowledge is the synthesis of subjective and objective factors. Popper a champion of objective knowledge denies classical view by saying that it involves subjectivity as subjective and there is no room for subjectivity in scientific investigation The belief centered traditional concept of knowledge is irrele vant because objective knowledge is characterised by logical content of scientific theories as conjectures or guesses. Scientific enterprise primarily involves falsification of a theory but not justification because falsification implies growth or evolution of scientific knowledge and consequently falsified theory implies or suggests a better theory. Popper's view of objective knowledge without a knowing subject clashes with his view of third world of scientific theories as human creations. Secondly reduction of epistemology to biology is shown to be untenable on the basis of the differentiating character of scientific knowledge. It is argued that scientific knowledge is to be understood in terms of truth, belief and justification.

The classical definition of knowledge as justified true belief is also applicable to apriori knowledge. Apriori knowledge implies necessary truths; logic and arithmatic are considered to be the sources of apriori knowledge. In the long tradition beginning from Plato, truths of reason constitute the genuine knowledge. For centuries deductive reasoning as a proof technique considered to be a paradigm of human thinking. However an axiomatic deductive model to gain apriori knowledge has been challenged by K. Gödel (1931). According to his discovery, a formal system like arithmatic cannot be considered to be a complete system because in that system certain non-axiomatic theorems as formulas cannot be deduced or proved within that system. In such a context the legitimacy of our knowledge claims about such undecidable but true propositions is considered. Certain recent interpretations of Gödel's theorems are also considered. An (apparent) inconsistency between Gödel's realism and his theory of proof has been resolved. An application of Gödels reasoning in the field of thinking machines (computers) is also considered. Further it is argued that even though certain true propositions in a system like arithmatic cannot be proved within the system, they are capable of being proved outside the system. In that case our knowledge claims about undecidable true propositions are justified ab extra, by means extrinsic factors in meta-systems. One of the reasons to incorporate last two units : 'the structure of scientific knowledge' and 'structure of apriori knowledge' from western epistemology is to explore the possibilities of interactions between Indian epistemology and western epistemology.

I
DEFINITION

1

The Concept of Definition (Laksana) in Nyāya and Advaita Systems

1.1. The Nyāya system well known for its epistemology and logic considers the technique of definition as an important aspect of a philosophical system. Although the term lakṣaṇa in Sanskrit has been used in several senses,[1] in the logical treatises it stands for 'definition.' The aim is to inquire into the structure and function of lakṣaṇa in the sense of definition. In the Nyāya-bhāṣya, uddeśa (enumeration of philosophical concepts), lakṣaṇa (definition) and parīkṣā (examination of the concepts) are considered to be the three main techniques of a philosophical system.[2]

1.2. Nyāya-bhāṣya (1.1.3) states the nature of definition (lakṣaṇa) as a means to differentiate an entity from that which does not possess the nature or essence (tattva) of that entity (uddiṣṭasya tattvavyavacchedako dharmo lakṣaṇam). Accordingly definition states the essential characteristic or nature (svarūpa) of a thing in order to differentiate it from others things. Thus the function of a definition is to differentiate the thing defined from other things.[3]

But the term 'essence' in the definition is vague in its meaning; the concept of lakṣaṇa with reference to 'essence' also remains vague. And vagueness may disappear if the meaning of essence is made precise. A criterion for precision in terms of the line of demarcation between essential and non-essential attributes or (properties) is implicit or presupposed.

1.3. However in the new school of Nyāya an attempt has been made to give a precise formulation of lakṣaṇa (definition). According to Tarka-dīpikā (3): Definition is that which distinguishes the definiendum (lakṣya) from all entities that are different from it—(vyāvartakasaiva lakṣaṇatvam).[4] There are three things in every case of defining: What is to be defined (lakṣya), the defining attribute (lakṣaṇa) and the definitional statement (lakṣaṇavākya). Or definitional statement (lakṣaṇa-vākya) usu-allyconsists of lakṣya (definiendum) and a lakṣaṇa (definiens). Definiens must be present in definiendum and must be absent in non-definiendum (a-lakṣya). Lakṣya or definiendum may designate a single thing or it may stand for many things coming under a class. In either case a defining property (definiens) must be present in definiendum (lakṣya) only and must be absent in non-definiendum.

1.4. Annaṃbhaṭṭa first states a defining property (definiens) as an 'un-common attribute' (asādhāraṇadharma).[5] But prima-facie there is a difficulty in equating definiens with an uncommon attribute. If the term 'uncommon' is the opposite of common then, common attribute must be found in both lakṣya (definiendum) and alakṣya (non-definiedum). The author of Tarka-dīpikā-prakāśa, Nīlakaṇṭha, points out the following flaws in the normal interpretation of 'uncommon attribute.' Firstly a certain inadequate characteristic may turn out to be an uncommon attribute. For example tawny colour' is absent in some cows (lakṣya) and non-cows (a lakṣya), and hence it is an uncommon property. But the definition of 'cow' having 'tawny colour' is an instance of too narrow definition, (avyāpti) for some cows are non-twany. Secondly a definition containing an uncommon attribute may be an instance of too wide definition (ativyāpti) also. For example 'having horns' is uncommon attribute to both lakṣya (say cows) and part of alakṣya (non-cows). Thirdly a definitional statement, having an attribute which is absent in the definiendum, is (asambhava) absurd definition. For example, a cow is animal having one hoof. Therefore it is not always possible to equate a defining attribute (lakṣaṇa) with asādhāraṇa dharma (uncommon attribute).

In order to clarify the notion of asādhāraṇya (uncommonness) Annaṃbhaṭṭa interpretes 'uncommonness' of an attribute' as 'its being co-extensive with the 'specific feature' (avacchedaka) of the things to be defined (lakṣyatāvācchedaka-samanīyatā). Accordingly 'uncommonness' is to be taken in the sense of 'being co-existensive with the specific feature of things to be defined', so that the difinition is flawless. For instance, 'Tawny colour' is not an uncommon attribute for it is not co-existensive with 'cowness' which is the specific characteristic of all cows. But tawny colour is not found in all cows. Therefore 'tawny colour' is not asādāraṇa dharma. According to Naiyāyikas samanīyatatvam has been analysed as follows.

X is samanīyata with Y if and only if X is pervaded by Y and also parvades of Y (tat samanīyatatvam tad vyāpyatve sati tad vyāpakatvam).[6] Two attributes are said to be co-extensive when their scope of extension is the same. For example in the case of a correct defining attribute for 'cow', namely 'a female quadruped having a dewlap' is co-extensive with cow.

There are two views regarding the function of a defining property: (i) The function of a 'defining attribute' is only to 'differentiate' (vyāvartana) i.e. to dimarcate something to be defined from what is not to be defined: (ii) The function of a defining attribute is to differentiate and control 'linguistic usage'. According to Annaṃbhaṭṭa the function of a defining attribute is both to differentiate and control linguistic usage (vyāvṛtteḥ api vyavahāra-sādhanatvāt).[7] For instance, the term 'cow' is to be defined with reference to its proper referent when one has the awareness of the difference of a cow from what is other than it. Normally linguistic usage pre-supposes such awareness of the difference in the facts. Thus the concept of vyāvṛtti specifies the exact function of adequate definition.[8]

According to Śivāditya and Vācaspati Miśra, defining is speaking of the unique reason or evidence what is technically called kevalavyatireki-hetu. That unique evidence determines the items of things to be defined by separating or differentiating them from similar as well as dissimilar things.[9] Accordingly definition is a means of supplying 'unique evidence' in order that inference becomes valid. Formally, a definition 'A has X' can be illustrated as follows :

Thesis	:	Everything that is A differs from non-A.
Reason	:	For each of them has X.
Rule	:	Whatever does not differ from non-A does not have X, e.g., that which is B.
Application	:	Everything that is an A has the absentee (pratiyogin) X whose absence pervades the absence of 'difference from non-A'.
Conclusion	:	Terefore, everything that is an A differs from non-A.[10]

Consider a concrete example of an adequate definition : 'A cow is an animial having dewlap.' The corresponding kevala-vyatireki (exclusive negative inference) is as follows :

1. A cow differs from non-cow.
2. Because a cow has dewlap.
3. Whatver does not differ non-cow does not have dewlap, e.g., a monkey.
4. A cow has the absentee (pratiyogin), dewlap, whose absence pervades the absence of difference from non cow.
5. Therefore a cow differs from non-cow.

1.5. A definition in Nyāya is a proposition specifying the differentiating feature of species or the thing to be defined. Vyāvṛtti or differentiation consists in the inference of difference from other things, for instance 'earth has smell' here 'having smell' is differentiating property which serves as a valid reason in the inference from non-earth. But in case of nameability (abhideyatvam) all things (padārtha) are to be covered by the definition and there is no differenting attribute between padārtha i.e. a thing and a non-thing which is beyond the universe of discourse. Consequently the only function of lakṣaṇa is designation (vyavahāra).[11] And the definition need not imply a search for the essence of the thing defined. But for Aristotle, a definition was the statement of the essence of a thing.[12] An essence of a thing is designated by its essential attribute (distinguished from non-essential attribute) such that a thing without its essential attribute ceases to be that thing. In orther words, essence of a thing means a property in virtue of which it is what it is. In Indian terminology the nearest equivalent of an essence would be svabhāva or svarūpa (own being or nature). But in Nyāya theory of definition there is no focus on the essential characteristic of a thing to be defined but a defining attribute must be unique and differentiating one.

1.6. According to Advaita system[13] there are two types of definition (lakṣaṇa) namely svarūpa-lakṣaṇa (essential definition) and taṭastha-lakṣaṇa (accidental definition). Svarūpa-lakṣaṇa reveals the essential nature of a thing under consideration. For example, Brahman as ultimate reality is defined as 'Brahman is sat-cit-ānanda'. The definiens 'sat+cit+ānanda' constitute the essential nature of Brahman. Consequently without those essential or defining properties Brahman cannot be understood. Similarly in ordinary paralance a thing or an object is defined in terms of its essential properties only. Some of the modern examples like 'water' is H_2O, and 'Gold is the element having atomic number 79[14] may be treated as the instances of essential definitions where there is an element of necessity and by virtue of that necessity a thing like gold cannot be called gold if it is devoid of that essential property of atomic number 79.

However taṭastha lakṣaṇa (accidental definition) unfolds only non-essential or accidantal properties of definiendum so that by means of those accidental features one can distinguish or differentiate the given thing from other things. For example, 'Devadatta's house is under that mango tree'.[15] In this example the property of being situated under the only mango tree in a given locality' functions as a distinguishing property. In practical affairs taṭastha-lakṣaṇa is often used. People learn to identity and reidentify on the basis of information based on taṭastha-lakṣaṇa. However any accidental characteristic cannot function as definiens in case of taṭastha lakṣaṇa because only unique type of accidental feature constitutes the definiens. In other words the definiens should be in the form of vyāvartaka-dharma (distinguishing property).

1.7. To the question whether svarūpa-lakṣaṇa and taṭastha-lakṣaṇas are mutually exclusive, the answer is both yes and no. Yes, because they are structurally different types of definitions. Of course no, because even svarūpa-lakṣaṇa may be used to distinguish one thing from another. In other words svarūpa-lakṣaṇa may function as a taṭastha lakṣaṇa but not conversely. But in that case svarūpa-lakṣaṇa is reducible to taṭastha lakṣaṇa. There are exclusive domains also. In such crucial cases both the definitions cannot convegse. For instance when svarūpa-lakṣaṇa uniformaly characterises number of things coming under certain class, it will be of no help to distinguish one member of species from another member in a given class. If in a certain village every house is built by stones, then essential characteristic of a house, in that place is 'stone built residence'. And such essential property as 'stone built residence' cannot function as a distinguishing property (vyāvartaka-dharma) in the given domain of stone houses. And in order to identify or distinguish a certain house in that locality for some practical purpose it is necessary to look for a peculiar feature of that house—'being situated under the mango tree' can function as a distinguish property if that house is only house being constructed under that mango tree.

1.8. There are certain similarities and differences between Nyāya and Advaita theories of definition. Since according to Nyāya the definiens is in the form of a distinguishing property and hence that distinguishing property need not be an essential property. And in this regard Nyāya view of definition resembles Advaitin's taṭastha-lakṣaṇa. In the example' 'A cow is an animal with dewlap', the distinguishing or unique property is 'an animal with dewlap' is not essential property of a cow. However Naiyāyikas in their general practice donot restric themselves to the definitions inolving non-essential (distinguishing) properties only; there are also cases where they frequenty formulate the essential definitions also. For example Gautama's definition of perception (pratyakṣa) as (indriyārtha sannikarṣotpannam jñānam, avyapadeśyam avyabhicāri, vyavasāyātmakam pratyakṣam' is an instance of svarūpa-lakṣaṇa. Similarly 'self is characterised by cognitive and conative faculties' is also an instance of the essential definition of self.

1.9. It is interesting to note that both Nyāya and Advaita systems employ ostensive definitions.[16] Even though an ostensive definition is paradoxically non-verbal, it has been frequently used. It is non-verbal, because an object is directly introduced in a given context of trustworthy speakers' (āpta) communications of direct information. Following are some of the ostensive definitions :

(i) 'This is silver' (ayam rajatam).

(ii) 'This is a pot' (ayam ghaṭah).

(iii) 'You are the tenth man (tvam daśamaḥ).

(iv) 'This ātman is brahman' (ayam ātmā brahmaḥ).

One of the distinguishing characteristics of ostensive definition is that it invariably contains demonstrative pronouns such as 'this' and a pronoun like 'you' which function as rigid designators directly referring to the corresponding objects. The logical frame woks of (i) and (ii) are the same because reliable speaker refers to a piece of silver, and a pot such that silver implies silver-ness and pot implies potness. Similarly-ātman-implies brahman ; silver-ness (rajatatva) and pot-ness (ghaṭa-tva) are the the essential properties. Thus (i), (ii), and (iv) function as essential ostensive definitions. However (iii) has a different logical status. The difference is due to its peculiar function namely distinguishing and/or identifying property. For clear understanding it is necessary to consider the context where (iii) has been formulated. Once a group of ten people had to cross a river. After crossing that river the leader of that group counted everybody except himself and falsely announced that tenth man was missing. Another person correetly counted and pointed to that leader as 'you are the tenth man'. So the leader realised that he was the tenthman. But in this, ostensive definiction 'You are the tenth man' the property of 'being the tenth man' even though specifies that leader, it cannot constitute as an essential property (svarūpa) of that person. Hence it may be called an accidental ostensive definition.

One of the virtues of ostensive definition is it that overcomes the difficulty of infinite-regress in the formulation of non-ostensive definitions. Given a non-ostensive verbal or real definition having a definiens say d_1, the possiblity of defining that d_1 interms of d_2 and d_2 in in terms of d_3 and so on leads to the fallacies of circular definition or infinite definitions. Thus ostensive-non-verbal definitions function as terminus for infinite regress.

1.10. In the western tradition[17] the older Aristotalean logical theory considers a definition as a delimitation of the species by stating the genus which includes it and the specfic differerce or distinguishing characteristic of the species. For example, the definition, 'a man is a rational animal' contains animal as genus and rationality as differentia. It is generally believed that such a theory of dfinition implies essentisalism. Accordingly a definition in order to be adequate must conform to the following rules :

1. A definition must state essence of the definiendum (that which is to be defined).
2. A definition must not be circular.
3. A definition must not be negative.
4. A definition must not be expressed in figurative and obscure language.

However a modern[18] logician expresses his dissatisfaction about such a theory of definition by saying that Aristotalean definition as 'per genus et differentiam' covers only real definitions as aganist nominal definitions. A real definition is not of words but of things. Consequently the definition of a thing is interms of the essence of that thing. The essence of thing is normally expressed in the form of defining characteristics. A defining character of thing in the form of physical thing, quality, action or relation etc, is a characteristic without which the term wolud not be applicable to the thing under consideration. For example the term triangle is not applicable to any triangle if it is devoid of the defining property of 'being a three sided figure.' It is to be noted that the analysis of a physical thing like water as H_2O is different from meanings of words or phrases. On the contrary there are nominal definitions used in formal sciences like logic and mathematics. The nominal or verbal definition helps to establish the meaning of an expression. Further a controversy in the western theory of definition is centered arround the question whether a definition is about a thing, a word or concept ? A suitable theory of definition has to give a satisfactory answer.

Normally nominal definition implies meaning. Authors like Quine have withdrawn ontological autonomy to meanigs in order to reduce them to linguistic entities. Authors like Matilal[19] express Quine's view about essentialism as follows :

Quine's fear of 'essentialism' seems to be overstressed. For it is not clear what is it that he wishes to avoid talking about . . . Although Quine goes to the extreme in his rejection of essentialism . . . it should be noted that he follows for the sake of science what I would call some minimal form of 'essentialism'.

1.11. One of the remifications of 'essentialism' is that the definitions as cognitive sentences are synthetic (based on observation) and necessary also.[20] But Nyāya theory of definition implies that the unique property need not always be essential property. Accordingly a defining property must be differentiating property of a thing defined. In the definition 'A cow is an animal having dewlap, implies the presence of dewlap as differentiating property of a cow. However this is not always so as I have pointed out, (S. 1.8) like Advaitins, Naiyāyikas also formulate essential definitions.

Both Nyāya and Advaita systems accommodate essential, and accidental definitions in their theories of definition. And their theories of definitions are liberal enough to extend their techniques of definitions from the fields of ontology to semantics and logic.

Notes and References

1. (i) Generally "lakṣaṇa" means a mark or an indicator or a characteristic and the corresponding "lakṣya" or "(lakṣita)" means an indicated entity. According to grammarians (Pāṇinīyas) the sūtras of Pāṇini as the rules of grammar are called lakṣaṇa, and consequently the correct forms derived in conformity with the sūtras (rules) are called lakṣya. Prof. Matilal, B. K. (1985; 164) in his recent work *Logic, Language and Reality*, (Motilal Banarsidass, Delhi) has made an interesting observation : "The scheme for a saṃjñā sūtra of Pāṇini roughly corresponds to the notion of nominal or syntactical definition of the modern formal logicians. Such definitions are explained as conventions which provide that certain symbols or expressions shall stand (as substitutes or abbreviations) for particular formulas of the system. (ii) Different senses attached to the "lakṣaṇa" are given in Jhalkikar, Bhimacharya (1974 : 691-701) : *Nyāya-kośa.* Bhandarkar Oriental Research Institute, Poona. Etymologically 'lakṣyate anenaity lakṣaṇaṃ (That by means of which something is adequately characterised is definition).
2. *Nyāya-bhāṣa* 1.1.3 in *Nyāya-sūtra with Nyāya-bhāṣya*, Edited by Ganganatha Jha and Dundi-raja Sastri (1925), Chaukhambha Sanskrit Series, Varanasi.
3. (i) *Nyāya-kośa* : 695 (op. cit).

(ii) *Tarka-dipikā* (5:3) in *Tarka-saṃgrah*, Edited by Athalye Y. V. and Bodas M. R., Bhandarkar Oriental Research Institute, Poona.

(iii) Radhakrishnan, S (1972) : *Indian Philosophy* (Vol. 2), Blackie and Sons, Bombay, p. 47.

(iv) *Sapta-padārthī*, Edited by D. Gurumurii (1932) Adyar Library, Madras, pp. 52-55.

4. (i) *Logic, Language and Reality* (op. cit); 166.

(ii) *Tarka-Saṃgraha-Dīpikā* on *Tarka-Saṃgrah*, Translated and elucidated by Bhattacharya, S (1983); Progressive Publishers, Calcutta, pp. 27-8.

5. *Tarka-Dīpikā* (S:3).

6. *Logic, Language and Reality* (op. cit), pp. 167.

7. *Tarka-Saṃgraha-Dīpikā* (op. cit) pp. 27.

8. (i) *Nyāya-kośa*, pp. 696.

(ii) *Logic, Language and Reality*, pp. 179-80.

9. (i) *Sapta-padārthī* : *Lakṣaṇa-khaṇda*, pp. 52-5.

(ii) Cited in *Logic, Language and Reality*, pp. 179-80.

(iii) *Nyāya-kośa* : 696.

10. *Logic, Language vnd Reality*, p. 189.

11. (i) *Tarka-saṃgraha-dīpikā* (op. cit), p. 21.

(ii) *A Primer of Indian Logic* (1963), Kuppuswami Sastri. The Kuppuswami Sastri Research Institute, Madras, pp. 12.

12. (i) *Aristotle* : Topics 1.5.

(ii) *Logic, Language and Reality* (op. cit), p. 125.

13. *Vedānta Paribhāṣā*, ed. by Swami Madhavananda (1972) Advaita Ashrama Calcutta, pp. 150-2. Nyāya-Kośa p. 696.

14. *Naming and Necessity* by S. Kripke (1980) : Basil Blackwell, Oxford, pp. 116-118.

15. *Indian Philosophical Studies* (Vol. I & II) by M. Hiriyanna (1957) Kavyalaya Publishers, Mysore, P. 803.

16. See *An Introduction to Philosophical Analysis* by J. Hospers (1971) Prentice Hall, India, pp. 56-7.

17. *Introduction to Logic* by P. Suppes (1957), East-West Publisher Madras, P. 151. *An Introduction to Philosophical Analysis* (op. cit), p. 25.
18. *Introductıon to Logic* (op. cit) p. 152.
19. *Logic, Language and Reality* (op. cit), p. 199.
20. Formulation of necessary aposterori proposition is a part of Kripke's modal semantics; *Naming and Nacessity* (op. cit), pp. 116-118.
    The Logical Structure of definitions is similar to necessary aposteriori propositions.

This unit on definition is thoroughly revised and enlarged version of 'The concept of definition (lakṣaṇa) in Nyāya system' ; *Philosophical* 1986-87; pp. 162-7. The Philosophica office Calcutta.

II
MEANING

2

Word and Meaning in Pāṇini's System

2.1. In Indian semantics the concept of meaning has been discussed in relation with a word and a sentence. In Indian tradition, the problem of meaning of an expression has become so important that various philosophical systems participated in the semantic dialectic. The problem of meaning may be stated as : what is the meaning of an expression ? Whether every meaningful expression has to refer to some thing ab extra?

2.2. Patañjali[1] in his *Mahābhāṣya* considers the question 'what is a word ?' For instance, there is an inquiry about the word 'cow'/(go), as distinguished from the animal cow. Accordingly the word 'cow' cannot be identified with substance (dravyam), action, (kriyā), quality (guṇa) or form (ākṛti). But the word 'cow' (go) is that which when uttered gives rise to knowledge of the individuals possessing dewlap, tail, hump, hoofs and horns. (yenochāritena sāsnālāṇgūla kakuda khuraviṣāṇinām sampratyayo bhavati sa śabdaḥ).[2] Consequetly a word (or articulated sound) is that which conventionally conveys a particular meaning (sense).[3]

2.3. Whether the meaning of an expression is an individual (dravya) or universal (jāti)? There are two different views held by early grammarians Vājapyāyana and Vyādi (prior to Patañjali). According to Vājapyāyana words express universal concepts (or attriributes), while according to Vyādi words express or refer to substances or particular things.[4] Vājapyāyana's universal theory implies that words like 'cow' designate a genus which resides in different substances by intimate relatation. Thus whenever genus is apprehended by virtue of intimate rela tion there is the apprehehension of corresponding particular substance in which it resides. Similarily the words like 'white' denote a genus which resides in particulars such that through inherence the quality is apperhended. Similarly in case of a word designating action, a genus is denoted. For example in 'paṭhati' (he reads) etc. a meaning is commonly shared by all those who read.[5] Thus meaning of an expression, primarily, stands for universal and only secondarily it refers to individuals.

2.4. In the theory of Vyādi the words primarily designate individual things (and not classes) while the genus is implied. The main object of this theory is to specify an individual in order to avoid indefiniteness about it. Consequently the principle of individuation is quantitatively determined so that the individual must have a physical body. Whenever an individual object is denoted by a certain word they do not refer to genus or universal according to the usage of mankind. For example an expression an like 'that cow is white' evidently means the individual cow. And it cannot refer to the genus 'cowness,' because genus or universal is one and eternal, which cannot be specified as this or that. This view is also adopted by Sāñkhyas.[6]

But individual theory has been rejected by Naiyāyikas on the basis of the following reasons. A word does not stand for an individual but a certain class of individuals. In an experession like 'that cow is white' the word cow does not merely designate the individual but the individual as distinguished by the generality of cowness.[7] However Nyāya theory of jāti-viśiṣta-vyakti vāda seems to reconcile the kevala-jāti and kevalavyakti-vādas (2.8).

2.5. The genus or universal theory has been adopted by Mīmāṁsakas and Vedāntins. The theory implies that the basis of similar cognitions in respect of different individuals belongs to a certain class. If one word has one inuividual then there is the violation of the law of parsimony, as there are infinite number of things. A word designates universal as its primary meaning also and denotes an individual as its secondary meaning. For example the word 'cow' means 'cowness' and by implication it also means the individual cow characterised by cowness as the generic attribute.[8]

2.6. Patañjali[9] under Pāṇini's rule 2.1.1, has considered certain relevant points regarding the differences between the views of Vājapyāyana and Vyādi. In case of nominal compounds (samāsa) like Vīraḥ-puruṣaḥ 'a brave man.' The two words 'vīraḥ' and 'puruṣaḥ' are compounded to yield a composite meaning. According to Vājapyāyana 'brave' (vīraḥ) means primarily the quality of being brave and puruṣaḥ 'man' means the quality of being a man. Even though two are different qualities, but related to each other by residing in the same locus or substance, technically called (samānādhikaraṇya). Hence by virtue of compatability of the two meanings the nominal compound vīra-puruṣaḥ 'a brave man' is justified.

But on Vyādi's theory both the words vīraḥ (brave) and puruṣaḥ (man) stand for the same particular (substance).

2.7. Patñjali has dealt the controverersy between Vājapyāyana and Vyādi's theories under Pāṇini's rule 1.2.58.[10] Pātañjali says that according to Pāṇini the meaning of a word has both the aspects namely a universal aspect and particularity or substantial aspect. Since in the rule 1.2.58 (jātyākhyāyāmekasmin bahuvacanamanyatarasyam) Pāṇini accepts the theory that a word means the genus but' he says 'when the singular is used to express the class, the plural may be optionally used. For example the sentence 'a cow has dewlap' is equivalent to 'all cows have dewlap."

2.8. There is another type of reconcilation between Vyakti theory and Jāti Theory as expressed in the Nyāya system. According to Naiyāyikas words do not mean universals only, for they cannot be understood apart from the individuals; a genus can be recognised through individuals only. Since a word has only one primary meaning constituted by universal and an individual, it is not correct to say that a word directly means the universal and indirectly the individual and vice-versa. According to the old Naiyāyikas a word means the universal, individual and some particular from even though one of these is predominant.[11] For instance whenever we want to give prominance to the universal or generality we have to stress the similarity of individuals, for example, 'a cow is an animal.' But in order to distringuish one individual from other, one has to stress individuality in the meaning of the word used, for example 'that cow is white.' Some modern Naiyāyikas like Jagadīśa subscribe to the view that a word means a individual as qualified by both the universal and configuration. (jātyākṛti viśiṣṭavyakti).[12] Other modern Naiyāyikas hold that the meaning of a word is an individual characterised by the universal (Jātiviśiṣṭavyakti).[13]

Above theories imply two important aspects of meaning of of a word namely meaning in denotation and meaning in connotation. A word denotes an individual and connotes a genus or universal.

2.9. In western symantics there is a referential theory of meaning according to which meaning of an expression is identified with that to which it refers.[14] According to this theory all meaningful expressions stand for something or the other in relation like designating or referring. Since above theories have a common denomination of referential element implied in the relation between a word and an individual or universal, it is possible treat these theories as the species of referential theory of meaning. Whether all meaningful expressions refer to something ? An affirmative answer may not be sought, for words like 'and', 'if', 'etc. do dot refer to anything though meaningful. But these words are treated as syncategorematic words subordinated to categorematic words. That is to say that syncategorematic words take their meanings only in relation to the categorematic words which are capable of referring to their referents.

2.10 According to Pāṇini, 'pada' or a word has either a verbal inflection or a nominal inflection (suptiñantam padaṃ;

Pāṇini Sūtra 1.4.14). Akṣapāda Gautama (2.2.60) also supports Pāṇini (Vibhaktyantāḥ padaṃ). Accordingly nāma pada (noun) and kriyāpada (verb) refer to their respective referents. But there are words like prepositions e.g., upasarga, nipāta etc. which do not have declensional inflections;[15] and such words find their meanings when they are used along with padas (words proper) in the meaningful sentences.

Notes and References

1. Patañjali : *Mahābhāṣya* (Paspaśā), edited and translated by Chatterjee, K. C. (1957), Mukherjee & Co., Calcutta, p. 1.
2. *Mahābhāṣya*, p. 2.
3. *Mahābhāṣya*, p. 4 : Pratītapadārthako loke dhvaniḥ śabda ityuchyate.
4. (i) *Mahābhāṣya*, pp. 46-7.
   (ii) Hiriyanna, M. (1957) : *Indian Philosophical Studies* (Vol. II, p. 73); Kavyalaya Publishers, Mysore.
   (iii) Matilal, B. K. (1971) : *Epistemology, Logic and Grammar in Indian Philosophical Analysis*, Moutan, The Hague, Paris, pp. 106-8.
   (iv) Mādhavācharya : Sarvadarśanasaṃgraha, translated by Cowell, G. B. and A. G. Gough (1961) : Chaukhamba Sanskrit Series Office, Varanasi, pp. 217-218.
5. (i) *Sarva-darśana-saṃgraha*, (op. cit.) p. 217.
   (ii) *Indian Philosophical Studies*, (op. cit.) pp. 73-74.
   (iii) *Mahābhāṣya*, (op. cit.) p. 47.
6. Chatterjee, S. C. (1931) : *Nyāya Theory of Knowledge*, Calcutta University, Calcutta, p. 358.
7. (i) Gautama : *Nyāya-darśana* (*Nyāya-sūtras* with *Nyāya Bhāṣya,*) edited by Ganganath Jha and Dundiraja Sastri (1925) : Chaukhambh Sanskrit Series, Varanasi. Nyāya-sūtras: 2-2.68-71.

(ii) Nyāya Sūtras : 2.2.63; Nyāya-bhāṣya 2.2.63, *Nyāya Theory af Knowledge*, (op. cit), p. 359.

8. (i) Dharma Rāja : *Vedānta Paribhāṣā*, edited and translated by Swāmi Mādhavānanda (1972), Advaita Ashrama, Calcutta, pp. 93-94.
   (ii) Śāstra-dīpikā Ch. I, referred in *Nyāya Theory of Knowledge*, (op. cit), p. 360.
9. (i) *Patañjali's Mahabhāṣya*. 2.1.1.
   (ii) *Epistemology, Logic and Grammar* (op. cit), p. 108.
10. (i) *Epistemology, Logic and Grammar* (op. cit), pp. 106-7.
   (ii) Raja K. (1969) : *Indian Theories of Meaning*, Adyar Library and Research Centre, Madras, pp. 75-76.
11. Nyāya-sūtra 2.2.68 : Vyaktyākṛti jātyastu padārthaḥ.
   Nyāya-sūtra 2.2.69 : Vyaktirguṇa viśeṣāśrayo mūrtiḥ.
   Nyāya-sūtra 2.2.70 : Ākṛtirjjātiliṅgakhyā.
   Form is the token of genus. The genus is recognised by certain collocation of the dowlap which is a form.
   Nyāya-sūtra 2.2.71. Samānaprasavātmrikājātiḥ. Genus is that which produces the concept.
12. (i) Bhāṣā-pariccheda and Nyāya-siddhānta-muktāvalī (Vol. II) of Viśvānātha ed. by Bhatta, V. M. Balaganapati, Mysore, S. 81.
   (ii) Śabdaśakti prakāśikā cited in *Nyāya Theory of Knowledge*, p. 361.
13. (i) *Tarka-saṃgraha with Tarka-dipikā* by Annaṁbhaṭṭa, edited by Athalye Y. V. and M. R. Bodas. Bandarkar Oriental Research Institute, Poona. S : 59.
14. Alston, W. P. (1964) : *Philosophy of Language*, Prentice Hall India, p. 12.
15. Matilal, B. K. (1985) : *Logic, Language and Reality*, Motilal Banarsidass, New Dehli, pp. 400-1.

3

Advaita Theory of Meaning

3.1. The Advaita theory of knowledge presupposes theory of meaning because understanding of a scriptural sentence depends upon the apprehension of the meaning (artha) of that sentence.[1] And the meaning of a given sentence is the product of the meanings of the component words of that sentence. Generally a word is any sound or combination of sounds or written/printed symbol. A word as a symbol is capable of conveying an idea. According to Advaita tradition meaning of an expression is characterised by a universal (jāti). Consequently there is the distinction between a word and its meaning. Śaṅkara says that the mere word does not constitute the object and word is different from denoted object (na śabdamātram artha svarūpam sambhavati śabdārthyor bhedāt).[2] For example the word 'Brahma' means a man who will be Brahman is not a mere sound.[3] There is an interesting argument concerning universal (jāti) theory of meaning in Brahma-sūtra-bhāṣya (1-3-28) : words designate not units or individuals but the universal and the universal is eternal (ākṛtibhiśca śabdānām sambandho na vyaktibhih ākṛtinām ca nityatvam).[4] Universal or generic attribute (jāti) is the common property which characterises all the individuals comprised in a given class. For example, the generic attribute 'cowhood' is found in all the cows. And it is in virtue of the manifestation of the universal 'cowhood' in a particular animal which is called as a cow distinguished from non-cows.

3.2. It may be asked if a word means a universal how does it denote an individual ? How does the word 'cow' is applicable to an individual cow if the word 'cow' means' cowness' ? In ordinary paralance when we say, "The cow is white", we mean only a particular cow, but not the entire class of cow.

It is replied that capacity of signifying individuals belongs to a generic attribute i.e. jyāti but not to individuals because individuals are infinite in number.[5] The relationship between cows and cowhood is eternal (beginningless) and the distinguishing characteristic i.e. genus of the cows is not created afresh every time an individual cow is born because individual forms of substances, qualities and actions alone can have origin but not so their distinguishing general characteristics (genus)[6]. Further individuals of a certain genus may be infinite in number and hence it is impossible to comprehend the relation of a word with all of them. Thus, even though many individuals are born in addition to the existing individuals of genus what remians constant is the generic character, and with reference that generic characteristic the corresponding word functions to designate it.

However the knowledge of the universal (jāti) which constitutes the meaning of a word also leads to the knowledge of a particular subsumed under it. Because in experience universal and particular are synthesised together as unsiversalized particular. To the question how are individuals known through generic character (jāti) ? the answer is that the same cognition that comprehends a generic attribute also comprehends the individuals.[7] That is to say that a direct mening (vācyārtha) is a generic attribute (jāti) and indiviuals are comprehended by implicatibn (lakṣaṇā). For example the word 'cow' primarily designates cowness and secondarily a particular cow. It is clear that the word 'cow' primarily stands for the universal concept, 'cowness', in other words the word 'cow' connotes cowness. To this effect Prof. D.M. Datta[8] observes : "the meaning of the word 'cow' being the concept that defines and determines the use of the word, can on no score be the particular animal, it must be essential common attribute which brings all such animals under the same category."

3.3. If universal (jāti) functions as a primary meaning of an expression, how is universal related to particular ? The question has global relevance. Long back Plato entertained such question to formulate his theory of Ideas. According to that theory, Ideas as universals have an independent existence and are not connected to corresponding particulars of experience. Ideas alone constitute the eternal transcendental realm of reality. Accodingly there is no bridge between a universal (Idea) and particular. But according to Advaita-vedāntins jāti or universal is not a mysterious eternal entity but consisted of the common denominator of essential characteristics actually existing in a set of individuals.

3.4. Although every word is capable of imparting a primary meaning, there are instances where a primary meaning of a certain word does not fit in a given context. Accordingly by reason of consistency contextual meaning is to be given to that word. That is to say the direct or primary meaning is to be set aside and secondary meaning is to be attached to the expression so that the word fits well in that context. To this effect Śaṃkara gives a precaution that "if literal meaning does not fit in, then alone the metaphorical meaning is to be adopted."[9]

Thus in Advaita tradition two types of meaning are postulated. The primary meaning or literal meaning (vācyārtha=śakyārtha=mukhyārtha=abhidheyārtha) and secondary meaning or metaphorical meaning (lakṣaṇā). A word functions metaphorically if it denotes a referent other than its normal one. A metaphoric usage is an application of name or descriptive term to an obect to which it is not literally applicable. Metaphoric usage is justified if the literal or primary meaning of an expresson leads to inadeqvate (meanigless) sentence. However the actual referent referred by the word is taken as different from its normal one but in some ways metaphorical meaning is to be related with primary meaning. The relation of metaphorical meaning to primary meaning is either through comparison or through some other relation. Thus the function of a word denoting a referent different from its usual or primary one, but related to primary meaning is called lakṣaṇā.[11]

3.5. C_1 : There are two types of implied meaning or metaphorical meaning (lakṣaṇā) : pure implication (kevala-lakṣaṇā) and double implication (lakṣita-lakṣaṇā).[12] In pure implication there is the direct relation to the primary meaning of word. For example in the sentence "The hamlet is on the Ganges" (Gaṅgāyām ghoṣaḥ) the word 'Ganges' refers by virtue of pure implication to the bank of the river although it is directly related to the stream, so that given metaphorical sentence turns out to be true but literally as it is false. In case of double implication (lakṣita-lokṣaṇā) indirect relation to the primary meaning is implied. Usual example given is the word 'dvirepha' which signifies two rs. The word 'dvirepha' by pure implication stands for the word 'bhramara'. Then by a second implication of the word dvirepha, through the intermediary word 'bhramara' we get its meaning, namely a bee (madhukara).[13]

3.6. There is another classification (C2) of lakṣaṇā according to which implied meanings are classified into three :[14] (i) Jahallakṣaṇā (exclusive implication), (ii) Ajahallakṣaṇā (inclusive implication) and (iii) Jahadjahallaksṇā (quasi inclusive implication). In different kinds of lakṣaṇās there is degree of relation to the primary meaning and consequently primary meaning of a word connot be excluded completely; but its retention may be to a greater or lesser extent.[15]

(i) Jahallakṣaṇā[16] (exclusive implication) : – In this type of lakṣanā there will be incompatability in the syntactical relation between terms, if the primary meaning of a word is considered. Consequently in order to make the sentence meaningful and also true primary sense has to be given up to a gteat extent so that another meaning connected with it fits in a given context. For exmample in a sentenc like 'gaṅgāyām ghoṣaḥ' (The hamlet is on the Ganges), the primary meaning of the term 'gaṅgā'

(Ganges) is to be set aside and the secondary meaning 'the bank of the Ganges' is to be adopted so that the given sentence turns out to be true. Thus by virtue of literal meaning of the word gaṅgā (Ganges) the entire sentence becomes paradoxical and false. However, what makes a given metaphorical sentence true is its correspondance with fact and every true proposition is capable of being exptessed in a literal sentence. Therefore a true metaphorical sentence can be equated to corresponding true literal sentence. Thus the given metaphorical sentence "gaṅgāyām ghoṣaḥ" (The hamlet is on the Ganges) is true if it is equivalent to true literal sentence "The hamlet is on the bank of the Ganges."

(ii) Ajahallakṣaṇā[17] (inclusive implication) :—The characteristic of this lakṣaṇā is that the primary meahing of an expression is retained and interpreted by implied meaning so that the given sentence turns out to be true. In other words the secondary meaning includes primary meaning. For example the sentence 'Chattriṇo-yānti' (umbrellas are going) implies through ajahallakṣaṇā that 'a group of people with umbrellas are going ? According to the primary meaning the sentence does not turn out to be true. Similarly the sentence 'śoṇo dhāvati' literally means 'red is running' which is false because red as a colour cannot run by itself. And consequently the word 'red' is interpreted as 'red horse' so that the resultant sentence 'the red horse is running' turns out to be a true sentence.

(iii) Jahadajahallakṣaṇā[18] (quasi-inclusive iimplication):—In this lakṣaṇā only a part of primary meaning is preserved while the other part is given up. Since the complete primary meaning leads to inconsistent sentence and partial meaning leads to true sentence, consequently that part of primary meaning leading to inconsistency is to be given up. Consider a sentence like "So' yam devadattaḥ." (This is that Devadatta), the term 'saḥ' (that) denotes to Devadatta as characterised by the past time and space, and other accidental properties and the term 'ayam' (this) has reference to the same Devadatta conditioned by present time, space and other personal features. Thus exclusive literal meaning of the sentence 'So' yam devadattaḥ' lead to inconsistency, for the components words 'saḥ' (that) and 'ayam' (this) refer to different sets of properties. And in order to resolve inconsistency, direct meanings of the terms 'sah and' 'ayam' are to be set aside and the primary meaning of 'Devadattaḥ' is retained because that meaning functions as a common denominator in changing personality.

3.7. In order to understand the import of 'great saying' (mahāvākya), tattvamasi (that thau art) incompatible primary meanings are to be given up and in virtue of the remaining part of primary meaning truth of that sentence is to be decided. The primary meanings themselves cannot characterse the truth of the sentence, for the primary meaning (vācyārtha) of tat (that) is akparokṣatvādi viśiṣṭa caitanya (consciousness characterised by immediacy) and the term tvam (thou) has the primary meaning parokṣatvādi viśiṣṭa caitanya (consciousness characterised by mediacy).[19] In order to arrive at true (yathārtha) tatvamasi vākya incompatable meanings are to be set aside. The remaing primary meaning characterises the truth of 'tatvamasi'. Mediacy and immediacy as parts of the primary meanings are to be removed so that pure conscioueness manifested through an individual and the consciousness of Īśvara are qualitatively identical. Therefore 'tatvamasi' (That thou art) means the consciousness of Īśvara (God) is the consciousness of an individual.

Above three types of secondary meaning (lakṣaṇā) are to be subsumed under pure implication (kevala-lakṣaṇā) because in each of the three secondary meanings (of C2) there is direct relation to a primary meaning. The relation of secondary meaning to the primary meaning is minimum in jahallakṣaṇā whereas it is maximum in ajahallakṣaṇā for in it primary meaning is combined with secondary meaning.

3.8. In western logic two types of terms are held to be non-connotative: (i) proper names and (ii) some abstract names. Examples of the former are 'John', 'London', 'England' etc. and of the latter are 'whitness', length', 'virtue' etc. A term is said to be non-connotative if it signifies an object only or an attribute only. A connotative term denotes object and implies an attribute.[20] A proper name has only denotation but no connotation (intension). However, a common noun like 'human being' has both a connotation and a denotation; it connotes those properties of animality and rationality which are specified in the definition of the term 'human' which denotes all humans. But proper name only denotes and lacks connotation. Abstract terms like whitness only connote but do not denote anything.

3.9. In Advaita semantics a proper name like 'Venus' become meningful by connoting 'Venusness' 'morning starness' and 'evening star-ness which constitute the primary meaning. To this effect the author of Sarvadarśana[22] Saṃgraha states: "The universal (jāti) connoted by a proper name (saṃjñā) like Devadatta is proved on the basis of the knowledge of his identity . . . through all the changing stages of childhood, boyhood and youth."

Another class of non-connotative terms are singular abstract terms. For example terms like 'whiteness', 'virtuousness' are non-connotative. Such terms signify attributes only. However in Indian context abstract terms are said to be connotative, that is to say that they possess both reference (denotation) and sense (connotation).

Importance of Advaita semantics becomes clearer in the consideration of the role of reason according to which criterion of intelligibility in the light of reoson functions as a semantic criterion to decide the nature of purportful scripture.

Notes and References

1. *Śāṅkarabhāṣya* on *Bṛhadāraṇyaka-upaniṣad*; 1.3.1 : Avipa-rītārthapratipatteḥ śreyaḥ praptyupapatteḥ lokavat. Śaṃkara analogically argues that as in secular matters correct understanding alone can lead to our well being so also in scriptural matters. Therefore correct understand-ing of the meaning of scriptural passages is necessary.

2. *Bṛhadāraṇyaka-upaniṣad-bhāṣya*. 1.4.10.
3. *Bṛhadāraṇyaka-upaniṣad-bhāṣya*. 1.4.10; Swami Madhavananda's translation, p. 102. (Advaita Ashrama, Calcutta).
4. *Śaṃkara's bhāṣya* on *Brahma-sūtra*. 1.3.28. Swami Gambhiranand's translation, p. 209. (Advaita Ashrama, Calcutta).
5. (I) *Vedānta-paribhāṣā*, p. 94. Tachha jātireva, na vyakteḥ, vyaktināmānantyena gurutvāt. Edited and translated by Swami Madhavananda, Advaita Ashrama, Calcutta,
   (ii) Śaṅkara's bhāṣya on Brahma-sūtra, 1.3.28.
6. Śaṅkara's bhāṣya on Brahma-sūtra, 1.3.28.
7. Vedānta-paribhāṣā (op. cit.); p. 94.
   Jātervyakti samāna saṃvitsamvedyatvaditi brumah.
8. Prof. D. M. Datta (1972) : *The Six ways of Knowlng*, Calcutta : University, Calcutta, p. 275.
9. (i) Śaṃkara's bhāṣya on Praśnopaniṣad. 6.3 : Tatra hi gauṇi kalpanā śabdasya yatra mukhyārtho na sambhavati.
   (ii) Swami Ātmānanda (1960) : *Sri Śaṃkara's Teachings in His Own Words*. Bharatiya Vidya Bhavan, Bombay, p. 86.
10. Vedānta paribhāṣā (op. cit.) p. 93.
    Padarthasca dvividhāḥ-śakyo laksyascheti tatra śaktirnām padānāmartheṣu mukhya vrttiḥ.
11. (i) Vedānta-paribhāṣā (op. cit); p. 96. Śakyasākrat sambandhaḥ kevalalakṣaṇā . . . śakya paramparāsambandhenarthantara pratitistatra lakṣita lakṣaṇā.
    (ii) Prof. K. Raja (1969). *Indian Theories of meaning*. Adyar Library and Research Centre, Madras, p. 231.
12. Vedānta paribhāṣā (op. cit) pp. 96-9; Laksaṇā ca dvividho kevala lakṣaṇā lakṣita lakṣaṇā ceti.
13. Vedānta-paribhāṣā (op. cit) pp. 96-7.
14. Vedānta-paribhāṣā (op. citd) pp. 97-98.
15. (i) Śaṅkara's Brahma-sūtra bhāṣya, 4.1.6 : Lakṣaṇā ca yathāsambhavam Samnikṛṣṭena viprakṛṣṭena vā svārtha sambandhena pravartate. Swami Gambhirananda's translation (op. cit) p. 829.
    (ii) *Indian Theories of meaning* (op. cit), p. 2S9.

16. Vedānta-paribhaṣā (op. cit), p. 97.
17. Vedānta-paribhāṣā op. cit, p. 97.
18. Vedānta-paribhāṣā op. cit, pp. 97-8.
19. *Vedānta-sāra* edited and translated with notes by Prof. M. Hiriyanna 1962 Oriental Book Agency, Poona, pp. 9-10; 36-39.
20. *The Six Ways of Knowing* (op. cit), p. 281.
21. *Sarva-darśana Saṃgraha* of Mādhavacārya, Pāṇini System. Translated by Cowell G.B. and A.G. Gough (1961) : Chaukhamba Sanskrit Series office, Varanasi, Pp. 272-218.
22. *The Six ways of knowing* op. cit), pp. 286-8.

4

Sense and Reference in Navya-Nyāya*

4.1. In Navya-nyāya semantics we find referential theory of meaning; accroding to that theory meaning of an expression or a word is due to its reference to certain object in the universe. However in its through going explication of śabdārth (word-meaning), Navya-nyāya subscribes to a peculiar theory of meaning technically called as : jāti-viśiṣṭa-vyakti-vāda (theory of meaning of an individual as qualiffied by universal). The theory implies that functional relation between a word and its referent is called śakti (denotative function), which is the conventional aspect of potentiality of a word.[1] And the meaning of an expression obtained through the relation of śakti is called śakyārtha or vācyārtha (primary meaning[2]). There is another aspect of meaning called lakṣaṇā or lakṣyārtha (secondary or metaphorical meaning). Lakṣaṇā is parasitic on vācyārtha.

4.2. One of the modern trends in understanding Navya-nyāya semantics is to interprete the concept of vācyārtha (primary meaning) in terms of theory of sense (sinn) and

* This paper was read in the 63rd Session of Indian Philosophical Congress, held, at Pondicherry University, Pondicherry, from 28th to 30th Dec. 1988.

reference (bedeutung) as formulated in Fregean semantics.[3] I wish to inquire about the adequacy of the claim that Nyāya concept of meaning can be understood in terms of sense and reference. However it is necessary to understand first the concepts of sense and reference as conceived by Frege.

4.3. The distinction between sense and reference was initially introduced by Gottlob Frege[4] in order to solve a puzzle about identity. His question was : whether identity is a relation between objects or between names or signs of objects. If we regard identity as a relation between objects, Frege reasons that the statment 'a=b' should mean the same thing as 'a=a' if 'a=b' is true. And in that case 'a' and 'b' are two names for the same object and consequently 'a=b' cannot tell anything more than 'a=a'. Since statements of the from 'a=b' if true are sometimes highly informative, however 'a=a' is never informative as it is a tautology. In other words 'a=b' and 'a=a' have different congnitive status. Hence above interpretation of identity as a relation in which a thing can stand only to itself is not correct. Frege illustrates the informative characteristic of 'a=b' by stating that it was an astronomical discovery that morning star and the evening star are one and the same planet namely, venus, Frege arrives at this distinction between sense and reference of signs on the ground that the reference of an expression is the object named or denoted by it and the sense of that expression contains the mode of presentation. For example two expressions : morning star' and 'evening star' have the same reference, the planet venus but different senses. By virtue of this difference in sense the statement 'morning star is eveing star' yields factual knowledge.

4.4. It may be suggested that the distinction between śakyārtha (primary meaning) and śakyārthavacchedaka of a word or name is parallel to reference and sense distinction. Another reason for such an interpretation is that in Navya nyāya semantics also there is the structural difference between 'morning star is morning star' and 'morning star is evening star' by virtue of the difference in their viṣayaytās (contentness).

4.5. However, I think the two distinctions donot coincide. Because śakyārtha as primary meaning is characterised by its denotative function and consequently denotes an individual (vyakti); and sakyātavacchedaka is just the limiting property or limitor of śakyārtha. In other words if śakyārtha is primary meaning (denotation) then śakyārthavacchedaka means primary meaning-ness i.e. denotationness. And primary meaning-ness as essence of denotation cannot be interpreted in terms of sense (sinn as conceived by Frege). Further sense-reference distriction seems to be valid only in case of singular terms like 'morning star' and 'evening star'. And it is difficult ro extend the alleged distinction to general terms.

4.6. I think there is some plausible way to understand Nyāya concept of meaning in terms of sense-reference distinction. Since the meaning of a word primarily stands for an individual; the denotative aspect of that meaning is similar to Frege's reference. And as Frege's reference of an expression refers to its referent so also a word (pada) denotes an object or individual. Meaning according to Nyāya is also to be a characterised by a certain sort of essential or generic character which may be treated as connotative aspect of a meaningful term.[6] To certain extent reference-sense distinction is analogous to denotation connotation distinction. In this way Nyāya theory of meaning accommodates sense and reference distinction. However certain differences between the two theories cannot be overlooked. Nyāya semantics as referential theory of meaning accomodates every meaningful expression, such as proper names, pronouns, common names and even verbs also. But Frege's theory of meaning has a limited application to proper names including, perhaps, definite descriptions. However Frege's theory has been challenged recently by the rival theory of direct reference without committing itself to the notion of sense.[7] The theory of direct reference does not deny the relationship between an expression and its referent but in this theory, there is no necessity of sense. On the controry Fregean theory of reference as a theory of indirect reference considers 'sense' as an indispensable factor for a reference. Accordingly every referring expressing must have sense and reference of an expression is parasitic on sense. However sense of an expression need not have reference or a non-referring expression may have sense. The theory of direct reference as a reactionary takes its point of departure by rejecting the orthodox Fregean semantics. And it is believed that theory of direct reference subscribes to the naive view held by Mill according to which proper names only denote but do not connote.[8]

Following are some of the important arguments advanced in favour of the theory of direct reference.[9] The arguments are in the forms of modal argument, epistemological argument and semantic argument. Let me consider these arguments briefly in the sequel for evaluation.

(i) *The modal agument* :—This kind of argument is due to Kripke. According to his theory of rigid designators a proper name just designates or denotes its referent without connoting any attribute. The proper name 'Shakespeare' is non-descriptional ; however it is a rigid designator because 'Shakespeare' designates the same individual in every possible world. Even though the name 'Shakespeare' means 'the person', who is the English Playwright who wrote *Hamlet*, *Macbeth* and *Romeo and Juliet*; according to modal argument the name Shakespeare continues to designate its referent without the alleged definite description mentioned above. Hence the name 'Shakespeare' is non descriptionl in terms of the proparties metnioned.

(ii) *The Epistemological argument*: According to this theory the proposition 'Shakespeare is the author of *Hamlet*, does not yield any apriori knowledge, because 'Shakespeare' does not necessarily imply the definite descriptions 'the author of *Hamlet*'. Thus orthodox Fregean theory is wrong in attributing the definite description to a proper name as a necessary property. In other words assuming that orthodox Freagean theory is correct then it would follow that the sentence 'Shakespeare is the author of *Hamlet*' should convey information that which is knowable a apriori solely by reflection on the concepts without sense-experience; however this is not so because the truth value of the sentence is a function of empirically observable fact.

Thus a name with respect to certain type of definite description is considered to be non-discriptional and it directly designates its referent even if does not satisfy the condition of definite descriptions.

(iii) *The Semantic Argument*:—This argument implies that in order to fix the referential meaning of a term there is no need to appeal to set of properties and without the cluster of properties one can understand the semantic structure of a given expression. Consequently to understand a certain sentence containing a proper name like 'Thales' one need not look into the descriptional aspect of that term. Consider a sentence 'Thales is the Greek philosopher who held that all is water'. According to Fregean theory of reference the associated definite description serves as sense which is indispensable to fix up the reference of the term (Thales). Thus on orthodox view, the name 'Thales, should have the description. However according to the semantic argument it might have happened due to strange coincidence that there was another Greek hermit philosopher who did in fact hold the view that 'all is walter.

4.7. According to these arguments names directly refer to the corresponding referents without the media of Fregean sense. But the question is whether these arguments totally dispense with Fregean sense in the postulation of reference of an expresion? However there is room for Fregean theory of sense in the theory of direct reference.

The theory of direct reference is not entirely independent of the theory of sense, because contextual factors in reference imply the need of sense components in the structure of reference. For instance according to Kripke,[10] the descriptional expression is used only to 'fiix the reference' of the non-discriptional term, but paradoxically not to supply it with a Fregean sense. In this paradoxical situation, Kripke imples that rigid designators as directly referring expressions need Fregean sense in the from of description. But, then Kripke seems to be inconsistent if he thinks that descriptional Fregean sense component is indispensable to fix up the reference of an experession. In a similar way it is said that historical chains of communications provide the reference for an expression.

Thus in the above three arguments there is an indirect reference to sense and the theory of rigid (direct) reference is not entirely free from Frege's concept of sense.

Eventhough the alleged Fregean sense-reference distinction is not clearly present in Nyāya semantics, it is there are least implicitly. The implicit sense-reference distinction can be made explicit along with the third essential semantic component namely a kind of relation that exists between sense and reference. In western semantic including that of Frege's one no attempt has been made to postulate a sort of relation that holds good between sense and reference. Praper names likes Devadatta refer to a certain individual characterised by Devadatt-hood. The semantic situation implies that an expression 'Devadatta' applies or refers to its referent to be called by the name 'Devadatta' whose characteristic nature is understood by another abstract noun—'Devadatta-hood'. Two relations are involved here are relation r_1 that holds between the name 'Devatta' and the person called Devadatta; and this relation is conventional; secondly the relation r_2 that which exists between two experessions 'Devadatta' and 'Devadatta-hood' is a necessary relation. And the abstract noun 'Devadatta-hood' is much more stronger than the definite description because it plays a cardinal role in identifying a person. Consider the following two sentences.

(i) Devadatta is the son of Śvetaketu.
(ii) This is that Devadatta.

In (i) the definite description 'the son of Śvetaketu' does not help to fix up the reference of the term Devdatta even though at some time it may help to identify that individual because even a person who is unaware of the said defiinite description can identify the person as Devatta. For instance in (ii) the same Devadatta is identified correctly eventhough 'this and 'that' refer to the same individual sperated by considerable gap of time. What has helped the identifier to identity the same person as Devadatta is 'Devadatta-hood'[11] which is not an adventitious property as definite description (s) because even in the absence of cluster of definite descriptions 'Devadatta-hood' remains constant. Devadatta is essentially qualified by Devadatta-hood. In case of natural kind terms like 'water', 'cow' etc., 'water-ness' and 'cow-hood'. stand for essences of respective referents.

4.8. In modal semantics general terms[12] like 'a cow', 'water', 'gold' etc. are analysed in the framework of proper names. Consequently it has been shown that general terms are like singular names or proper names. Even in such a theory of general terms along with the referential aspect there is also sense-component which is again indispensible to the structure of a general term. There are several descriptions attributed to general term. For example in natural kind term like 'water' there are cluster of descriptions such as 'a colourless liquid', 'used for quenching thirst', 'falls from the the clouds' etc. Of course all these properties are not necessarily the properties of water only. There may be some other liquid or substance possessing the said properties. However the sentence 'water is H_2O'[13] implies that the essence of water as water-hood which is understood in the form of its micro-structure charcterised as a set of water molecules where each molecule is structured by the combination of two atoms of hydrogen and an atom of oxygen. Similary a general term 'gold' reveals its essence in the from of a unique definite description, 'the element having atomic member 79'. Thus general terms like proper names not only refer to their referents but also reveal essence of the referents. And the characterisation of essences in case of general terms function as senses.[14] Thus in case of theory of direct reference the thoeory of sense is indispensable. And this kind of understanding of joint theory of sense-and reference fits in the framwork of Nyaya semantics qualified by certain essential or generic character, which is cannotative aspect of a meaning-ful term.

Notes and References

1. Tarka-dīpika : (TD) 59; Siddhānta-muktāvalī (SM) 81.
2. TD : 59; SM : 81.
3. Prof. B. K. Matilal is optimistic about the interaction between Nyāya semantics and Gottlob Frege's classical

distinction between sense and reference. He has made some interesting attempt in that direction in his works :

i *Navya-nyāya Doctrine of Negation*
Harvard University Press, 1968 pp. 26-27.

ii *Epistemology, Logic and Grammer in Indian Philosophical Analysis*, Mount, The Hague, Paris, 1971, pp. 119-122.

Although in this work the author has made an attempt to analyse Vyādi's (old Grammarian) theory of meaning in Frege's terminology, the approach is relevant to Nyāya semantics also because of certain similarity between Nyāya semantics and Vyādi's theory of meaning. However my treatment differs from Matilal's interpretation (see 4.5-6).

4. "On Sense and Reference' in *Philosophical Writings of Gottlob Frege* Translated by Geach P.T and Max. Black, Blackwell, Oxford 1960, pp. 56-78.
5. Matilal 1968, pp. 26-27.
6. *A Primer of Indian Logic* by K. Sastri. Kuppuswami Sastri Research Institute, Madras 1961, pp. 259-60.
7. Authors like Donnellan, Kaplan, Putnam and Kripke have brought considerable resistance to orthodox Fregean sense-reference distinction. Brief accounts of these theories have been stated by Salmon. N. U. in his *Reference and Essence* 1982 Basil Black Well, Oxford.
8. It is said that Mill is more-or-less right about singular' names but wrong about general names. Kripke, S. 1980 : *Naming and Nacessity* Basil, Blackwell, Oxford.
9. The three arguments referred here have been elaborately considered by Salmon cited above , pp. 23-32.
10. Kripke 1980 op. cit thinks that reference fixers are normally in the form of definite descriptions qualified as Fregean sense. However there are also definite descriptions which are indispensable as they imply the essence of a thing. To this effect Kripke's distinction between ordinary definite descriptions and necessary definite descriptions is not clearly brought out.

11. *In Sarva-darśana-saṃgraha,* Madhavācārya states the Nyāya position in Akṣapāda adhyāya that proper names like Devadatta possess Devadatta-hood.
12. See Salmon 1982 : op. cit pp. 42-68.
13. Putnam, H 1975 *Mind, Language and Reality* Cambridge University Press, gives interesting analysis of 'Water is H_2O', pp. 223-5. See also Salmon 1982 (op cit pp. 94-99.
14. Salmon 1982 negates commitment of essentialism in modal semantic as affirmed by Kripke, Putnam etc., but tries to argue against essentialist claims in modal semantics. However Salmon's arguments are not convincing because realistic modal semantic ought to presuppose essence.

5

The Concept of Viṣayāta in Navya-Nyāya*

5.1. A cardinal tenet of Navya-nyāya system is that every cognition (*jñāna*) must have *viṣayatā* (contentness).[1] Epistemology of Navya-nyāya implies that every cognition refers to an object (*viṣaya*) and consequently the realism of Navya-nyāya postulates a relation between a cognition and corresponding object, so that every cognition is explicated by virtue of contentness or *viṣayatā*. By virtue of *viṣayatā* a truth value of a cognition (*jñāna*) may be explicated; *i.e.* a cognition is true if the *viṣayatā* of that cognition reveals the structure of reality or state of affair; even false cognition has *viṣayatā* for the negation of true cognition is false cognition and the denial of *viṣayatā* of false cognition gives rise to the *viṣayatā* of true cognition. But what is the logical status of *viṣayatā* in Navya-nyāya system? The specific object of this inquiry is to analyze the notion of *viṣayatā* (contentness) in terms of contemporary conceptual framework.

5.2. Jñānas (cognitions) are classified into *savikalpaka jñāna* (qualificative congnition) and *nivikalpaka jñāna* (non-

* This article is reprinted with the permission from the Editor of *Brahma-vidya. The Adyar Library Research Bulletin* 1984, Vol, 48 ; Pp. 65-67 ; The Adyar Library and Research Centre, Madras.

qulificative cognition or indeterminate cognition).[2] Normally qualificative cognitions are capable of being expressed in language but *nirvikalaka jñāna* or indeterminate cognition is, in principle, incapable of being characterized in language.[3] But both *savikalpaka* and *nirvikalpaka jñāna-s* possess *viṣayatā* (contentness). Let us first consider qualificative cognition in order to begin an inquiry into the nature of *viṣayatā*. A qualificative cognition is necessarily propositional because it is a bearer of truth value and consequently a qualificative cognition is expressed in cognitive language in the form of a declarative sentence, true or false. A declarative sentence is true if the corresponding cognition is true, otherwise the sentence is false.

5.3. A qualificative cognition consists of three elements namely, *viśeṣyatā* (qualificandness) *prakāratā* (qualifierness) and *saṃsargatā* (relationness) holding between *viśeṣyatā* and *prakāratā* (*viśeṣaṇatā*). And these three elements are known as *viṣayatās*,[4] that is to say, the three elements of cognition come under a common category of *viṣayatā* (contentness). For example, in the cognition 'The pot is blue', the word 'pot' designates qualificand, the term 'blue' stands for qualifier and the inherence is the relation by virtue of which blue colour resides in the pot. Thus *viṣayatā* as a cognitive content has three sub-categeries in which *viśeṣyatā*, *prakāratā* and *saṃsargatā* are the class names for the contents referred to the qualificand qualifier and relation respectively.

It may be asked whether 'qualificand'-qualifier relation is the same as substance and attribute relation. But as a matter of fact, the ideas of qualificandum and qualifier are to be differentiated from the ontological notions of substances and corresponding qualifying attributes,[5] because according to Nyāya thinkers qualificand is 'that which is characterized' by that which is a qualifier or character' (*prakāratā*). The concept of qualifier, (character), is wider than that of quality. It is true that in a cognition. 'The pot is blue', the pot is a substance, while blue is a quality which characterizes the pot. But in the cognition, 'The blue is different from white' it is not correct to say that blue is a substance and 'different from white' is a quality of blue. Blue as a quality remains as a quality without being the locus of another quality even if it functions as a qualificand. Thus qualificand and qualifier may function as substance. quality, activity relation or any other.[6]

In the thorough-going analysis of *viṣayatā* of a given qualificative cognition, Nyāya thinkers postulate several cognate species of *viṣayatā.* I think fuller analysis of a cognition like 'The pot is blue' reveals the following species of *viṣayatā* (contentness). (For slightly different denominations of *viṣayatā* see *Gaṅgeśa's Theory of Truth*, p. 36)

(i) The pot as *viśeṣya*, is the locus of pot-ness as viśeṣyatā.
(ii) The pot is *prakāra* (in 'potness is in pot').
(iii) The potness is the *prakāratā* of the pot.
(iv) Blue is *prakāra* of the pot.
(v) Blue is *viśesya* of blueness
(vi) Blueness is the *prakāratā* of blue.
(vii) The relation of inherence by virtue of which 'potness' and 'pot', 'blueness' and 'blue' and blue and 'pot' are related, so that in herence-ness is a relational viṣayatā.

However, ultimately there are three species of *viṣayatā*, namely, qualificand-ness qualifier-ness and relation-hood.

5.4. *Viṣayatā of nirvikalpaka jñāna* (or indeterminate cognition) is without characterization or qualifier (*niṣprakāraka*); and hence there is no qualifier and qualificand distinction in such a cognition. But that does not mean that *nirvikalpaka jñāna* has no *viṣayatā*; it must have *viṣayatā*, otherwise it ceases to be a *jñāna* or cognition. But how are we to understand the nature of *viṣayatā* in non-qualificative cognition ? It is normally believed that non-qualificative or indeterminate cognition is logically prior to determinate cognition and hence it is pre-judgmental in character.[7] Even in indeterminate cognition the corresponding object is experienced, but without conceptualization of that experience, so that only *sattā* or essence is apprehended without an apprehension of the properties. Every detrerminate cognition presupposes indeterminate cognition as a necessary condition. In a determinate cognition like 'This is a pot' there must have been the indeterminate cognition of pothood, without which determinate cognition is not possible. Gaṅgeśa in his *Tattva-cintāmaṇi*[8] observes that the cognition of cowhood is indeterminate in the determinate cognition, 'This is a cow.' Gaṅgeśa implies that the *viṣayatā* of every determinate cognition is grounded in the *viṣayatā* of indeterminate cognition. Accordingly, the *viṣaytā* of *nirvikalpaka* cognition is characterised as an entity of essence in the form of universal. In a cognition 'The pot is blue', potness' and 'blueness' are the *viṣayatā-s* of indeterminate cognition.

5.5. Now it is fairly clear that postulation of *viṣayatā* is indispensable in every conceivable form of cognition. It is true that *viṣayatā* of a cognition has certain bearing on objective reality according to Nyāya realism. Objective counterpart of a cognition may suggest the following possibilities.

(i) *Viṣayatā* is the same as the cognition.
(ii) *Viṣayatā* is the same as the object.[9]
(iii) *Viṣayatā* is the same as the relation.

Let us examine the possibilities in the sequel in order to understand the nature of *viṣayatā*.

(i) If *viṣayatā* is the same as the cognition then a certain true cognition may turn out to be false. Prof. B.K. Matilal has argued that true cognition like 'there are pot and cloth' may turn out to be false because the cognition has *viṣayatā* that is delimited by potness since cognition of a pot is component cognition of the given conjuction (*samūhālambana*). If (i) is true, the contentness present in pot would be identical with the contentness (*viṣayatā*) of cloth which is the same as cognition. But *viṣayatā* delimited by potness may occur in a locus other than the pot, say in the locus of cloth, which confirms the characterization of false cognition that 'a cognition is false if it has *viṣayatā* that is delimited by a certain property but occurs in a locus where that property does not occur.' The second possibility also leads to a certain difficulty, that objects may be the same but cognitions are different. It is possible to cognize separately a tree and a monkey and a relation of contact as discrete individuals at the same. But corresponding to three discrete individuals following two different cognitions take place :

(a) A cognition that 'a contact and a tree that has a monkey (on it)'.

(b) A cognition that 'a tree and a monkey and a contact.'

But Nyāya postulates that contentness or *viṣayatā* is a criterion to distinguish one cognition from another cognition. And the criterion of identity states that two cognitions are identical if and only if their *viṣayatās* as relational abstracts are identical but not when their objects are identical (Matilal 1966:64).

5.6. Now according to the third alternative, *viṣayatā* must be relation (or relational abstract). But what sort of relation is suitable to characterize *viṣayatā* ? The concept of relation arises in a cognitive situation regarding certain objective state-of-affair. Given an object like 'blue pot' there is a corresponding cognition that 'the pot is blue'. The relation between the object 'blue pot' and cognition 'the pot is blue' is not one of inherence (*sāmavāya*) because a cognition (*jñāna*) is a quality of the self[10] so that self is the locus of cognition but 'blue pot' is not the locus of the cognition. Nor does the relation of contact (*saṃyoga*) holds good between a cognition and its objects because the relation of contact operates only in the case of substances; but cognition is a quality. Nevertheless there must be some relation existing between an object and its cognition because for a given object certain cognition takes place. The relation is called *svrūapa-sambandha* (self-linking relation). And consequently the relation between cognition and object is known as *viṣayatā* (contentness).[11] Gaṅgeśa gives a negative characterization of *svarūpasaṃbandha* as follows :

'The relation which must be held to exist in a case where a determinate cognition (*viśiṣṭa-jñāna*) could not have been effected by another relation (*samavāya* or *saṃyoga*).[12]

The specific nature of self linking relation (*svarūpasambandha*) is further explicated as a species *vṛttiniyāmaka saṃ-*

bandha (*Nyāya-Kośa* 921) which is characterized as form of relation in which something functions as a locus for something else. For example in the relation of qualificand and qualifier, qualificand is the locus for the qualifier. In the cognition 'the pot is blue', the qualificand 'pot' is the locus for the qualifier 'blue' so that we may paraphrase the experssion as the qualifier 'blue' resides in the qualificand 'the pot'.

Gaṅgeśa's explicit charactarization of *viṣayatā* is as follows :

Jñāna-viṣaya-svarūpa-sambandhātiriktā yā viṣayatā.[13] (contentness is the from of self-linking relation pertaining to cognitive-content).

The definition implies that contentness as the relational abstract is abstracted from the content (*viṣaya*) of a cognition (*jñāna*). A defining property namely *jñāna-viṣaya* (cognitive content) imples that contentness is cognitive in character even though it is not indentical with the cognition.

5.7. The idea o*f viṣayatā* may be understood in another way, that is from the semantic standpoint, because only meaningful experession possesses *viṣayatā.* Normally an expression 'meaning of a cognition' equal to 'cognition' itself because *jñāna* or 'cognition' captures the sense of proposition or meaning. But the 'meaning' of an expression cannot be identified with the contentness or *viṣayatā* of that expression for the obvious reason that as seen above (i), it leads to certain odd results. If the meaning of an expression is synonymous with 'cognition' then it makes good sense to say that meaning (as a cognition) must possesses contentness or *viṣayatā.* Since every cognition has contentness and cognition is a bearer of truth value; both true and false cognitions must have *viṣayatā.* A cognition is true if the qualifier (*prakāra*) is related to the qualificand (*viśeṣaya*) throught *appropriate* relation (*saṃsarga*). Traditional thinkers are not explicit on the point concerning the role of *saṃsargatā* (relation-ness) in the characterization of truth value of a given cognition. However following C. Bhattacharya,[14] one may be inclined to say that the existence of a relation qualifies a cognitton as true non-existence of the relation makes it false.

5.8. For fuller understanding of the logical status of the concept of *viṣayatā* it is also desirable to consider the ontological status of *viṣyatā*. It is necessary to understand whether '*viṣayatā*' claims an independent status of category or it is to be subsumed under the category of cognition itself. There are two camps : According to Gaṅgeśa, *viṣayatā* is not an independent catagory, for it is considered as *svarūpa-saṃbandha* relation; according to Reghunātha, *viṣayatā*, a relational abstract as a separate entity canstitutes additional category.[15] Prof. Matilal thinks that there is an inclination of Raghunātha to accept new entities forming new categories (or *padārtha*) apart from the traditional scheme of seven categories. Gaṅgeśaa refutes the additional postulation of *viṣayatā* as an independent category. According to Gaṅgeśa[16] the recognition of additional category for *viṣayatā* leads to infinite regress (*anavsthā*) and hence he treats *viṣayatā* (contentenss) as relational abstract. Since a cognition implies contentness or *viṣayatā* postulation of *viṣayatā* to understand the nature of cognition is indispensable. Consequently a cognition cannot be thought of or formulated without the presupposition of *viṣayatā* (contentness). To this effect Prof. Matilal[17] thinks that contentness (*viṣayatā*) as a self-linking relation may belong to the same category as the cognition.

We may deduce the following important consequences from the above theory of *viṣayatā*:

(i) *Viṣayatā* (conteness) of a cognition gives the picture of a cognition in relation to reality or state-of-affair. That is to say *viṣayatā* is normally an object oriented factor pertaining to cognition.

(ii) *Viṣayatā* serves as a matrix of a cognition and a truth value of a given cognition emerges from the configuration of *viṣayatā* of that congnition; in other words, a specific mode of arrangement or configuration of qualificand-qualifier and relation determines the truth-value of that cognition.

(iii) Only cognitives sentences (declarative sentences) possess contentness or *viṣayatā*, for a cognition (*jñāna*) is capable of being expressed through declarative sentence only.

(iv) Certain semantic paradoxes like the 'laiar's paradox' may very easily be resolved by means of the postulation of *viṣayatā*. The liar's paradox is formulated in the sentence 'I am lying'. If the sentence is true then it is false. Or, if the sentence is false then it is true. The paradox is resolved by saying that the sentence about lying has no cognitive content or there is no *viṣayatā*. The paradox, therefore, disappears if the absence of contentness is made explicit.[18]

(v) Epistemologically[19] contentness of a cognition forms the nucleus of our knowledge claims. The reconstruction of this important point is as follows :

Viṣayatā or contentness is a from of *svarūpa-sambandha* (self-linking relation) by virtue of which a cognition reflects the nature of reality or a fact. *Viṣayatā* provides a conceptual scheme for a cognition so that a cognition functions as a bearer of truth value. Logical operations like affirmation and denial of a cognition are made possible through self-linking characteristic of contentness. Further, *viṣayatā* in an epistemologial situation exhibits a sort of transition to cognizer's belief. In other words, a *viṣayatā* in a logicals situation reveals a self-linking relation of its cognition to the respective object, in an epistemological or knowing situation *viṣayatā* or contentness of a knowledge claim implies self-linking relation of its cognition to the respective object through the cognizer's belief. For instance, *pramā* or knowledge implies true cognition (*yathārtha-jñāna*) justifled by means of its *pramāṇa*[20] used by the *pramātṛ* (knowing subject). *Viṣayatā* of true cognition must exhibit a relation to a knowing subject so that *pramā* or knowledge is formed.

Notes and References

1. The Sanskrit word '*Viṣayatā*' has been rendered as 'objectness' or 'contentness'. '*Viṣaya*' is a cognate word for '*Viṣayatā*' and '*Viṣaya*' captures the sense of the word

'object'. Therefore *viṣayatā* is rendered as 'objectness'. But a more accurate rendering of '*viṣayatā*' is 'contentness', for the word 'content' means the stuff of cognition and '*viṣayatā*' also stands for the elements of cognition. Thus I follow Prof. B. K. Matilal's rendering of viṣayatā as 'contentness' in his research monograph *The Navya Nyāya Doctrine of Negation*: Harvard University Press, Cambridge, Masschussetts, 1968, pp. 62-4.

Cf; *Nyāya Kośaḥ* by Jhalkikar Bhimacharya, Bhandarkar Oriental Research Institute, Poona, 1978, pp. 791-2: *Viṣayatā viṣayatāvān yathā ayam ghaṭaḥ iti jñāne ghaṭatvaṃ viṣayaḥ viṣayatā cātra viṣayaḥ ityākārakapratītisākṣikaḥ svarūpasambandhaviśeṣaḥ.*

2. *Tattva-cintāmaṇi Pratyakṣa-khaṇda* of Gaṅgeśa, edited by Shree Kamakhyanatha Tarka-vagisa; Motilal Banarsidass, New-Delhi, 1974, p. 809. Cf. *Tarka-saṃgraha* with *Tarka-dīpikā* of Annambhaṭṭa edited by Y. V. Athalye and M.R. Bodas, Bhandarkar Oriental Research Institute, Poona, 1974, verse 42.
3. *Niṣprakārakaṃ jñānaṃ nirvikalpakam, saprakārakaṃ jñānaṃ savikalpakam Tarka saṃgraha* 42. Cf. *Tattva-cintāmaṇi* pp. 809.
4. *Viṣayatā trividhā, viśeṣyatā, prakāratā, saṃsargatā ceti. Nyāya-kusumāñjali* of Udayana in *Nyāya-Kośaḥ*, pp. 791-2. *Tattvacintāmaṇī* pp. 401-2. *Navya-Nyāya Doctrine of Negation*, pp. 16-17.
5. *Gaṅgeśa's Theory of Truth*: by J. N. Mohanty, Viśva Bhārati, Santiniketan, 1966, pp. 33-4.
6. *The Elements of Indian Logic and Epistemology*, by Chandrodaya Bhattacharya, Modern Book Agency, Calcutta, 1975, p. 10.
7. *The Elements of Indian Logic and Epistemology*, pp. 38-9.
8. *Tattva-cintāmāṇi*, p. 823.
   Gaur iti savikalpakam api gotvāṃśe nirvikalpakam eva. The Elemente of Indian Logic and Epistemologi, p. 39, fn. 18.
9. I have borrowed the alternatives (i) and (ii) along with their analysis from *The Navya-Nyāya Doctrine of*

Negation, p. 63, but I have used (i) and (ii) along with (iii) which I have added for a different purpose, namely to inquire into the logical status of *viṣayatā* whereas Prof. Matilal has considered (i) and (ii) to evaluate the ontological status of *viṣayatā*.

10. *Jñanādhikaraṇam ātmā*: *Tarka-Saṃgraha*, 19. *Dravyāśritā jñeyā nirguṇā niṣkriyā guṇāḥ*: *Bhāṣāpariccheda*, 86.
11. *Indian Philosophy* Vol. II by Prof. S. Radhakrishnan, Blackie and Sons, Bombay, 1977, p. 124, fn. 3.
12. *Saṃbandhāntareṇa viśiṣṭapratītijanana-yogyatvam*. Cited in *Nyāya-Kośaḥ*. p. 1057. Cf. *Indian Philosophy* (Vol. II), p. 124.
13. *Tattva-cintāmaṇi*, p. 816.
14. *The Elements of Indian Logic and Epistemology*, p. 11.
15. *The Navya-nyāya Doctrine of Negation*,p. 62.
16. ibid.
17. ibid. p. 64.
18. Generally a paradoxical statement seems to be absurd and also false. In western tradition several attempts have been made to suggest the solutions to liar's paradox. Traditionally the paradox is related to Epimenides, the Cretan, who said that 'All Cretans were liars'. If Epimenides spoke the truth, he was a liar. But paradox may be vanished if he occasionally spoke the truth. But the sentence 'This sentence is false' is paradoxical in the form of antinomy. Accordingly a sentence is true if and only if it is false. The phrase 'This sentence' is vacuous, for it refers to nothing. According to Nyāya thinkers the sentence lacks 'qualificand' and 'qualifier' and hence there is no contentness (*viṣayatā*) in the sentence 'This sentence is false'. And a sentence without contentness (viṣayatā) cannot be a bearer of truth value. Different paradoxes have been discussed in. *The ways of paradox and other essays* by W. V. Quine, Harvard University Press, Cambridge, Massachusetts, 1976 pp. 1-18.
19. Epistemology or Theory of knowledge may be distinguished from logical theory. Epistemology is mainly

concerned with knowledge (*pramā*) and its sources (*pramāṇa-s*). *Paamāṇa-s* may be inferential or non-inferential. Logical inquiry is narrower, for it is mainly concerned with *anumāna-pramāṇa* or inference. From logical point of view, a congnition is objective and universal and hence its contentness or *viṣayatā*. But epistemologically a knowing subject under appropriate conditions acknowledges or entertains a belief towards a given cognition so that he may claim to have knowledge (*pramā*). A cognition may be true *yathārtha* or false (*ayathārtha*). But knowledge (*pramā*), is necessarily true because *prāmāṇya* or truth is a defining property of knowledge. Further knowledge claim is justified by its *pramāṇa-s* or sources of knowledge. *Pramā* or knowledge implies truth or true cognition and true cognition has contentness *viṣayatā* : therefore *pramā* or knowledge is also characterised by (*viṣayatā*) or contentness.

20. Traditionally, the Nyāya thinkers have formulated pramāṇa-śāstra as a science of the sources of knowledge. *Pramāṇa* is an instrumental cause of *pramā* (knowledge). *Pramā* is invariably related to *pramāṇa*; in other words, *pramā* as a form of *yathārtha-jñāna* is grounded in *pramāṇa* so that it is justified by means of that *pramāṇa*. A *pramāṇa* as a faculty of knowing presupposes a knower technically named as a *pramātṛ* i.e., knowing subject. The concept of *pramā* also presupposes a knowable object (*prameya*). Thus the system of Nyāya has postulated four inter-related entities in an epistemic situation. The four epistemic entities, namely, *pramāṇa*, *pramātṛ*, *prameya and pramā* play the role of necessary and sufficient conditions for the comprehension of reality.

6

Sambandha (Relation) in Navya-Nyāya

6.1. The concept of relation (sambandha)[1] plays an important role especially in the structural analysis of facts and propositions. Although modern writers[2] like Profs. Matilal, Ingalls, Potter and others have made some attempt to understand the concept of sambandha (relation) in terms of contemporary ideas, there is no comprehensive understanding of the notion of sambandha (relation). The aim is to explicate the concept of sambandha (relation) in terms of modern theory of relation as expressed in modern logic and epistemology. In the sequel I shall present the cardinal features of the modern theory of relations. And then follows the treatement of relation in Navya-nyāya. Afterwords I have to sort out may observations in comparative perspective.

6.2. What is a relation ? In ordinary paralance the word relation stands for connection, bond, tie or link. However in technical sense:

D_1 : 'A relation is a set of ordered pairs.'[3]

D_1 serves as most widely accepted definition of a binary relation or relation in general. A relation may be binary, ternary, quadranary and so on. A relation containing orders n-tuples is reducible to a binary relation in the following fashion :

An ordered pairs or an ordered couples simply means two objects say x and y given in a fixed order. By using pointed brackets an ordered pair is conventionally expressed as $<x, y>$ where x is the first member and y the second member of the ordered pair. An ordered pair $<x, y>$ is sharply distinguished from the set $\{x, y\}$; $<x, y>$ may or may not be equal to $<y\ x>$.

$<x, y> = <y, x> \equiv (x=y,\ y=x)$, otherwise identity does not hold good.[4] However $\{x, y\}=\{y, x\}$. And x and y may take any value in a given set. Thus an identity condition for $\{x, y\}= \{y, x\}$ is more liberal then that of $<x, y> = <y, x>$.

It is possible to define, ordered triples containing (i) x, y, z and (ii) ordered quadruples of x, y, z ; w and in general (iii) ordered n-tuples respectively as :

(i) $<x, y, z> = \ll x, y> , z>$,

(ii) $<x, y, z, w> = \ll x, y, z,> , w>$;

(iii) $<x_1, x_2, \ldots\ x_n> = \ll x_1, x_2, \ldots\ x_n—1>, xn>$.

However (i) to (iii) are only ordered pairs but not relations, for a relation is a set of ordered pairs. Hence as per D_1 $<x, y, z>$ or $\ll x, y>, z>$ is not a relation but $\{<x,y,z>\}$ or $\{\gg x, y>, z>\}$ is a relation (Suppes 1978:211).

6.3 However the reducibility of (i) to (iii) to their respective ordered pairs may be questioned, for they are capable of having alternative reductions. For instance an order triple $<x, y, z>$ may also be expressed as $<x, <y, z\gg$, which is also an ordered pair. Similarly an ordered n-tuple as an order couple is $\gg x_1, <x_2, \ldots x_n<$. But these alternative formulations are not logically equivalent. For instance :

(iv) $\ll x, y>, z> \neq <x, <y, z\gg$ and

(v) $\ll x_1, x_2 \ldots x_{n-1}>, x_n> \neq {}^{\vee} x_1 < x_2 \ldots x_n \gg$.

Let me explore more about (iv) and (v) by going further into the notion of an ordered pair. Authors like Quine (1960:258) have expressed their moderate sketptical attitude towards a notion of an ordered pair by qulifying it as defective noun in the sense that corresponing to the idea of an ordered pair there need not be an object on par with other objects. However, Quine (1976 : 24-6) does not deny the utility of an ordered pair in handling things as one—the ordered pair of x and y i.e. $\langle x, y\rangle$ whether x and y be numbers or other things. An important property of an ordered pairs is that if $\langle x, y\rangle$ is $\langle z, w\rangle$ then $x=z$ and $y=w$. In other words.

$$\langle x, y\rangle = \langle z, w\rangle \equiv (x=z.\ y=w).$$

Similarly for an ordered triple —

$\langle x, y, z\rangle = \langle u, v, w\rangle \equiv (x=u.\ y=v.\ z=w)$, which in turn is the same as—

$$\langle\langle x, y\rangle\ z\rangle = \langle\langle u.\ v\rangle, w\rangle \equiv (x=u,\ y=v.\ z=w).$$

To the question what things are ordered pairs, Quine (1970b; 58-9) seeks answer from the versions of Norbert Wiener and Casimir Kuratowski who offer set theoretical characterisations of an ordered pairs i.e. to say that both prefer to understand an ordered pair as a class of classes. According to Wiener:

$$\langle x, y\rangle = \{\{x\}, \{y. \Lambda\}\}$$

Accordingly an ordered pair '$\langle x, y\rangle$' is expressed in terms of a set of two sub sets $\{x\}$; $\{y, \Lambda\}$ where Λ is a null element. Kurutoski's version is slightly different from Weiner's according to which

$$\langle x, y\rangle = \{\{x\}, \{x, y\}\}$$

This version is pereferred by Quine for it is more adequate for a number theory. Thus an ordered pair is reduced to unordered class of classes.

Now let me take up the question whether

$\langle\langle x, y\rangle, z\rangle$ equals to $\langle x, \langle y, z\rangle\rangle$ if each ordered pair has the corresponding ordered triple $\langle x, y, z\rangle$.

Following Kurutowski :

$\langle\langle x, y\rangle, z\rangle = \{\{\langle x, y\rangle\}, \{\langle x, y\rangle, z\}\}$...$S_{-1}$

Whereas

$\langle x \langle y, z\rangle / \rangle = \{\{x\} \{x, \langle y,z\rangle\}\}$...$S_2$

(For complete expansion see fn. 5).

Since the sets in S_1 and S_2 are different the corresponding ordered pairs are also different. Same reasoning holds good for n-tuples also. An ordered n-tuple x_1, x_2, x_3,...x_n may be expressed as two different ordered pairs, namely,

$\langle\langle x_1, x_2 \ldots x_{n-1}\rangle, x_n\rangle$ which is not equal to

$\langle x_1, \langle x_2, x_3 \ldots x_n\rangle\rangle$

Thus an ordered n-tuple give rise to two different relations corresponding to two different ordered pairs mentioned above.

6.4. There are certain important characteristic features of relations. In a relational proposition having a form xRy 'R' stands for the relation whereas 'x' and 'y' indicate terms. If $x \neq y$ then xRy denotes a different proposition from yRx. And that characteristic of a relation by virtue of which a particular relation is uniquely determined is called a sense of that relation.[6] In a relation what is important is its order or direction. Two propositions like 'John called Jones' and 'Jones called John' have exactly the same terms, yet they are two different propositions, for in each case the order of terms between which the relation holds is different. In the former case the direction of the relation of calling is from John to Jones and in the second case the relation is from Jones to John.[7] However in some relations such as equality, identity or difference, the direction or the order remains the same. For example two propositions: 'Jones is the same age as John' and 'John is the same age as Jones' are equivalent.

Given a relation R the converse of R symbolised as $\breve{R}$ is obtained by reversing the order of R. The converse relation of of xRy is the relation such that yRx if and only if xRy for all values of x and y. For example the converse of 'x is taller than y' is 'y is smaller than x'. In some cases like symmetry

U U
R=R iff (xRy=yRx).

There are two aspects of a relation R namely domain (D) of R and counter domain (C) or range of R.[8] If R is a relation, then the domain of R is symbolised by DR as

$\{x/$ for some $y, \langle x, y\rangle \in R\}$. And CR. the counter domain (range) of R is

$\{y/$ for some $x, \langle x, y\rangle \in R\}$.

In the relation of motherhood the realtion is the set of all mothers and range or the counter domain is the set of all people. A relation R may also be understaood in terms of the cartesian product X.Y where X is some fixed set such that $x \in X$ and $y \in Y$ i.e. y is a member some fixed set Y. In case of the simplest types of binary relations as the set of all pairs $\langle x, y\rangle$ where $x \in X$; $y \in Y$ the relation R is the cartesion product :[9]

$$X.Y=\{\langle x,y\rangle/x \in X, y \in Y\}.$$

It is to be noted that a relatson R as set of ordered pairs is is further undertood in terms of a Cartesian product in whch there is also reference to set of ordered pairs; however memberships of x and y are made explicit in the cartesian product.

6.5. Now let me take up the concept of sambandh having its synonym 'saṃsarga'. The word sambandha generally means connection, union, association, relation and relationship. But whether 'sambandha' captures the technical sense of relation. discussed above (6.2) as a set of ordered pairs or relation as class of classes? An answer to this question must begin with generally accepted definition of sambandh in Navya-Nyāya literature. Following is the technical formulation of sambandha.[10]

D2 : "A relation is that which determines or conditions an adjunct-hood '*a*' and a subjunct-hood '*b*' such that '*a*' and '*b*' are of specific type and also that one of them delimits the other" : (sambandhatvaṃ ca parasaparāvacchedyāvacchedaka bhāvapanna vilakṣaṇa—pratiyogy/anuyogitānirūpakatvam), (Matilal 1968:37).

6.6. For clearer understanding of D 2 it is necessary to inquire into the nature of anuyogitā (subjuncthood) and pratiyogitā (adjuncthood) which are essential ingrediants of D 2. Both anuyogitā (subjuncthood) and pratiyogitā (adjuncthood) are the abstractions of anuyogi (subjunct) and pratiyogi (adjunct). In the characterisation of sambandha (relation) certain relata (sambandhi) are postulated. In a relation characterised as "the relation of x to y", the relata are x and y; the relatum x is the pratiyogin (adjunct) and the relatum y is anuyogin (subjunct).[11] For example in the relation of contact between a pot and the ground (floor); pot is the pratiyogi (adjunct) and the ground is the anuyogi (subjunct) of that relation. It may be asked : is it always the case in the locution "the relation of x to y" x stands for pratiyogi (adjunct) only ? Traditionally relations are classified into (a) vrtti-niyāmaka sambandha (occurrance exactting relation) and (b) vratti-aniyāmaka-sambandha (non-occurrence exacting relation).[12] (a) if an entity or a thing is said occur in or on another, the relation is vrtti-niyāmaka. For example, 'the pat is on the ground' where there is supporter and supported relation (ādhāra-ādheya-sambaddh). In case of (b) an entity does not occur in or on another in other words there is no supporter and supported relation (ādhāra-adheya samdandha.) For example "right hand is in contact with left hand", right hand is the pratiyogi (adjunct) and left hand is anuyogi (subjunct). In the pair of anuyogi and pratiyogi it is the direction of a relation which is characterised by the definite orders of pratīyogi and anuyogi. Of the two relata say x and y in xRy where the direction is from x to y, x is pratiyogi (adjunct) and in case of y R x the direction of R is from y to x and in that case the relatum y is pratiyogi and x functions as anuyogi (subjunct). Thus in a relational situation two entities designated by x and y must always be kept in the order—'pratiyogi and anuyogi.'

6.7. Next 'nirūpaka' (conditioner), another important concept in D2, is to be assimilated into that of adjunct (pratiyogin) (Matilal, 1968 : 33). There is also a talk about reducibility of relations to properties. Authors like Matilal (1985 : 116; 1968: 32-4) think that a relation (a connector) may sometimes be treated as a property (in Navya-nyāya). Of the two relata in a relational situations if a relation itself is attached to one relatum then that complex (of relatum+relation) functions as a qualifier of other relatum. For example in the case of a cup being placed on a table can be treated as a property or qualifier of that table. In a clear case of relational form like "x is the father of y", the relational abstract fatherhood (pitrtva) is in the locus x and is conditioned by y. In otherwords "Fatherhood resident in x is conditioned by y." However such a reducibility of relations to properties needs a closer look by considering the question whether every relation is reducible to a property ? and whether such a reducibility is justified ? However not all relations are reducible to properties. Non-occurrance-exacting relations (vitti-aniyāmaka sambandha) are irreducible to properties (Matial 1968:67-9, Ingalls 1951:44, 73). And reducible relations have pattern of 'x is a locus of y, or x supports y (ādhāra-ādheya-bhāva). In such cases it is somewhat interesting to see how propositions having the form x R y are reducible to the form Fx. A proposition like 'Devadatta is fat (pīno devadaṭṭah) take the form Fx; whereas a proposition' A gavaya is like a cow' (go sadrśyo gavayaḥ) has the structure of x Ry. F and R are characterised as one place predicate and two place predicates respectively. Given a proposition having the form 'Fx', and given that 'Devadatta is actually fat, we can say that 'F' is predicated of x. Predicating 'F' of x may yield a false proposition so that it may not be the case that x is F i.e.$\neg$Fx. Similarly in case of relational forms. If xRy is true then$\neg$(xRy) is false and conversely.

Regarding what portions of propositions one has to account for predicates, there seems to be three alternatives.[13] According to the first, words such as 'fat' and a phrases such as 'to the right of' are treated as predicates. The second alternative incorporates the corresponding verbs also so that the above expressions become the phrases : 'is fat' and 'is to the right of'. The third view implies the identification of predicates with sentence frames such as"...is fat" and "...is to the right of...". However the first alternative is suitable for Nyāya-theory of propositions, for often propositions do not contain verbs perhaps it is due to peculiarity of Sanskrit syntax or language. It is quite possible that in certain propositions there may be subject and verb only and in that case mere verb itself may be treated as a predicate [14] In case of a sentence containing an intransitive verb, the sentence makes a sense; and the verb itself functions as a predicate, for example 'Devadatta stands' contains the verb 'stands' which itself functions as a predicate. So properties or attributes are designated by adjectives, nouns and verbs also.

6.8. One of the distinctions between properties and relations is that properties are monadic whereas relations are dyadic, triadic and n-adic predicates. According to the principle of instantiation of properties, for each property, P, there is a particular x such that Px.[15] And in case of instantition of relations, for each R, there are x and y such that xRy or yRx.

Regarding the relational properties, one may say that, the admission of such properties is of little ontological importance for it is possible to reduce relational properties in terms of non-relational properties and relations. For instance the predicate 'revolves around a star' applies to a particular, a. And the reductive account of this predicate is a as follows :

(i) There exists '*a*' and x is such that x is a star,

(ii) that '*a*' revolves around x.

This kind of analysis disolves the predicate 'revolves around a star' in favour of 'being a star' which is one place predicate and 'revolves around' the two place predicate. Former indicates non-relational properties of x, the second is characterised by relation holding between a and x.

An argument in favour of admitting relations fundamental is that relational properties are complex properties having the components of relations and non-relational properties. However, if relations are required as constituents for relational properties then our account of relations cannot be given in terms of relational properties. Further relational properties are normally monadic in nature but analysis of such complex monadic properties involves a relation which is polyadic predicate and relations holds part between the particulars having the relational property and other particulars.

Again consider the following a relational argument whose elements are relational propositions :

A : 1. A gavaya is like a cow.
2. A cow is like an ox.
∴ 3. A gavaya is like an ox.

This argument is valid. But if A is transformed in predicative argument, it turns out to be invalid as shown below :

1. A gavaya is that which has the property of similarity with a cow.
2. A cow is that which has property of similarity with an ox.
∴ 3. A gavaya is that which has the property of similarity with an ox.

Therefore relations cannot be reduced to properties for their structures are different.

6.9. Now let me sort out certain similarities and differences between two charactertstions (D 1 (6. 2) and D 2 (6. 5) of a relation. A concise formulation of D2 as a relation is that which determines or conditions an adjuncthood '*a*' and a subjuncthood '*b*'. (samban dhatvaṃ...pratiyogya anuyogita nirūpakatvam). D2 captures the sense of D 1 namely 'a relation is a set of ordered pairs'. Because D 2 like D 1 contains a pair of adjuncthood and subjuncthood to form a couple. Further such pair is also ordered as shown above (6. 6). Accordingly in a relation (sambandha) the direction is from pratiyogi (adjunct) to anuyogi (subjunct), so that pratiyogi is always the first member of the pair and anuyogi takes the second place in that pair. The order of pratiyogi and anuyogi also implies the sequence of domain and counter domain (range) of a relation. That is to say that pratiyogi is always an element of a domain and anuyogi belongs to counter domain or range as shown below :

Domain of relation = {x/for some y, <x, y>ϵR};
(DR)
where x = pratiyogi
y = anuyogi

And Counter domain or range (CR)={y/for some x, <x, y> ε R}. In a concrete example like 'a gavaya is similar to a cow) symbolised as gRc (g=a gavaya, R=is similar to; c=a cow) the domain of the relation is in the class of all gavaya (wild oxen) and the range (counter domain) is the class of all cows.

6.10 It can also be shown that Nyāya theory of relations exhibit some properties of binary relations such as symmetry, asymmetry; non-symmetry, transitivity, intransititvity, non-transitivity, reflexivity, irreflexivity, non refflexivity etc.. Some clear cases of relational propositions are as follows :

(1) Relation of contact has the form (xRy) i.e. x is in contact with y, for examdle "a pot is in contact with cloth". This relation is symmetrical because the converse of y is in contact with x (y=cloth; x=pot) also turns out to be true.

(2) Similarly 'a gavaya is like a cow' is also symmetrical. But it is also transitive for that 'a gavaya is like a cow' and 'a cow is like an ox' together imply that 'a gavaya is like an ox, so that it satisfies the rule of transitivity.

(3) In case of a causal relation (kāraṇatā sambandha) the relation is asymmetrical. In the formula 'x causes y' cannot be equivalent to its converse 'y causes x' which would be false if x stands for a cause (an antecedent) whereas y is the consequent. It is non-transitive for even if y causes some z, x may or may not be the cause of z.

(4) Logical relation between premissess and the conclusion is asymmetrical for premisses imply a conclusion (anumiti) whereas converse is not true unless it is biconditionally related to the premisses. The relation of implication is also transitive.

(5) Relation of identity (tādātmya sambandha) such as 'pot is pot'; 'he is the same Devadatta' exhibit the properties of symmetry, transitvity and reflexivity.

6.11. There are certain differences between the two theories of relations. The Nyāya theory of relations tries to accomodate every proposition and a fact as relational which is due to its peculiar realistic framework. According to that framework the world of reals is constituted by dharama (property), dharmi (possesser of a property) and sambandha (relation) each having its own order of reality.[16] In order to constitute a fact as a relation between two or more particulars, the postulation of relation is indispensable. And the structural analysis of a cognition (savikalpaka jñāna) also reveals viśeṣya (qualificand), prakāra (qualifier) and sambandha (relation connecting qualificand and qualifier). However, modern theory of relations focusses on study of relational term, relational propositions and relational arguments. This kind of theory of relations is also implied in Nyāya theory of relations but not in well developed forms. Modern theory of relations seems to be compatible with the claims of free logic according to which there are no ontic presuppositions such as existence of class or ordered pairs. Nyāya iheory of relations seems to be bound to its realistic framework. However in a thorough going abstract articulations the of concept of relation in Navya-nyāya one may also find certain liberty to achieve formalisations parallel to realistic commitments.

Notes

1. An etymological characterisation of 'sambandhah' is samyagbandhaḥ (legitimate bond). See Jhalkikar, 1978 Nyāya-kośa : p. 921. Although sambandhatvam (relationhood) is the avacchedaka (limitor) of sambandha

(relation) authors like Matilal (1968 : 31-44) use them interchangeably for practical convenience.

2. Authors like Ingalls (1951 : 72) intuitively felt the possibility of interaction between modern logic of relations and Nyāya theory of relations by way of sāying, "mathematical logic distinguishes relations as dyadic . . . etc. . . Navya-nyāya distinction is similar but differently conceived." See Matilal (1968 : 31-44), Potter (1977 : 48); Guha (1968 : 60).
3. Quine (1970 a : 42); Quine (1970 b: 58) also prefers to define a relation as classes of pairs. See Supues (1978:211); Stoll (1976 : 23).
4. Quine (1970b : 58); Suppes (1978 : 208), Stoll (1976 : 23).
5. $S1=\{\{\langle x, y\rangle\}, \{\langle x, y\rangle, z\}\}=\{\{\{\{x\}, \{x, y\}\}\}, \{\{\{x\}. \{x, y\}\}, z\}\}$

   $S2=\{\{x\}, \{x\langle y, z\rangle\}\}=\{\{x\}, \{x \{\{y\}, \{y, z\}\}\}\}.$

   Now it is clear that sets S1 and S2 possess uncommon subsets as members.
6. Russell (1951 : 95-6).
7. Woozley (1967 : 111).
8. Suppes (1978 : 211-2); Stoll (1976 : 26).
9. Suppes (1978 : 209-10); Stoll (1976 : 26).
10. Prof. Matilal 1968 : 35-7 examines different definitions D1-D4 which are inadequate, and considers D5 as an adequate definition of a relation. I have treated D5 a D2 in my convention.
11. Matilal (1968 : 32); Ingalls (1957 : 44).
12. Matilal (1968 : 49-41); Ingalls (1951 : 73); Jhalkikar (1978 : 921).
13. Armstrong (1978a : 2).
14. Copi (1973 : 64).
15. Armstrong (1978, b : 76).
16. Potter (1977 : 48).

References

1. Armstrong, D. M. (1978a, I Edn.) : *Nominalism and Realism*. Combridge University Press, Cambridge.
2. Armstrong, D. M. (1978, b) : *A Theory of Universals*. Combridge University Press, Combridge.
3. Copi, I. M. (1973, IV Edn.) : *Symbolic Logic*. Macmillan Publisher, New York.
4. Guha, D. C. (1968, I Edn.) : *Navya-nyāya System of Logic*. Bharatiya Vidya Prakashana, Varanasi.
5. Ingalls, D. H. H. (1951, I Edn.) : *Materials for the Study of Navya-nyāya Logic*. Harvard University Press, Cambridge, Mass.
6. Jhalkikar, Bhimacharya (1978) : *Nyāya-kośa*. Bhandarkar Oriental Rercarch Institute, Poona.
7. Matilal, B. K. (1968, I Edn.) : *The Navya-nyāya Doctrine of negation*. Harvard University Press, Camb. Mass.
8. Matilal, B. K. (1985, I Edn.) : *Logic, Language and Reality*. Motilal Banarsidass, Delhi.
9. Potter, K. H. (1977; I edn.) ; *The Encyclopedia of Indian Philosophies : Nyāya-Vaiśeṣika*. Motilal Banarsidass, Delhi.
10. Quine, W. V. O. (1960) : *Word and Object*. Harward University, Cambridge, Mass.
11. Quine, W. V. O. (1970a) : *Philosophy of Logic*. Indian Reprint 1977 Prentice Hall, Delhi.
12. Quine, W. V. O. 1970b : *Set Theory and its Logic*. Harvard University Press, Cambridge, Mass.
13. Quine W. V. O. (1975, II Edn.) : *The Ways of Paradox and other essays*. Harvard University, Combridge, Mass.
14. Russell B. (1951, II Edn.): *The Principles of Mathematics*. George Allen and Unwin, London.
15. Stoll, R. R. 1976, II reprint : *Set Theory and Logic*. Eureshia Publisher, Delhi.
16. Suppes, P. (1957, I Edn. ; 1978, Rpt.) : *Introduction to Logic*. Affiliated East-West, Madras.
17. Woozley, A. D. (1949, I Edn.; 1967, Rpt.) : *Theory of Knowledge*. Hutchinson University, London.

7

The Concept of Laksana in Navya-Nyāyā and Advaita-Vedānta

7.1. The Navya-nyāya and Advaita systems consider two types of meaning namely primary meaning (Vācyārtha) and secondary meaning (lakṣyārtha).[1] An expression is a bearer of primay meaning if that expression gives some literal meaning by virtue of its direct reference to an intended object. On the contrary secondary meaning is parasitic on primary meaning. And an expression bears a secondary meaning if that expression is used in some sense other than its normal or established sense. Traditionally 'lakṣaṇā' is considered as a bearer of secondary meaning. An expression is used literally if its meaning is conventionaly fixed up. By virtue of convention, literal expression possesses standard meaning (s). But the concept of 'lakṣaṇā' presents a problem concerning the semantic status of 'lakṣaṇā' as a bearer of secondary meaning where there is no inter-subjectively stabilised usages of 'lakṣaṇā'. Lakṣaṇā as a linguistic phenomenon in its aesthetic aspects belongs to rhetoric and poetics; but at present the cognitive status of 'lakṣaṇā' is to be investigated. An inquiry about the cognitive aspect of 'lakṣaṇā' hinges on the question whether lakṣaṇā is a means for acquisition and communication of knowledge.

7.2. The word 'lakṣaṇā' has been normally rendered as 'metaphor'.[2] The word 'metaphor' seems to be an adequate rendering of 'lakṣaṇā'. However in order to justify this sort of rendering it is desirable to dwell upon the meaning of 'metaphor'. After considering the characterisation of metaphor it is relatively easier to see whether 'lakṣaṇā' captures the sense of 'metaphor' in its western counterpart. According to *The Concise Oxford Dictionary* (p. 763) the word metaphor means 'application of a name or descriptive term to an object to which it is not literally applicable'. Thus lexicographically 'metaphor' is constasted with literal expression in the form of words and sentences. Alston (*Philosophy of Language* (p. 96)) Characterises 'metaphor' as that sort of figurative use in which the extension is on the basis of similarity. To this effect Hospers[3] thinks that 'metaphor' operates by similarity and by virtue of metaphorical expression it is possible to sort out similarity or likeness in apparently unlike or dissimilar things so that our perception of the world is heightened. Professor K.K. Raja in his book *Indian Theories of Meaning* (p. 229) renders 'lakṣanā' as 'metaphor' and then acknowledges certain relevant points of similarity between 'lakṣaṇā' and 'metaphor'. He acknowledges the view that in a metaphoric usage, an expression is used to denote a referent other than its normal one. That is to say that an expression is used metaphorically if that expression is used in none of its established senses (vācyārthas). Accordingly in a metaphorical usage there is a transfer of meaning both in intension and extension.[4]

7.3. According to Annaṃbhaṭṭa, Vśvanātha and Dharmarāja, 'Śakya sambandho lakṣaṇāh'[5] (lakṣaṇā is that which is related to primay meaning). On Raja's interpretation lakṣaṇā has no direct power to convey the sense intended, for its power is derived from the primary meaning. Śaṃkarācārya[6] indicates the relation of secondary meaning to primary meaning: as "in a transfer one cannot exclude completely the primary meaning of the word; but its retention may be to a greater or lesser extent."

7.4. According to Dharmarja there are two types of lakṣaṇās (metaphors) namely kevala lakṣaṇā (exclusive metaphor) and lakṣita lakṣaṇā (implied metaphor).[7] Normally exclusive metaphor is characterised by its direct relation to the primary meaning (vācyārtha). For example "The cowherd colony is in the Ganges" (Gaṅgāyām ghoṣḥ) ; the word 'Ganges' as an exclusive metaphorical word refers to the bank of the river but the direct meaning of the word 'Ganges' consists in its normal usage to denote the stream. But the 'implied metaphor' indirectly refers to primary meaning to denote certain object. For example the metaphorical word 'dvirepha' signifies to 'r' s referring to a bee by an indrect relation through the intermediary word 'bhramara'. Another convincing example is in the form of metaphorical sentence, "The boy is a lion".[8] Literally the sentence is self contradictory for, the ṣubject term 'the boy' stands for a biped whereas the predicate term 'a lion' denotes a quadruped. But the metaphorical word 'a lion' denotes ferocity so that 'the boy' is known through his relation to ferocity which is also associated with primary meaning of a 'lion'.

The classification of lakṣanā into jahallakṣaṇā (exclusive metaphor), ajahallakṣaṇā (inclusive metaphor), and jahadajah lakṣaṇā (quasiexclusive-inclusive metaphor) cutts across Advaitin's former classification of lakṣanā into kevala-lakṣaṇā and lakṣita-lakṣaṇā.

7.5. Both Advaitins aud Naiyāyikas seem to advocate similar theory of metaphor; but as a matter of fact there is a difference in their view points. Their difference concerning semantic status of metaphor is implied by an alleged difference in the semantic status of non-metaphorical, (literal) words. According to Advaitins 'a word' is directly or literally meaningful if it refers to 'universal' and thereby it also denotes an individual.[9] In other words a word is literally meaningful if it connotes a class character and denotes a particular individual of that class. Because the same cognition that comprehends a generic attribute also comprehends the individuals. The literal meaning of a word used must be primarily due to its capacity to signify a class character but not to individual because individuals are infinete in number. But thinkers of Navya-nyāya system try to formulate an opposite argument. Accardingly the literal meaning of an expression is due to its direct reference to an individul but not universal because in ordinary paralance elder's usage of words like "Bring the cow" refers to an individual cow as qualified by a generic character.[10]

But logically it makes no difference whether 'literal meaning' of an expression primarily signifies generic character or refers to an individual, because every meaningful expression is characterised by sense pertaining to essence or intrinsic character and reference or capacity to denote individuals. To this effect we find a compromising tendency in *Siddhāntamuktāvalī*[11] that the same denotative function is held to be with regard to all individuals and it can be urged that denotative function can be presented as an attribute common to all the individuals, for cowhood etc. do constitute that.

I am going to argue that an apparent divergence of two views of primary meaning likely to converge in the explication of cognitive status of metaphorical statements. In order to analyse the cognitive status of metaphorical statements it is desirable to consider the paradigms given by Nyāya and Advaita thinkers.

7.6. "Gaṅgāyām ghoṣaḥ"[12] literally means 'there is a herdsman's hamlet in the Ganges' which is false because houses cannot be built on stream of water. An incompatibility is resolved by abandoning the literal sense of 'Ganges' as stream but metaphorical or indirect meaning namely 'the bank of Ganges' is accepted. Hence it is an example of exclusive metaphor where primary meaning is comletely set adide. The metaphorical sentence 'Gaṅgāyām ghoaṣḥ' is paraphrased into 'there is a hamlet the bank of the Ganges.' The sentence 'there is a hamlet on on the bank of the Ganges' is ture if as a matter of fact there is a hamlet on the bank of Ganges. On Navya-nyāya analysis of a true cognition, a cognition is true if and only if the qualifier belogs to the qualificand otherwise it is false. Consequently the cognition 'There is a hamlet on the bank of the Ganges' is true if and only if 'the bank of Ganges' i.e., (the qualificand) is the locus of 'the existence of a hamlet' (the qualifier). Secondly as an instance of ajahallakṣaṇā (inclusive metaphor) a metaphorical sentence 'chatriṇo gacchanti', (umbrellas are going) may be considered. Again literally the sentence makes no sense. Metaphorically the sentence means that 'persons with umbrellas are going'. In this expression literal meaning of 'umbrellas' is retained and combined with another compatible word 'persons' so that the resultant sentence is meaningful.

7.7. The nature of third type of metaphor, namley, quasi-exclusive inclusive metaphor (jahadajallakṣaṇā) is illustrated by 'sóyam Devadattaḥ' (this is that Devadatta) and 'Tat tvam asi' (that thou art). The sentence 'this is that Devadatta' is contradictory if taken literally as 'the present fat Devadatta is the lean Devadatta seen in the past'. To avoid incompatibility it is necessary to set aside conflicting terms like 'fat' and 'lean' so that the sentence turns out to be a meaningful expression. Similarly the sentence 'that thou art' : 'Individual self is God' is literlly self-contradiciory because God is omnipresent, omnis-scient and omnipotent but these qualities are absent in an individual self. After discarding incomptible attributes like 'limited power'—'unlimited power' 'Omniscient and non-omnis-cient, etc. the basic consciousness as the ground of individual self and God remains the same. Thus 'That thou art' implies 'the eternal consciousness of an individual self is the same as the basic consiousness in God'.

But Dharmarāja, the author of *Vedānta-paribhāṣā* maintains that 'sóyam Devadatta' and 'tatvamasi' need not be treated as metaphorical sentences because literally they are meaningful and there is no syntactical incompatibility when two substantives posit their identity. This view hinges on the presupposition that words directly refer to substantives and not to the attributes of substantives which are indirectly referred.[13]

7.8. On the contrary Sadānanda[14] in *Vedāntasāra* argues for the metaphorical characteristic of 'sóyam Devattaḥ' and 'tattvamasi' as foollows : This argument presupposes three types of relations namely samānādhikarṇya – the relation between two words having the same substratum, viśeṣana-viséṣyabhāva or the relation between the imports of two words qualifying each other; and lakṣyā-lakṣaṇa bhāva—the relation between two words where an identical thing is implied by them. According to samānādhikaraṇya in the sentence 'this is that Devadatta' the word 'that' signifies Devadatta associated with the past and the word 'this' denotes Devadatta associated with the present but both refer to one and the same person called Davadatta. In the same way in the sentence 'thou art that' the word 'that' stands for consciousness characterised by remoteness etc. and the word 'thou' signifies consciousness characterised by immediacy etc.; but the same consciousness (Brahman) is referred by both the terms. Similarly by virtue of other two relations identity of the metaphorical statements is established. To this effect Professor T.M.P. Mahadevan[15] thinks that 'This is that Devadatta' is an instance of jahadajahallakṣaṇā. And in construing the sense of the major texts like 'that thou art' and 'I am Brahman' jahadajahalakṣaṇā is employed.

Tarka-dīpika (59) refers to the views of orther thinkers where gauni and vyañjanā are different from lakṣaṇā. But Annaṃbhaṭṭa argues for the reducibility of 'gauni' and 'vyañjanā' to lakṣaṇā. The term 'gauni' captures the sense of metaphor in western rhetoric. For example the sentence "this boy is (veritable) fire", the word 'fire' cannot have its literal sense namely the burning substance. But metaphorical sense of purity or brightness of fire is taken so that the resulting sentence 'this boy is as pure or bright as fire' may turn out to be true. According to rhetoricians (alankārika) vyañjanā plays quite distinctive role than 'lakṣaṇā'. They argue that the statement 'there is a hamlet on the Ganges' means that there is such a hamlet on the bank of the stream of Ganges, is an instance of lakṣanā. But by virtue of vyañjanā we understand that the hamlet is situated in an atmosphere of holiness and coolness.

But Nyāya thinkers on the basis of the definition of lakṣaṇā as the relation with what is literally signified (śakhya-sambandha) and logical parsimony reduce 'gauni' and 'vyañjanā' to 'lakṣaṇā'.

7.9. Thus a linguistic expression may be metaphorical or or non-metaphorical. A word is to be taken in its metaporical sense if its literal meaning leads to inconsistency or unintelligibility. Metaphorical usage resolves the inconsistency and consequently the statement turns out to be cognitively meaningful if it is translatable into literal sentence and consequently the literal sentence is cofirmed by virtue of confirming instances based on experience. Otherwise it is confuted due to a contrary fact. For instnce the metaphorical statement 'there is a hamlet in the Ganges' is testable when the resultant sentence 'there is a hamlet on the bank of the Ganges' is confired by direct observation of the corresponding state of affair.

7.10. It may be asked if it is possible to express our ideas in a straight forward literal language what makes us to rely on metaphorical language ? Firstly a metaphor is a convenient and flexible device for extending the resources of our language.[16] Accordingly metaphorical expressions are means for creating novel senses of word for particular puposes. Secondly metaphor has potentiality to point out a relevant and surprising similarity between apparently unlike things.[17] Normally metaphors are invariably used in theological or religious discourses to construct and express intuitional experience in terms of intersubjectively stabilised language. Professor S. Radhakrisnan[18] thinks that we can describe spiritual experience by metaphors. In a metaphorical expression 'prajñā netro lokaḥ' (Aitareya Upanishad 3.1.3) (the universe has consciousness (God) as its eye) there is an inclination to take up the picture presented by the whole sentence so that one may see how that expression functions as a way of expressing a feeling of security. Consequently such an expression is a way to represent or unfold the insight that entities in the manifold world may be used to enrich human life. Thus in such contexts it is true that metaphor is a medium of fuller and riper knowing of a fact and it is capable of expressing trans empirical or intuitive truths.

7.11. Metaphors also play significant role in scientific literature, as it is evidenced by its role in the historical development of empirical science. For example in the early stages of scientific knowledge terms like "field" "force" etc. are metaphorically used. It is true that an ideal form of empirical language is formalised language where a chance for metaphorical usage is kept at minimum. Nevertheless science cannot get on without metaphors because more often than not metaphor is considered as a model to express certain novel state-of-affair or fact. For example metaphorical statement like "electricity is a fluid" is probably a legitimate description of the nature of electricity when the statement is paraphrased as electricity behaves, in certain ways like a fluid".

Certain precautions in the usage of metaphorical expression are indispensable. Metaphors possess complexity of meaning, there may be ambiguity or obscurity imposed on that expression; it is necessary to fix up precise sense to a given metaphor. A decision concerning metaphorical usage depends upon the contextual suitability of that expression. A given expression is to be treated metaphorically if the litetal usage of that expression leads to contradiction but its non-literal or metaphorical usage qualifies the expression as meaningful and true depending upon the satisfaction of the relation of correspondence between a statement and its fact.

Notes and References

1. (i) 'Padārthaşca dvividhaḥ—śakyo-lakṣyasceti' in '*Vedānta-Paribhāṣā*' of Dharmaraja; edited and translated by Swami Madhavananda, Advaita Ashrama, Calcutta : 1972, pp. 93.
   (ii) *Siddhānka-muktāvalī* (verse 81) of Viśvanātha and *Tarka-Dīpika* (59) of Annambaṭṭa.
2. *Indian Theories of Meaning* by K. Kunjunni Raja. The Adyar Library and Research Centre, Madras : 1969, pp: 229-73.
3. *An Introduction to Philosophical Analysis* by J. Hospers : Allied Publishers, New Delhi, 1971; pp. 94.
4. Normally intension (sense) and extension (denotation) are considered to be the two aspects of literal meaning. An expression denotes or applies to large number of similar things and also reveals certain essential characteristics. See *Primer of Indian Logic* by Kuppuswami Sastri.

Kuppuswami Sastri Research Institute Madras, 1196; pp. 259-60.

5. *Tarka-dīpikā* : 59; *Siddhāntamuktāvalī* 81; *Vedānta Paribhāṣā* pp. 96-97.
6. *Vedānta-sūtra bhāṣya* (4.1.6) of Sri Śaṃkarācārya : 'Lakṣaṇā ca yathāsaṃbhavam saṃnikṛśṭena viprakṛiṣṭena vā svārtha saṃbandena pravartate'.
7. *Vedānta-paribhāṣā* : p. 96.
8. Ibid.
9. Ibid p. 94.
10. *Tarka-dīpikā*. 52 and *Siddhānta-muktāvalī* : 81.
11. *Siddhānta-muktāvalī* : verse 81 : "It cannot be urged that denotative function cannot be presented as an atrribute common to all the individuals". Translated by Swami Mādhavānanda. *Bhāsā-pariccheda with Siddhānta-muktāvalī*. Advaita Ashrama, Calcutta : 1977; pp. 155.
12. *Vedānta-paribhāṣā* p. 96: *Tarka-dīpika* 59; *Siddhānta-muktāvalī* : 82.
13. *Vedānta-paribhāṣā* : p. 99.
14. *Vedānta-sāra of Sadānanda*, translated and edited by Swami Nikhilananda, Advaita Ashrama, Calcutta : 1974 pp. 86-95.
15. *The Philosophy of Advaita* by Dr. T. M. Mahadevan, Arnold Heinemann Delhi : 1976 : p. 51.
16. "Metaphor" by M. C. Beardsley in *Encyclopedia of Philosophy* : edited by P. Edwards, The Macmillan Publishing Co,, Newyork; 1967 Vol. 5. pp. 284-289.
17. *An Introduction to Philosophical Analysis* : by J. Hospers. pp. 94.
18. *Indian Philosophy* (Vol. I) by Sir S. Radhakrishnan, Blackie and Sons Bombay : 1977 : p. 178.

Kuppuswami Sastri Research Institute, Madras, 1990, pp. 259-60.

6. *Tarkadīpikā* on *Siddhāntamuktāvalī*, 81, *Vedānta Paribhāṣā*, pp. 96-97.

7. *Vedānta-paribhāṣā* [illegible]
'Lakṣaṇā ca vākyārthānupapattau [illegible] sambandhena [illegible] [illegible].'
Vedānta-paribhāṣā, p. 96.

8. Ibid., 98.

9. Ibid., p. 94.

10. *Tarka-saṅgraha* 57 and *Siddhānta-muktāvalī*, 81.

11. *Siddhānta-muktāvalī*, verse 81.
It cannot be urged that denotative function cannot be presented as an attribute common to all the individuals.

12. Translated by Swami Madhavananda, *Vedānta-paribhāṣā with Sanskrit text*, Advaita Ashrama, Calcutta 1972, pp. 135.

13. *Vedānta-paribhāṣā*, p. 96; *Tarkasaṅgraha*, 59; *Siddhānta-muktāvalī*, 82.

14. *Vedānta-paribhāṣā*, p. 99.

15. *Vedāntasāra of Sadānanda*, translated and edited by Swami Nikhilananda, Advaita Ashrama, Calcutta: 1974 pp. [illegible]

16. *The Philosophy of Advaita* by Dr. T. M. P. Mahadevan, Arnold Heinemann, Delhi, 1976, p. 31.

17. "Metaphor" by M. C. Beardsley in *Encyclopedia of Philosophy*, edited by P. Edwards, The Macmillan Publishing Co., New York 1967, Vol. 5, pp. 284-289.

18. *An Introduction to Philosophical Analysis*, by J. Hospers, pp. [illegible]

19. *Human Knowledge* [illegible] Bertrand Russell, Blackie and Son, Bombay, 1977, p. 128.

III

TRUTH (Satyam)

8

The Advaita Conception of Truth (Satyam)

8.1. The concept of truth (satyam) is an essential ingradient of the conceptual framework of Advaitic epistemology. Both 'truth' (satyam) and 'knowledge' (jñānam) play the cardinal roles, for (even) the ultimate reality is characterised in terms of truth and knowledge (satyam jñānam anantam brahmah).[1] But what is truth (satyam) ? Is there any difference between truth (satyam) and knowledge (jñānam) ? In contemporary epistemology knowledge is defined as justified truth (or true belief). This definition is called the classical definition of knowledge. And the roots of this definition are to be traced out in Platos' Dialogues. The definition of knowledge implies truth condition, belief conditton and justification condition.[2] For instance if a knowing subject S knows that P (a true proposition) then S believes in that P and that P is true and S has adequate grounds for believing that P. Thus the truth is a necessary condition but not sufficient condition for knowledge. In otherwords knowledge necessarily involves truth. But whether truth involves knowledge? Of course not, for truth is independent of knowledge. For example, the truth expressed by the true proposition that 'Gauriśaṅkara is the tallest mountain' is (timelessly) true independent of human experience, reason or belief. Consequently belief or disbelief in truth (proposition(s)) is not going to alter the structure of truths. However if truths are adepuately apprehended by mind or reason via beliefs, there is knowledge for knowing subjects. Similarly the upaniṣadic statement 'satyam jñānam . . . brahmaḥ' seems to imply the distinctions between stayam and jñānam. For clearer understanding it is necessary to explicate the concepts of satyam and jñānam.

8.2. Etymologically the term 'satya' designates an existing things that is not sublated and the word 'jñāna' stands for the awareness of truth or true cognitions. Śrī Śaṅkara[3] characterises 'satyam' as that which accords with what is grasped through the means of knowledge. Similarly speaking of things as they are is truth.[4] Śaṅkara implies that truth is the actual state of affair and is capable of being confirmed by human experience; a person having such apprehension is able to communicate his experience of truth to his fellow beings. However what is communicated through the instrument of language is correct information or knowledge of that truth. Consequently the imperative 'satyam vada'[5] (Speak the truth) means 'make reliable or thurstworthy assertions". Further implications of 'satyam vada' is that a speaker of truth must be truthful that is to say that a reliable or thrustworthy person alone is capable of communicating the true facts without twisting the information about true states of affairs.

Further "satyameva jayate" on Śaṅkara's interpretaton, entails the fact that truthful man wins and untruthful man is defeated by a truthful one.[6] Credibility or trustworthiness is a moral consideration blended with epistemic factor in 'speak the truth'. Thus in the sequel the Rṣi of the Upaniṣad[7] states 'dharmam cara' (practice righteousness). Practice of righteousness is a necessary condition for a speaker of truth because unreliable speaker by chance may utter the truth which has no legitimate consequence. Since righteousness or virtuous nature of a person qualifies him as speaker of truth (yathārtha vaktā); such person alone is able to convey the right sort of information about the truth he grasped through a source of knowledge (pramāṇa) such as perception (pratyakṣa) or śabda (testimony). In the long run the practice of righteousness makes a person morally perfect and spiritually adequate. Moral perfection qualifies the person to grasp the truth intvitively or by means of pramāṇas. Otherwise due to the digration from the practice of righteousness there will be negligence about truth. Thus the Upaniṣad[8] states that there should be no negligence about truth (satyāt na pramāditavyam). To this effect Śri Śaṅkara thinks that 'inadvertance about truth is tantamount to falsehood'.[9] An inadvertance means falsehood, because of indifference or negligence, truth is not properly grasped. Due to inadvertance what is to be grasped or understood as it is may not be grasped as it is. Consequently misapprohenison of a fact due to ignorance distorts the correct apprehension of truth.

8.3. The mahāvākya (cardinal sentence) 'satyam, jñānam, anantam brahmaḥ'—'Reality (Bsahman) is truth. knowledge and infinite' functions as a definition (lakṣaṇa) of Brahman.[10] The component terms Syatam, jñānam and anantam are distinguishing caracteristics of the substantive-Brahman. Accordingly for 'satyam' (truth) and 'jñānam' (knowledge) function as adjectives because Brahman, the substantive is qualified by the definiens. However the expressions satyam and jñānam stand for the essential or defining properties (*svarūpa dharma*) because the concept of Brahman is inconceivable apart from such essential attributes. The Mahāvākya implies 'satyam brahma', 'jñānam brahma' and 'anantam brahma'. The term satya (truth) designates the actual state of affair or a thing which is not subject to spatial and temrpoal changes. In otherwords satyam (truth) implies traikālikābādhitatva (timeless coherence or non-contradictoriness).

8.4. Śrī Śaṅkara offers an interesting semantic analysis of the expression 'satyam'. The term 'satyam' (truth) has the same case ending as other two jñānam and anantam and they stand in opposition i.e. (having syntactic) parallelism with each other. The logical function of these terms is to serve as defining properties of 'Brahman' so that the entity-Brahman under definition can be distinguished or differentiated from other things. Here Śrī-Śaṅkara is using the principle of individuating the Brahman, from non-brahman. The principle of individuation is necessary for specifying an object with reference to essential characteristics so that the object under consideration can be known or grasped through awarenes. For example in common paralance, a particular thing, say, a lotus 'L_1' is claimed to be known on the principle of individuation as applied to that lotus 'L_1'. Accordingly the lotus 'L_1' by virtue of its individuating characteirstics like 'blue', 'big' and 'sweet smelling', the lotus L_1 is said to be known so that the corresponding knowledge claim takes the form of the judgement. 'The lotus L_1 is big, blue and sweet smelling'. This kind of empirical model set up for understanding the non-sencuous object like Brahman may be considered as inadequate according to an opponent, because there is a single Brahman and there donot exsit other Brahmans from which it can be distinguished. Brahman is unlike a blue lotus 'L_1' that can be marked off from non-blue lotuses. Thus a noun like a 'lotus' (L_1) can be distinguished only when there is the possibility of deliminating some other adjective qualifying some other noun for instance a 'white lotus' can be distinguished from red or blue one. And, as a matter of fact an adjective like 'white' is meaningful eventhough there are many nouns (like rose', jasmine etc.) which belong to the same class of white objects which in turn are capable of having many other adjectives such as big, sweet smelling etc. But a single or singular noun like 'Brahman' has no counterpart as it is unique and non-dual. Thus principle of individuation cannot be applied in the case of Brahman. There is an interesting encounter :[11] Since the adjectives designating essential attributes constitute defining properties of the concept under consideration and other adjectives designating accidental properties donot serve as defining properties. Eventhough a certain adjective distinguishes a noun from things of its own kind, a definition demarkates the thing defined from other things. For example, the definition of 'ākāśa' 'as that which provides space' uniquelly characterises ākāśa.

8.5. Eventhough the terms 'satyam', jñānam' and 'anantam' occur in a certain syntactic order, each of them are related to Brahman independently of others, such as 'satyam brahma' and 'jñānam brahm. In this context Śrī Śaṅkara[12] offers an interesting characterisation of satyam (truth), perhaps in continuation of earlier characterisation of truth referred above (8 : 2). Following is the characterisation of satyam (truth).

". . .a thing is said to be satyam, when it does not change the nature that is ascertained to be its own; and a thing is said to be unreal (asatyam) when it changes the nature that is ascertained to be its own."

According to the above characterisation, 'satyam' implies that primarily a thing (or fact) is said to be the bearer of truth values such as satyam and asatyam; that is to say that a thing is either true or false (but not both). If a thing is characterised as true thing then it cannot be false and viceversa. To this effect, the text (Ch. 1.4) says that "a mutable thing (like a pot) exists only in name depending on speech; the earth alone is real."[13] The two cardinal concepts 'truth' and 'existence' are intimately related. Truth means existence and existence implies unchanging characteristics in all the possible world situations (traikālika abādhita). Thus necessary existence is contrasted with contigent existence. A thing such as a pot has contigent existence because discontinuity of it in its absence before manufacturing it out of clay and again that pot will be devoid of existencc in the state of pradhvaṃsabhāva (posterior absence) i.e. after breaking the pot. However the clay remains the same as true stuff as compared to the fluctuating states of the pot—the fluctuing states of the pot are prior non-existence, existence and posterior non-existence. However an analogy that Brahman is like the earth (clay) as unchaning stuff has certain limitations. The limitation is that analogy only serves as model of explanation for understanding the true nature of Brahman. However the clay is insentient whereas Brahman is sentient (cetana viśiṣtaḥ), hence further qualification : jñānam brahmah.

8.6. It may be objected[14] since the term satyam (truth) logically negates its contradictory untruth (asatyam) and Brahman as reality is not a wellknown entity like a lotus and hence the words in 'satyam, jñānam, anantam brahman' are vacuous terms like the vacuous words in the sentence 'there goes the son of a barren woman having bathed in the water of the mirage and having put a crown of sky flowers on his head, assumed with a bow made of hare's horn'.

Śrī Śaṅkara's reply is quite illuminating one. Since the sentence under consideration is meant as a definition (lakṣaṇa-vākya) of Brahman. And consequently he defines 'satyam', 'jñanam' and 'ananta' as defining properties of Brahman. And definiens function as differentia having positive import without relating to a non-entity, otherwise terms like satyam cease to be meaningful. As a matter of fact the words satya etc. are quite meaningful and one can logically distinguish their substantive from other substantives possessing opposite qualities. And even the word Brahman has its own individual meaning. Etymologically the word 'Brahman' is derived from the root bṛḥ which means growth or vastness. And the word 'Brahman' refers to the entity Brahman which is beyond space, time and causation. Thus the word Bradman has positive imoprt. Even in ordinary paraldnce the word satyam is used with positive import. For example the earth, in relation to a pot made up of earth, is called real entity. Thus from semantical point of view 'satyam', 'jñānam, 'anantam' and 'Brahman' are meaningful termsas they refer to positive entities.

Śrī Saṅkara makes the distinction between the nature of truth and the criterion or test of the truths. Logically the nature of truth characterised by its unique feature or structure as explicated above, (8.2) is prior to the criteria (tests) of that truth. *The principle of non-contradiction* (*abādha*) has been formulated by Śaṅkara as the criterion of truth[15] The function of the criterion of truth is to serve as a practical device for sorting out the correct beliefs (in truths) from false beliefs in the contexts of human experiences. Thus a legitimate criterion of truth (or reality) must imply its applicability in human cognitive enterprises along with its capacity to explain away the familiar cases of human errors. For example the straight stick partially immersed in the water appears bent. Eventhough its crookedness in water on account of the phenomenon of refraction is as real to the eye as its straightness to the touch, it is only touch that rectifies the false visual judgement. Thus abādha as a criterion of truth implies the coherence aspect of truth as the systematic character or harmonius nature of truth. Human knowledge in its evolutionary process is subject to constant modification and revison. In the domain of human experience, dream states are contradicted by waking experiences which in trun are contradicted by the dawn of 'self-knowledge (ātma-jñāna). Since the top logical priority is attributed to ātma-jñāna or ātmānubhava; there is no other cognition or experience that can contradict it. (bādhakajñānāntarābhāvāt).[16] Sir Radhakrishanan observes: 'Logical proof arises only in the empirical world, where the ultimate one-ness of the observer and the observed is obscured by the clogging psychological hindrances which are summed up in the word avidya. Logical proof enables us to break down the obstructing veils and reveals the self-evident character of truth.[17] It may be asked; "if the Brahman is unknown it cannot at all be desired to be known" (opponent's view in Śaṅkara-bhāṣya of Brahma sūtra 1.1.1).[18] This objection implies that if there is absence of human cognitive faculties such as reason and the like towards an ultimate reality then such a reality is beyond humau comprehension. This objection has been effectively raplied by Śaṅkara[18] by saying that the ultimate reality (Ātman) is not altogether unknown and since knowable must be within experience; the ultimate reality is within the reach of human comprehension. And hence there is jiñāsā (spiritual inquiry) about the nature of ultimate reality. Śaṅkara being a champion of reason does recognise the importance of reason as source of the criteria of truth. Reason must be qualified as sutarka (legitimate reasoning) which ought to function within the frame work of śruti. Thus an inquiry into truth (satyam) through the criterion of truth ends up with the actual experience of that Truth.

Notes and References

1. Taittirīya-upaniṣad. II. 1.1 in *Eight Upaniṣads* (Vol. One) with Śaṅkārācārya's commentray, translated by Swami Gambnirananda, Advaita Ashrama Calcutta, P.286.
2. In the present context 'jñāna' is synonymous with pramā

(adequate or true cognition) which in turn captures the sense of 'knowledge'. The structural similarities between pramā and knowledge have been investigated thoroughly in *Śabda-pramāna-An Epistemological Analysis* by Dr. Rachappa I. Ingalalli; Indian Books Centre, Shakti Nagar, Delhi. PP-8.58.

3. Taittirīya-upaniṣad-bhāsya of Śaṅkārācarya. 1. x. 1.2. Swami Gambhirananda's translation, Pp266-267.
4. Muṇḍ akopaniṣad-bhāṣya of Śaṅkarācārya 111. 1.6 in Gambhirananda Vol. (two) P.153.
5. Taittirīya-upanisad 1. xi. 1.
6. Taittiriya-upanisad 1. xi. 1.
7. Muṇḍakopaniṣad-bhāsya of Śaṅkarācārya 111. 1.6 P. 153'
8. Taittirīya-upnisad 1 x. 1.2, P. 265.
9. Taittirīya-upaniṣad-Śāṅkarabhāṣya 1. x. 1.2 P. 267.
10. Taittirīya-upaniṣad-Śāṅkarabhāṣya 11. 1.1, P. 290.
11. Taittirīya-upaniṣad-Śāṅkarabhāṣya II. 1.1 Pp. 290.
12. Taittirīya-upaniṣad-Śāṅkarabhāṣya II. 1.1 Pp. 291.
13. Taittirīya-upaniṣad-Śāṅkarabhāṣya II. 1.1 Pp. 291.
14. Taittirīya-upaniṣad-Śāṅkara-bhāṣya II. 1.1 Pp. 294-5.
15. (a) Indian philosophy (Vol. II) by S. Radhakrishnan, Blackie & sons Bombay, 1977. P. 501.
    (b) *An Introduction to Śaṅkara's Theory of Knowledge* by N.K. Devaraja, Motilal Banarsidass, New Delhi, P-130.
16. Braḥmasūtra-śāṅkara-bhāṣya : ii. 1.4.
17. Indian Philosophy (Vol. II) Op. Cit. Pp. 501-2.
18. Brahma-sūtra-śāṅkara-bhāṣya : 1.1.1.

9

Navya-Nyāya Conception of Truth

9.1. An inquiry into truth (prāmāṇya as satyam) in Navya-Nyāya ought to begin with the analysis of a qualificative cognition (savikalpaka-jñāna)[1] for according to Navya-Nyāya (Nn) primarily a qualificative cognition is a bearer of truth value. A qualificative cognition is capable of being expressed in the form of a declarative sentence so that at the level of expression a declarative sentence functions as bearer of truth value. Thus primarily truth and falsity are the properties of true and false cognitions respectively.

9.2. In contemporary epistemology the distinction is made between 'truth' and 'knowledge'. Generally accepted definition of knowledge is that knowledge is justified true belief.[2] This definition implies that 'truth' is a necessary condition of knowledge. Accordingly 'S (subject) knows that P (proposition) then that P is true' is analytic. Truth is only a ncessary but not sufficient condition. 'Truth', belief and 'justification' together constitute necessary and sufficient condition for knowledge. However every form of truth or true proposition may not be considered as an instance of knowledge unless it is justified or adequately supported by means of proper grounds or reasons.

9.3. In order to appreciate the distinction between the concepts of knowledge and truth in Navya-Nyāya system it is necessary to find out the cognate concepts in that system. The concept of 'pramā' captures the sense of knowledge for the following reasons.

9.4. Gaṅgeśa formulates the definition of pramā as :

(D_1) : tadvatitatprakārakānubhavopramā (*Tattva-cintāmaṇi* : 401) "Pramā (knowledge) is true apprehension of reality as it is".

Like the classical definition of knowledge namely 'knowledge is justified true belief' (S:2), Gaṅgeśa's definition (D_1) implies truth condition in the form of 'tadvati tatprakārakatvam' and belief condition is implicit in 'anubhava'. Although reference to 'justification' condition is not explicit, it is implied through the notion of 'pramā'. Because pramā is grounded in pramāṇa (pramā karaṇa pramāṇaṃ). Four forms of pramā (TC : 538) namely pratyakṣa, (perceptual knowledge) anumiti (inferential knowledge), upamiti (identificational knowledge) and śābda (testimonial knowledge) are justified by respective pamāṇās namely pratyakṣa (perception), anumāna (inference), upamāṇa (identification) and śabda (testimony) (*Tattva-cintāmaṇi* : 538).

There is some textual evidence to say that yathārthajñāna (anubhava) is to be equated to pramā. The component concept 'yarhārtha' does not function to give actual characterisation of pramā or truth. Because Gaṅgeśa criticises the definition of yadhārtha vijñānam sa pramā. Gaṅgeśa's criticism implies that there is no similarity between cognition and its corresponding object. For instance in the cognition,[8] this is a pot the word 'yathā' does not exhibit any similarity with the object (artha) namely pot (jñāna, ghatatvādina yathāśabdārtha sādraśyabhāvāt, (TC-374). It seems to me that Gaṅgeśa's argument is directed against a copy theory of truth.[3] Structure of a true cognition cannot adequately be expressed through yathā+artha because true cognition and the corresponding fact belong to different orders of reality or categories. For instance 'cognition' (jñāna) belongs to the category of guṇa (quality) where as an object of cognition may be substance, quality, relation etc.

Gaṅgeśa gives the following definition of truth:

D_2: Tadvati tatprakārakatvam prāmāṇyam (TC: 226) "Truth is the property (of a cognition) of having a qualifier which is present in the qualificandum". I think D_2 is an exclusive characterisation of truth (prāmāṇya) for the following reasons. Firstly the defining property of truth (prāmāṇya) namely 'tadvati tatprakārkatvam' is an impersonal characterisation and hence independent of any belief operation by a cogniser. In an epistemic relation of knowing that P, reference to subjective belief in the form of 'anubhava' (jñāna) is necessary. If anubhave presupposes the operation of cognitive faculties such as perception, inference etc. then the reference to anubhava does not imply exclusive characterisation of truth but knowledge or belief. To this effect D_2 may be contrasted with D_1 in which epitstemic relation is involved. I wish to distinguish between D_1 and D_2 on the ground that according to Gaṅgeśa D_1 has its component 'anubhava' and D_2 is free from that component. For Gangeśa D_1 is the epistemic definition of pramā which involves belief component anubhava as its necessary condition where as D_2 is a logical characterisation of truth (prāmāṇya) only.

Secondly pramā necessarily presupposes its antecedent pramāṇa (pramā karaṇa) where as prāmānya as truth does not presuppose any epistemic relation with pramāṇa for the simple reason that D_2 is logical characterisation of truth (pramāṇya) only. And in order to apprehend truth of true cognition, dual theories of criteria of truth have been formulated. As a matter of fact both parataḥ-prāmāṇya-vāda (PPV) and svataḥ-prāmāṇya-vāda (SPV) presuppose D_2 i.e. to say both accept 'tadvati tatprakārakatva' as the defining property of truth but they differ in the ways of apprehension of that truth. Given a true cognition C The pot is blue/such that truth of C is prior to the functioning of prāmāṇas, how are we to decide in that case whether C is true or not ? In order to justify the knowledge claim reference to prāmāna is necessary so that apprehension of truth becomes knowledge.

According to Gaṅgeśa (TC: 382) fruitful activity involved in SPV or PPV cannot be considered as the characterisation of.

truth because certain species of pramā need not give rise to any fruitful activity. And at best it constitutes a test or a criterion of truth; truth of a cognition is prior to successful activity.

Another indirect evidence regarding the distinction between truth and knowledge is derived from the theory of cognition (jñāna). Although 'jñāna' is a quality of the soul, when it is interpreted as an objective entity like Frege's 'thought' (or proposition) having the status of Plato's Ideas, jñāna or cognition could be the bearer of truth values. Thus on implied classification of jñāna (cognition) may be expressed in the form of the following table :

Jñāna (Cognition)

Yathārtha-jñāna — ayathārtha-jñāna

as — as

(A) Satyajñana Pramā (Sj) — Asatya-jñāna (Aj) (B) (uncaused) — apramā

SJ (independent of pramātra) — (caused by pramāṇa) pratyakṣa anumiti upamiti śābda — aj (independent of a belief in the form of negation of satya-jñāna) — caused by defective cognitive faculties

In the above table, some species of true cognition (A) possibly remain as the cognitions unknown of any knowing subject and hence their negations constituted by the species (B) of false cognitions. Thus it is clear that truth of a true cognition is independent of knower's subjective conditions such as belief and technique of adducing good grounds in support of that belief.

9.5. The meaning of D_2 is more precisely paraphrased as follows:

D3 : A cognition is true if and only if the qualifier of the cognition is legitimately related to its qualificand.

But what are these qualificand (qd) and qualifier (qr)? Are they logical, epistemological or ontological entities? Some times they are treated as straight forward ontic entities say, categories of the world such as substance quality etc. Consider an instance of a true cognition/The pot is blue/the qualificand is pot which is substance and qualifier blue is a quality. And the qualificand pot and the qualifier blue are related to each other by virtue of the relation of inherence (samavāya sambabandha). Of course qualificand need need not always be substance nor qualifier exclusively stands for a quality. They (qd and qr) may belong to any domain of categories say, substance, quality etc.[4] For example in the cognition/the pot is on the ground/both qd and qr are substances but the relation is contact (saṃyoga).

9.6. I think the above treatment of qd and qr as ontic entities or referents is somewhat odd and ambiguous. Because in the structural analysis of a true cognition in terms of its constiu-ents qd, and qr, it is reasonable to treat qd, qr and r., as cognitive elements, but not actual objects referred by qd and qr. Ambi-guity attached to qd or qr is due to double functioning of qd or qr as cognitive element and ontic entity. If qd qr, and r are the constituents of a cognition, then they are cognitive elements. If we understand a true cognition much in the fashion of Frege's thought (or proposition) similar to Platonic Ideas[5] the consti-tuents qd, qr and r should be treated as the concepts but not as objects. Of course propositions and concepts have their own ontic realms of different orders other than domains of physical objects.

It may be asked if qd and qr are treated as concepts whether they could function as subject and predicate of sentence., or what is the grammatical status of qd and qr?

I think NNS do distinguish between a concept and a term. Because for them jñānas or cognitions are prelinguistic (or non-linguistic) and capable of being expressed in language. Thus only at the level of expression a concept appears as a term. A term is a linguistic entity in which a concept is encapsuled. The possibility of expressing the non-linguistic jñānas in terms linguistic entites like declarative sentences gives rise to the consideration of true-sentence in order to understand the concept of truth, which I consider later (9.15-16).

Qualificand as a concept functions a locus such that qualifier resides in the qualificand through the self-linking relation (svarūpa sambandha). However it is wrong to suppose that qd designates substance only. The phrase 'qualifier resides in the qualificand' appears to be figurative because, it is odd to say that one concept resides in another concept. It would be an adequate understanding if qualificand is treated as a principal concept and qualifier as a subordinate concept such that qr is a function of qd. In D2 'tat' occurs twice and functions as a variable like x so that a dummy schemata yields a determinate entity if the variable x has been given a value.[6] For example rajatatvavati rajatatva prakārakatvam prāmānyam (The truth of the cognition is that property of the cognition having silverness as qualifier(ness) being present in the qualificand of silver). In this particular instance 'rajatatvavati' is the value for 'tadvati'. D2 is not satisfied by an instance of its negation. D^12 (where D^12-D2). The formulation of D^12 is as follows :

D^12: tadabhāvavati tatprakāraka jñānam apramā TC: 401. "Falsity is that property of a cognition having a qulifier which is absent in the qualificandum."

An instance of D^12 such as 'This is silver' does not satisfy D2. Because the qualifier silverness does not belong to its qualifi cand 'this' namely shell. In other words 'idam rajatatvābhāvavati rajatatva prakarakam', idam is the locus for the absence of (rajatatva) silverness. Hence the cognition is false and does not point to reality or a fact.

The expression 'tadvati' designates logical or epistemic correlative implying ontologcal situation such that the qualifier of a given cognition underconsideration in relation to its qualificand of a true cognition also hinges on the analysis of the corresponding fact.

Since a true cognition and corresponding fact belong to different orders of reality; the corresponding analysis namely cognitive and factual analysis ought to be different eventhough they are closely related to each other.

9.7. In order to have a clearer understanding of the nature of true cognition it is desirable to inqure into the distinction between a true cognition and the fact which makes that cognition true.

Although D2 implies correspondence view of truth, it may be asked whether structural correspondence of one to one relation is implied. Firstly there is difference between a logical structure of a true cognition in terms of the configuration of qd, qr and r where qd, qr and r are the concepts capable of referring to the referents of the real world. Since a referent is that entity referred by the corresponding concept and referrent belongs to a different order of reality; it is necessary to conceive the distinction between a true cognition and the fact. The analysis of a fact as factual analysis of an ontic reality differs from the logical and epistemological structure of a true cognition Given a true cognition C, an objective or impersonal characterisation of the nature of that true cognition is logical or conceptual characterisation in which there is no reference to knower's or believer's subjective phenomenon like believing, stating, saying, justifying etc For instance the true cognition/the pot is blue/reveals the following logical characteristic or structure (LS)

Truth value status	Concept 1 qd	Concept 2 Verb implying r	Concept qr
True	(The) pot	is	blue

Firstly, a logical structure should reveal the truth value status of a cognition so that a bearer of a truth value is distinguished from non-bearers of truth values such a objects and facts.

Secondly the structure of a true cognition is unchangeable and hence impersonal. Because it is independent of the cogniser but capable of being grasped or understood by many cognisers. At the level of understanding and communication of a cognition, the cognition acquires the epistemic structure (ES) as shown below :

Subjective status:— Belief or disbelief	Objective status : (Logical status) qd + r+qr
S (a knowing subject) (believes) says or reports that	'the pot is blue'

However the fact that 'the pot is blue' reveals the follwing factual structure (FS):

Ontological status:— substance, quality action etc.		Factual elements : objects and relations
A catagory of substance (fact)	'The pot is dravya or relationship substance of inherence Anuyogi= (lower correlate)	blue' quality of blue colour pratiyogi = upper correlates.

In the cases whenever two entities are related to each othar by virtue of occurrance exacting-relation (vrtti-niyāmaka-sambandha) there adhār-ādheya-bhāva (locus-located-relation) is implied. For exampie 'ghatvad bhūtalm' (The floor has pot), is the fact in which the object ground is ontologically characterised as adhāra (locus) or anuyogi (lower-correlate) where as another object 'pot' is an entity having the status of adheyatā or (locatedness) or pratiyogitā i.e. upper-correlatedness; the object pot is ādheya (located entity) or pratiyogi (upper correlate).

9.8. If there is one-to-one correspondence between the factual structure (FS) and the cognitive structure or logical structure (LS) of the true cognition that/the pot is blue/then it is necessarily the case that for a given fact (f) there is only one true cognition (c) such that fact (f) is described by that true cognition (c) only. But the upholders of one-to-one correspondence view subscribe to the theory that for a given a fact (f) there may be alternative true cognitions say C1, C_2, such that $C_1 \neq C_2$. If $C_1 \neq C_2$ due to difference in their contentness (Viṣayatā-bheda), neither C1 nor C2 imply any one-to-one correspondence with the fact (f). Thus Nns donot advocate correspondence in terms of one-to-one relation although they subscribe to the specific type of correspondence theory of truth.

But what is viṣayatā (content-ness) of a true cognition? A qualificative cognition is composed of three elements namely qualificand, qualifier and relation and each element possesses relational abstract namely qualificand-ness qualifier-ness and relation-ness respectively. Totality of relational abstracts is known as viṣayatā or contentness of that cognition. For example the viṣayatā or contentness of the true cognition/the pot is blue/is stated interms of the sum of potness, blueness and inherence-ness In other words blueness and potness are related by virtue of inherence-(ness). The theory of visayata implies that (i) for a given fact there may be more than one true cognitions which differ in their visayatā's and (ii) cognitions are identical when their viṣayatas are identical but not when their objects are identical.

The following two true cognitions referring to the same fact differ in their viṣayatas (contentness).

(i) C1:/ghaṭvad-bhūtalam/=The floor has a pot on it; (S_1);
(ii) C2:/bhutalea-ghaṭo-asti/=There is a pot on the floor (S_2).

In case of (i) qualificand-ness : floor-ness (bhūtalatva)+relation-ness of contactness (samyogatva) + qualifier-ness-potness (ghatatva) constitute contentness for of C1; where as C2 (ii) is constituted by the pot-ness (as qualificand-ness) contact-ness (samyogatva and floor-ness (qualifier-ness). Although contact-ness is same for C1 and C2, the different configuration of other elements makes the difference between C1 and C2. I think this kind of difference is analogous to the difference of grammatical construction in S1 and S2 which are the linguistic expressions of C1 and C2 respectively. Yet there is the difference: grammatically speaking S1 and S2 have different syntactic structures but semantically both give the same meaning.

9.9. Referring to the notion of viṣayatā one may understand the notion of true cognition interms of viṣayatā. A cognition is true if the qualificand-ness and qualifier-ness possess appropriate relation-ness.

9.10. Sometimes it is objected[7] that 'D2' does not cover all types of cognitions but only non-relational (S-P) type of cognitions and relational type of cognitions of (SRP) type are covered by another alternative definition of truth given by Gaṅgeśa, that :

D3: tadvati tadvaiśiṣtya jñānatvam vā prāmāṇyam (TC 170) "Truth is that specific property of a cognition having a qualifier which is present in the qualificand". I think D_2 and D_3 are not mutually exclusive because Gaṅges'a treats them synonymously. According to Gaṅgeśa 'tat-prakārakatvam' is paraphrased as tadvaiśiṣtya prakārakatvam (TC:401-2).

And even in actual practice Gaṅges'a employs D_2 itself to characterise different forms of pramā, such that 'tadvati tat-prakārakam' is a necessary condition of pramā. It appears that D2/D3 as a definition of truth is applicable to certain species of true cognition namely atomic or individual cognitions such as 'The pot is blue' in which qualificand refers to single entity 'the pot'. In case of existential and universal generalisations it is unclear as to what sort of an entity is to be conceived as referrent of a qualificand. Regarding universal generalization there are two ways of specifying a qualificand. One is interms of converting or paraphrasing a given universal cogition interms to its negative equivalent. For example the universal cognition/All the cases of smoke are the eases of fiere/is expressed into/smokeness is absent from the locus in which there is the absence of fire-ness.

Annaṃbhaṭṭa (17th century) and Viśvanātha (17th century) accept Gaṅges"a's definition of truth. In the above definition, D_2 the defining property consists of the variable the wor ;

'tat' which occurs twice. By using a name of an individual object in the place of 'tat' we formulate a particular true cognition, so that we can very easily see that the definition is applicable to the cases of true cognition but not to false cognitions. For example in the true cognition 'This is silver', there are three qualifiers namely 'thisness' 'silver' and 'silverness; If we take the qualifier 'silverness' as the value of the variable 'tat' then the cognition in that case is such that it has 'rajatatva-prakāra', i.e. it has 'silver-ness' as its qualifier. Since the word 'this' in the true cognition denotes a real silver and hence possesses silverness (rajatatvavat). The true cognition is thus characterised by the property of rajatatvavati rajatatva prakāra-katva which is, equivalent to the cognition 'This is silver'.

9.11. In the definition (D2), the defining of property of truth is 'tadvati tat prakārakatvam'. However mere 'tat prakārkatvam' cannot be the defining property of true cognition because even false cognition also possesses tatprakāra-katvam. For instance in the following joint-definition of truth and falsity qualifierness is common as given in *Tattva-cintāmaṇi* (p.401).

D4: A qualificative cognition is false if and only if the qualifier does not occur in, or is not contained in the qualificand, otherwise it is true.

According to this definition "qualifier does not occur in the qualificand" is the defining property of false cognition. That is to say a qualificative cognition 'x is y' is false if y does not occur in x. For example in the false cognition 'This is silver', the cognition has 'silverness, for its qualifier which does not occur or belong to the qualificand '*this*'. In other words in the false cognition 'this is silver', the qualifier (prakārata) is rajatatvavat (silverness) which does not occur in the qualificand 'this'. Or the qualificand 'this', is not the possesser of silverness (rajatatvavat). Therefore the false cognition does not possesses the property of rajatatvavati rajatatvaprakārakatva which is equivalent to the false cognition *This is silver*.

9.12. Now it is somewhat easier to contrast a true cognition (truth) with a false cognition (error). In a cognition 'x is y', qualifier 'y' is common to true and false cognitions where 'x' is the qualificandum. **But the difference** between false cognition and true cognition is that the negation of true conition implies false cognition and conversely. *Negation of a true* cognition 'x is y'; which is equivalent to 'the qualificand x has the qualifier 'y' or 'y occurs in x', gives rise to the corresponding false cognition that 'x is y' which is equivalent to 'the qualificand x has no qualifier y' or 'y does not occur in x'. A distinguishing characteristic of a true cogntion is tadvati which implies presence of something; where as 'tadabhāvavati', the negation of tadvati, is the hallmark of false cognitions. 'Abhāvatva' (absentia) in tadābhāvavati may suggest an idea that a false cognition is necessarily negative in character, and the definition of false cognition may not cover a false cognition having the form 'x is not y'. However this is not so. Because according the definition of false cognition (in D4), a cognition ('x is not y') is false if the qualificand x has not that y (absence of y). In otherwords 'x is not y' is false if and only if not y (absence of y) does not occur in x. However a cognition 'x is not-y' is true if and only if absence of y i.e. 'not y' occurs in x.

9.13. It is interesting to consider Annaṃbhaṭṭa's reply to a subtle objection to D1 and D2. The definition D1 appears to be too narrow for it is not applicable to the true cognition 'potness is in pot'. Because the potness as the qualificand cannot be said to be the locus of the pot (the qualifier). On the contrary pot is the locus for potness. But this objection is not valid; Annambhatta's reply is that:

> For what is meant (by the definition D1) is that it (true cognition) is the cognition of the relation of a certain character (tatsambandhānubhava) in respect of that subject (tatra) in which there is the relation of that character and certainly there is in pothood the relation of a pot (although the pot cannot be said to be in pothood. (Tarkadipika : 35).

Annambhaṭṭa's interpretation of D1 and D2 in terms of tatsambandhānubhava (cognition of the relation of a certain character in respect of that subject) implies that

D1 and D2 cover all sorts of true cognitions. If so

D2 and D3 are not mutually exclusive and

D3 is just the paraphrase of D2.

9.14. Since a true declarative sentence expresses a true cognition, it is desirable to understand the structure of true sentence. But what are the conditions or criteria of a true sentence? Or under what conditions a declarative sentence functions as a legitimate vehicle for true cognition? There are four criteria that a true sentence must satisfy: akāṅkṣā (expectancy), yogyatā (competency), āsatti, or sannidhi (proximity) and tātparya (intention). First three conditions are general conditions of any sentence true or false. The addition of fourth necessary condition tātparya and the first three conditions together constitute necessary and sufficient conditions for a true sentence, thus:

'A sentence is true if and only if it has expectancy, competency, proximity and intention'.

A true sentence like 'the pot is blue' is true as it satisfies criteria mentioned above. The first requirement of expectancy is satisfied interms of structural or syntactical adequacy. The component words fite in the structure of sentence to make that sentence grammatically adequate, otherwise mere grouping of words such as 'The pot, blue, is' lacks syntactical expectancy.

The second criterion of competency or compatibility avoids internal inconsistency among words within the structure of a given sentence. A sentence must be formally consistent whether it is materially true or false because competency is a necessary condition of an adequate sentence.

The third criterion, proximity implies proper order and relevance of the component terms in the sentence. An irrelevant and disordered collection of words does not yield any sense to the sentence and consequently sentence becomes inadequate. The formulation of any adequate sentence (true or false) must be in accordance with the first three criteria. An adequate sentence becomes a true sentence by virtue of the addition of fourth condition, tātparya or intension. In the Nyāya theory of communícation, speaker's sayings or utterances presuppose certain type of intention., such that with reference to his intention certain type of verbal reports function as true sentence. Contextually tātparya or intension presupposes reliable person's reports. And it is the reliability or trustworthiness of the speaker which qualifies a given utterance as true eventhough ultimately what makes a sentence true is the true cognition which corresponds to a fact.

A true sentence may be redefined with reference to D2 as follows:

A sentence is true if and only if qualifier-term is relaled to qualificand-term through appropriate verb. That is to say that a sentence is true if it describes a fact as it is.

9.15. Navya-naiyāyikas' definition of truth (D2) may be compared and contrasted with semantic theory of truth. Tarski's[8] semantic theory of truth is normally claimed to be a sophisticated version of traditional correspondence theory of truth. Traditional view of truth interms of correspondence involves many ambiguous and obscure notions such as 'reality', 'fact' and 'corresponds. Tarski's originality in his formulation of the semantic definition of truth, lies in the fact that he uses precisely the semantic concept namely satisfaction which is the defining property of the concept of truth. The word 'truth' is also a semantic concept, it is a property of a true declarative sentence. The concept of truth is also meta-linguistic for the concept of truth is explicable in meta-language,

Tarski has made an attempt to give satisfactory definition of truth interms of material adequacy and formal correctness. Both material adequacy and formal correctness constitute necessary and sufficient conditions for the definition of truth.

The criterion for material adequacy is expressed in the form of the following schema:

(T) : 'X' is true if and only if p.

Where p is to be replaced by any declarative sentence of object language 'X' stands for a name of the sentnece (p) which occupies p. A definition of truth should have the consequences of all the instances of the schema (T). For example

(i) 'Snow is white' is true if and only if snow is white. It is an instance of T, where the expression on the right hand side is the sentence and its quotation mark is a name of that sentence. Quotation mark distinguishes between talking about snow on the right hand side and talking about words on the left and side. The sentence 'snow is white' is true because as a matter of fact snow is white. However Tarski's paradigm (i) cannot be generalised as :

'p' is true if and only if p.

for the letter 'p' is only a sixteenth letter of English alphabet and hence there is no generalization and an attempt at generalization would result in explicit contradiction. Authors like Prior (1967:230)[9] for instance have shown contradiction as as follows :

(ii) The sixteenth letter of the alphabet is a true sentence if and only if 'snow is white', and

(iii) the sixteenth letter of the alphabet is a true sentence if and only if snow is not white.

(i) and (ii) entail the contradiction that 'snow is white' if and only if snow is not white. For Tarski neither the expression (T) itself nor any particular instanace of (T) is to be regarded as the definition of truth. Every equivalence of the schema T obtained by replecing p by a particular sentence and 'X' by the name of that sentence may be considered as a partial definitron of truth and the conjunction of all such partial definitions constitute the general definition of truth. But there is a difficulty about infinite number of conjuncts. Of course Tarski is aware of this difficulty of infinite conjuncts and tries to over come it by incorporating the notion of sequence.(—)

The word 'true' in (T) is a metalinguistic concept because truth value of sentence is expressed in metalanguage.

The second requirement is the formal correctness. It is about the structure of a language in which the definition of truth is to be given. Tarksi (1944 : 586-7) draws the distinction between semantically closed and semantically open language. Semantically closed language consists of certain expressions and names of those expressions. And there is also the belief that laws of logic operate in that language. Semantically closed language is a source of semantical paradoxes. Samantically open language on the other hand is normally an object language for which the concept of truth is defined in metalanguage.

After the formulations material adequacy and formal correctness Tarski[24] formulates semantic definition of truth. This definition of truth involves characterisation of true sentence as follows :

S1 'A sentence is true if it is satisfied by all objects and false otherwise.

Concept of satisfaction in this definition is a relation between open sentence and its object. Quine (Philosophy of Logic) (1970) : 36-7) characterise the concept of satisfaction by the notion of ordered pairs, triples and so. Given function 'x is white' is satisfiedby an object snow and turns out to be true sentence. But a technical difficulty faced, by Tarki is that a sentintial function may contain any number of free variables and the notion of satisfaction with one variable represents a binary relation between the function and a single object. Function with two variables become a ternary relation between functions and couples of objects and so on ad infinitum Tarski (1944 : 591) overcomes this difficulty by introducing another semantic notion of sequence, and redefines true sentence as follows :

A true sentence is that which is satisfied by every sequence.

Now in this definition satisfaction is not considered as a many termed relation between sentential functions and an infinite number of objects but as a *binary relation* between functions and sequence of objects. But what is a sequence ? Singles, pairs, triples and so on are collectively known as sequences (Quine 1970 : 37). A sequence satitfies a sentential function if the sentence comes out true when we take the first thing of the sequence as the value of 'x' in the sentence and the second thing of the sequence as the value of the variable 'y' in the sentence, and so on.

9.16. So far I have given the important aspects of Tarski's semantic concept of truth for the purpose of comparative understanding. Authors like Prof. Mohanty[10a(i)] and Prof. B.K. Matilal[10b] think that Navya-nyāya conception of truth especially Gaṅgeśa's concept of truth differs from Tarski's semantic concept of truth for the following reasons.

R1: According to Navya-nyāya a qualificative cognition is a bearer of truth value. A cognition (or proposition) is capable of being expressed through a declarative sentence, and a cognition is prior to language. But Tarśki's notion of truth is applicable to declarative sentence and is always related to a specific language.

R3: Semantic theory of truth requires the distinction between object language and meta-language but no such distinction is made in Nyāya theory of truth.

R3 : Gaṅgeśa's concept of truth consists of both epistemic and ontological components. 'Viśeṣyatā (qualificand) is an epistemological notion, but the idea of 'tadvattva' seems ontological in nature; 'tadvati' may be construed as 'tadvadviśesyakatve sati' which means 'having viśeśya' which possesses 'tat'.

However it is desirable to evaluate the weight of the reasons R1 to R3 towards the difference between the alleged theories of truth· Nyāya view of truth, that truth is the property of a true qualificative cognition (R1) does not make significant difference with semantic concept of turth. Because a qualificative congnition in principle is capable of being expressed in a language. Normally characterisation of truth is at the level of expressions in the form of cognitive language.

Regarding (R2)—It is possible to formulate meta-languistic sentence within the framework of Nyāya theory of truth. The same can be shown by expressing Tarski's paradigm as an inatance of Nyāya definition of truth D2.

Tarski's paradigm namelly 'Snow is white' is true if and only if Snow is white' may be expressed from the Nyāya point of view as follows :

The cognition 'Snow is white' is true if and only if whiteness (the qualifier) occurs in snow (qualificand).

It is to be noted that like Nyāya definition of turth, semantic definition truth is also an attempt to characterise the notion of truth within the realistie framework of metaphysics.

Nevertheless it is possible to point put certain significant differences between the Nyāya definition and semantic definition of truth.

The defining properity of Nyāya conception of truth is tadvati tatprakārakatvam, 'a legitimate relationship between qualificand and qualifier but the defining property of semantic conception of truth is 'satisfaction by every sequence'. Tarski himself has put the limitation to the semantic concept of truth by saying that it is not applicable to natural language.

Further the notions involved in the defining property of truth in Navya-nyāya are capable of being expressed in the system of language in which no adequate distinction of semantically closed and semantically open language is sought. Navya-nyāya conception of truth and the criteria of truth provide an adequate frame work for realistic epistemology. The ramifications of this type of theory of truth find their relevance in formal and material sciences and also in practical life.

Notes and References

1 Sarvavyavahāraheturbuddhirjñanam Sa dvividhā smṛti-ranubhavasch Sā (anubhavaḥ) dvividhā yatharth āyathārthasch; Tarka-samgrah: 34·5. Smrtirapi dvividhā yathārthā yatharthasca Tarka Samgrha 65 in *Tarka Saṃgraha of Annambhatta with authors own Dipika and Govardhana's Nyāya Bodhini* Edited by Y.V. Athalye and M.R. Bodas (1974) Bhandarkar Oriental Research Institute poona,

apramā cha pramā cheti jñānam dvividhamiṣyate Bhasaparicheda : 126 in *Bhāsā-pariccheda with Siddhānta Mukātavalī by Visvanātha Edtor Swami Madhavananda Advaita Ashrama Calcutta 1977.* The root jña yields the cognate words like jñāna, jñapti (understanding), jñātam (knowledge or (cognised), jñāta viṣayatvam jñātata-taccha svarūpa samandhameva, yathā jñāto ghatah iti pratīti viṣayo jñātateti Naiyāyikaḥ. *Nyāya-Kosa* Bhimacharya Jhalkikar (1977) Bhandarkar Oriential Research Institute, Poona Pp-300-1. Barlingay S.S. (1976) : *A Modern Introduction to Logic* National Publisher House, New Delhi, Keith, A.B. (1977): *Indian Logic and Atomism*, Oriental Reprint Book Corporation, New Delhi, Pp-42-5. Potter, K.H. (1977): *Encyclopedea of Indian Philosophies Vol. I. 145-9.* Keith does not distinguish between cognition and knowledge, he almost uses them synonymously.

Unlike Keith, Potter gives another rendering namely judgement for jñāna. But even the word 'judgement' does not capture the sence of jñāna which has more wider sense than that of judgement.

2. In contemporary epistemology S knows that p if and only if.
   (i) S believes in p
   (ii) p is true and
   (iii) S is justified in believing that p *Theory of knowledge* (1977) by R.M. Chisholm, Prentice Hall India; Pp-102-4.
3. Gaṅgeśa Upādhyaya (1300) : *Tattva-Cintāmaṇi* with Shri Mathuranatha tarkavagīsāviracitayā rahasyakhyaya tīkayo sahitah: prathamo bhāgaḥ Pratyakṣa khaṇdam Shri Kamakhya natha tarka vagiseṇa pariśodhitam (1974) Motilal Banarasidas Delhi, See the chapter on Pramā laksaṇa pūrvapakṣa. A brief summary of a few incorrect definitions rejected by Gaṅgesa is given by Prof. J.N. Mohanty (1961) in his book '*Gāngesa's Theory of truth*' Pp. 40-2. Shanti Niketan Visvabharti.
4. *The Elements of Indian Logic and Epistemology* (1974) by C Bhattacharya, Modern Book Agency Calcutta p, 10.

5. *The Navya Nyāya Theory of Inference* 1977 by L.C Mullati Karnatak University, Dharwad. P. 156.
6. Mohanty J.N. (1966): *Gangesa's theory of Truth* Visva-Bharati, Santiniketan, P.33.
7. Mohanty J.N. (1966) : *Gangesa's Theory of Truth* P.43-4. Mohanty J.N. (1966) Op. cited 111-2.
8. (i) Tarski, A (1931): 'The Concept of Truth in formalised languages *in Logic, semantic and mathematics* Edited translated by Woodges (J.H. (1956) The Clarendon Press Oxford. P 152-278.
   (ii) Tarski, A (1944) : 'The Semantic Conception of Truth' in *Problems in the Philosophy of Language* Ed. by T.M. Olshewsky (1969) Hatt, Rinchart and Winston Inc New York Pp 578-610.
9. Prior A.N. "Correspondence Theory of Truth" in *Encyclopedia of Philosophy* Nos 152 Pp 230-1, Collier Macmillan NewYork, 1967.
10. (a) (i) J.N. Mohanty (1966) : Op. cit Pp 45-6.
   (ii) B.K. Matilal (1968) : Op. cit (Note No. 12 b Pp 332).
   (b) Matilal, B.K. (1968: 'Indian Theories of knowladge and Truth' in *Philosophy* East *and West* Vol. XVIII No. 4; Pp. 322.

IV
KNOWLEDGE

10

Gaṅgeśa's Concept of Knowledge (Pramā)*

10.1. Gaṅgeśa's *Tattva-cintāmaṇi*, the magnum-opus of Navya-Nyāya is the paradigm of pramāṇa-śāstra, because *Tattva-ciatāmaṇi*, deals exclusively with pramāṇa (source of knowledge) as its subject matter. Following the Nyāya tradition of Gautama, Gaṅgeśa identifies four pramāṇas, pratyakṣa, anumāna upamāna and śabda[1] in order to explicate the structure of each pramāṇa under separate section. Since pramāṇa is the instrumental cause of pramā (pramā karaṇam pramāṇam),[2] in this paper an attempt has been made to understand the nature of pramā as explicated by Gaṅgeśa.

10.2. Pramā (Yathārthānubhava) is a species of jñāna. Accordingly jñāna (cognition) is either yathārtha (true) or ayathārtha (bhrama). Pramā (knowledge) is sharply distinguished from bhrama (error) by virtue of pramātva (knowledgeness) technically called the avacchedaka (limitor) of pramā.[3]

10.3. Gaṅgeśa in the chapter on pramālakṣaṇa pūrvapakṣa (pp 373-400) considers various views abuot the notion of pramā held by other schools. Subsequently in the section : Pramā-

* Reprinted from *Pathway to God* 1988, Pp. 25-35, Academy of Comparative Philosophy and Religion, Belgaum.

lakṣaṇa-siddhānta, (pp. 401-429) Gaṅgeśa formulates adequate definitions of knowledge in order to explicate the structure of pramā as distingushed from apramā.

(1) To the question what is pramātva (prāmāṇya) mainly Prabhākara's views are considered in the pūrvapakṣa. Prābhākaras regard every jñāna as true. That is to say that every jñāna is pramā characterised by pramātva (prāmāṇya). Since jñānatva or anubhavatva, according to Prābhākaras is not a jāti (universal) pramātva or prāmāṇya is not jāti. Further pramātva is not generic character or jāti because it is not free from sāmkarya (cross division) which is jātibādhaka. That is to say that pramātva is not vyāpyavṛtti (complete occurrence). Sometimes part of error may consist of knowledge (bhramāme pramā). Thus pramātva and bhramatva may reside in the same locus as in the case of interference of two or more cognitions (samūhālambana jñāna).[4] The above objection reflects Prābhākara's metaphysical standpoint regarding the nature of jāti. According to that standpoint jāti can be present only in perceptible individual as instances of substance.[5] Hence jāti is absent in other categories like guṇa and karma. And jñāna or pramā is not viewed as substance, hence pramātva or jñānatva is not a jāti.

10.4. But the above objection does not stand to reason, for in the tradition of Nyāya four forms of pramā namely, pratyakṣa (perceptual knowledge), anumiti (inferential knowledge), upamiti (identificational knowledge and śabda (testimonical knowladge) have been recognised. Since pramā is caused by pramāṇa, pramātva is considered to be kāryatāvacchedaka (limitor of pramā which is the consequence of pramāṇa). Pramā is a species of jñāna which is an instance of guṇa (quality). And guṇa according to Nyāya can possess guṇatva as its jāti. Therefore pramātya is jāti or universal and is manifested in the four forms of pramā.[6] Since pramātva also functions as limitor or avacchedaka for each pramā, there is no possibility of sāṇkarya or overlapping of knowledge (pramā) and apramā (error). And even apramā (error) is also clearly demarketed by virtue of its limitor apramātva or bhramatva.

Thus pramātva as jāti is present only in pramā and is absent in apramā.

10.5. Gaṅgeśa considers some definitions of pramātva given by different schools along with the criticisms.

D1. Bhāṭṭas formulate the definition of pramātva in terms of the property of apprehension of previously unapprehended true cognition hāyathārthāgṛhīta-grāhitvaṁ). According to this definition pramā as knowledge is a new understanding of a true cognition. Hence novelty (anadhigatattva) as defining property of pramā (knowledge) negates true memory cognition as pramā.

But D1 is too narrow as it is not applicable to a series of true cognitions about the same objeet. For example in the perception of a pillar, even though there is no novelty of perception, perceptual knowledge is obtained.[7]

Subsequently (D2) yathārthānubhavatvam is also not satisfactory. According to D2: Pramā (knowledge) is apprehension of that true cognition resembling its object (yathārtha). But possibly there could he no resemblance between true cognition and its object,[8] because cognition as a quality and object as substance belong to different orders of reality. For example there is no structural similtarity between the true cognition 'this is a pot' and the object 'pot'. But if similarity between a cognition and its object is taken for granted, in that case one has to accept the similarity between false cognition and its object, however this is not so.

D3. Pramātva cannot be defined as the proparty of being uncontradicted experience (abādhitānubhavatvam)[9] because it is possible that contradictory cognition (bādha) is itself true, through contradictory relation (bādhakajñā) for instance the fact that p is contradicted by p it does not follow that p is true or that-p is false. For example a proposition 'some swans are quadrupeds' is false and its contradictory 'No swan is a quadruped' is true because every swan is a biped.

D4: Pramātva cannot be defined in terms of saṁvādyanubhavatvam (experience of coherence), because coherence which is 'being mentioned as consistent with another cognition' may also be found in cases of error also.[10] Accordingly D4 is too wide as it is applicable to true and false cognitions.

D5 : Pramātva cannot be defined in terms of samarthapravṛttijanakatvam (means of successful activity) for the definition does not accomodate an instance of pramā where due to some reason no fruitful activity follows. For instance cases of upekṣāpramā do not cause any pragmatic activity.[11]

D6 : Pramātva as tettvānubhavatvam (the property of being experience of the real) excludes the the species of pramā about non existence of facts.[12] Hence the definition is too narrow.

D7 : Pramātva cannot be defined as the characteristic property of an experience of the qualifier as a property which is not the counter positive of an absolute absence, residing in the qulificandum (viśeṣyaniṣṭātyantābhāvāpratiyogi-dharmaprakārakānubhavatvam). Because D7 is not applicable to a certain type of pramā (knowledge) of conjunction which is characterised by incomplete occurrence (avyāpyavṛtti). And in case of conjunctive knowledge, conjunction may be absent in the qualificandum and consequently there may be the counter-positive of an absence residing in the qualificandum.[13] Avyāpyavṛtti (incomplete occurance) is a relation such that qualifier occurs in only part of qualificandum. In the case of a monkey on a tree, the monkey is related to a part of the tree, say one of its branches, by virtue of its contact. And constant absence of contact related to the other parts of the tree such as the roots having absolute absence of the monkey is considered to be avyāpya-vṛtti (incomplete occurrence).

D8 : Pramātva cannot be defined in terms of viśeṣyavṛttyanyonyābhāva-pratiyogitāvacchedaka- dharmprakārakānubhavatvam (the property of on experience where qualifier is not a property which limits the counterpositiveness of a mutual absence residing in the qualificandum).[14] In other words pramā (knowledge) cannot be defined as an experience of qualities as related to its qualificandum where qualifier is not a property which limits the counter-positiveness of mutual absence residing in the qualificandum. The inadequacy of D8 becomes clearer by the following illustration. The true cognition (p) that 'This tree has conjunction with monkey, has qualifier namely conjunction with monkey' whose absence is in the qualificandum namely 'This tree' because there is also another true cognition with the same qualificandum namely 'This tree is one having no conjunction with the monkey in another part of the tree.' Consequently there is in the qualificandum (this tree) also a mutual absence (or differenc) whose counter-positive is one having conjunction with monkey' And the limitor of the counterpositiveness is the property of being the conjunction which is the qualifier of the true cognition that 'this tree has the conjunction with the monkey.'

D9 : Pramā or knowledge cannot be defined in terms of an experience of a cognition which does not have a qualifier non-resident in the qualificandum (viśesyāvrttya prakāratānubhava). Because the definition is not applicable to the conjunction of true cognitions namely 'These are pot and cloth.[15] Here the qualifier 'potness' is absent in the cloth and the qualifier 'clothness' is absent in the pot. Hence the D9 is too narrow. And D9 is also too wide as it is applicable to the conjunction of true and false cognitions or knowledge and error (pramā-apramā samūha) combined.

D10 : Pramā cannot be defined as an experience of a cognition whose qualifier is a part of the contentness of that cognition (Viṣayatāsamānādhikarṇa prakārakānubhavaḥ). This is so because D 10 is not applicable to non-qualificative cognition (nirvikalpakajñāna)[16] which is devoid of a qualificer (prakāra). Secondly D 10 is also applicable to error partially containing knowledge (bhramatvaṃśe pramā). Thus characterisation of pramā in terms of prakāra (qualifier) is an instance of incomplete definition for it is not applicable to non-qualificative (nirvikalpakajñāna) which has no qualifier (prakāra).

10.6 But since according to Gaṅgeśa (nirvikalpaka-jñāna) is excluded from the distinction of pramā and apramā, or it is neutral to truth values,[17] the defination may not be defective due to the presence of prakāra (qualifier). As a matter of fact

Gaṅgeśa formulates the definition of pramā containing qualifier as one of the elements in the definiens.

Gaṅgeśa's pramāṇa-lakṣaṇa siddhānta begins with the formulation of adequate definition of pramā as follows:

D=Pramā (knowledge) is an experience of a fact as it is.[18] Technical formulation of this definition is:

D=Pramā (knowledge) is an experience of the qualifier belonging to its qualificand through appropriate relation.[19] Or more formally, pramā (knowledge) is an apprehension of a true cognition such that its qualifier (prakāra) is appropriately related to its qualificand.

An important component com of pramā (knowledge) is a true congnition. The structure of true congnition consists of qualificand, qualifier and relation which relates qualifier to its qualificand. For example the true congition that 'the pot is blue' consists of 'pot' as qualificand and 'blue' as the qualifier of the qualificand 'pot', the relation of blue to pot is known as inherence.

10.7 But it may be objected that the definition (D) applies to a cognition of ghaṭa (pot) when tadvati is interpreted as ghaṭatvādhikaraṇa (locus of potness) but it is not applicable to a cognition that 'ghaṭatva is in ghaṭa' for ghaṭatva in not the adhikaraṇa of ghaṭa. Thus the expression 'tadvati' cannot function in this case and consequently the definition D is too narrow as it is not applicable to certain cases of pramā.[20] This objection is not correct because in the alleged true cognition 'the pot-hood is in pot', the viśeṣya, is 'pot-hood' and prakāra is pot. The appropriate relation which holds good between 'pot-hood' and 'pot' is inherence (samavāya). And tadvati means tatsambandhavati.[21] In other words viśeṣya must possess a legitimate relation with its prakāra and hence D is applicable to the above type of knowledge (pramā).

Now it is interesting to see how the definition (**D**) applies to cases of pramā (knowledge) only, but does not apply to error (apramā) or false belief. Consider an instance of knowledge that 'This is silver.' This knowledge is constituted by 'This' as viśeṣya and the three qualifiers 'thisness', 'silver' and 'silverness'. If we take the qualifier 'silverness' as the value of the variable 'tat' then in that case the knowledge is one which has 'silverness' as its qualifier. Accordingly knowledge is rajatava-prakāraka. Since the qualificand 'this' refers to a real silver, consequently this possesses silverness. Thus the knowledge (pramā) that this is silver' is equivalent to the pramā as charācrtred by the sion, rajatava-prakārakānubhava.[22] In other words the expres pramātva in the present context, is characterised by the property of rajatava-prakārakatva.

10 8 Let us take a case of error where a piece of shell is mistaken for silver. The erroneous cognition is expressed as 'this is silver', This cognition has also 'silverness' as its prakāra (qualifier). But the qualifier 'silverness' does not belong to the qualificand this; that is to say that this is not rajatatvavat. Similarly a doubtful cognition as an instance of apramā is not satisfied by D as mutually incompatible properties cannot belong to the thing designated by 'this'. Hence the definition D does not apply to erroneous and doubtful cogitions. Both erroneous and doudtful cognitions are satisfied by the definition of apramā (D′):

D′ : tadabhāvavati tatprakārka jñānam apramā.[23]

=Apramā (false belief) is an apprehension of (a false) cognition in which qualifier (prakāra) is not appropriately related to qualificand (viśeṣya).

10.9 Since the definitions of knowledge (D) and error (D′) are mutually incompatible, it is not the case that D and D′ function towards the same cognition, because they are applicable to mutually exclusive cognitions. In other words D is applicable only to pramā whereas D′, is applicable to apramā only.

Pramā in relation to pramāṇa, prameya and pramātṛ is to be analysed as follows :

Pramā is justified true congnition because primā is grounded in pramāṇa and hence pramā is justified by pramāṇa.

Pramātṛ possesses pramā if and only if

(i) there is a true cognition of a prameya (object);
(ii) Pramatṛ apprehends that true cognition
and (iii) that true cogninition is justified by a pramāṇa.

The structure of pramā is similar to the structure of knowledge in western epistemology in which knowledge is justified true belief.[24] Thus pratyakṣa-pramā (perceptual knowledge) is justified by pratyakṣa-pramāṇa ; anumiti (inferntial knowledge is justified by anumāna (inference). Upamiti and śābda are also justified by the respective pramāṇas, namely upamāna and śabda.[25] Hence pramāṇa as a means of justificātion clearly distinguishes apramā from pramā, because only pramā is justifiable by a pramāṇa.

Notes and References

1. Gaṅgeśa (1947) : Tattvacintāmaṇi with Mathurānātha's Tattvacintāmaṇirahasya. Edited by K. Tarkavagish, Motilal Banarsidas, New Delhi, Pratyakṣa-khaṇḍa, p. 538.
2. (i) Tattvacintāmaṇirahsya, pp. 116-117.
   (ii) Jhalkikar Bhimacharya (1974) : Nyāya-koṣa Bhandarkar Oriental Research Institute, Poona, pp. 553-556.
3. Guha, D. C. (1968) : Navya-nyāya-system of Logic, Bharatiya Vidya Prakasana, Varanasi, pp. 34-36.
4. Na tāvajjātiḥ, yogyavyaktivṛttitvena pratyakṣatva pramātva-samśayānupapatteh......sākṣātvādinā sankarāpatteṣca.
5. Radhakrishnan, S. (1977) : Indian Philosophy (Vol. II), Blackie and Sons, Bombay, p. 415.
6. (i) Tattvacintāmaṇi, (TC) pp. 538.
   (ii) Tattvacintāmaṇi-rahasya, pp. 538-539.
7. नापि यथायार्थगृहीतग्राहित्वं, धारावाहिकबुद्धयव्याप्ते:
   T.C. 379.
8 नापि यथार्थानुभवत्वं, ज्ञाते घटत्वादिना यथाशब्दार्थ-
सादृश्याभावात्। सादृश्यात्रस्य भ्रमेऽपि गतत्वात् ।
   T.C. 381.

9. नाप्यबाधितानुभवत्वं, बाधस्य विपरीतप्रमात्वात् । T.C. 382.
10. नापि संवाद्यनुभवत्वं, ज्ञानान्तरेण तथोल्लिख्यमानत्वस्य संवादित्वस्यभ्रमसाधारणत्वात् । T.C. 382
11. नापि समर्थप्रवृत्तिजनकानुभवत्व, उपेक्षाप्रमायामव्याप्तेः । T.C. 382. 3.
12. नापि तत्वानुभवत्वं, अवस्तुनोऽभानात् । T.C. 383.
13. नापि विशेष्यनिष्ठात्यन्ताभावाप्रतियोगिधर्मप्रकारकानुभवत्वं, संयोगादि-प्रमाऽव्याप्तिः । T.C. 383–4
14. नापि विशेष्यवृत्यन्योन्याभावप्रतियोगितावच्छेदक-धर्माप्रकारकानुभवत्वं, अव्याप्यवृत्तिप्रमानुपग्रहात् । मूले वृक्षः कपिसंयोगवान्नाग्रे इत्यबाधितानुभवात् । T.C. 384.
15. नापि विज्ञष्यावृत्यप्रकारकानुभवत्व, एकैक-विशेष्यावृत्तिनानाप्रकारकसमूहालम्बनाऽव्याप्तेः । T.C. 386.
16. विषयतासमानाधिकरणप्रकारकानुभवः······ न, निर्विकल्पकाव्याप्तेः······भ्रमस्तत्रांशे प्रमैवेति । T.C. 390—1.
17. निर्विकल्पकञ्च प्रमाप्रमाबहिर्भतमेवः T.C. 402.
18. यत्र यदस्ति तत्र तस्यानुभवः प्रमा । T.C. 401.
19. तद्वति तत्प्रकारकानुभवः । T.C. 401.
20. Tarka-Samgraha with Tarka-dipika (Section. 35) Edited by Athalye Y. V. and Bodas M. R. Bhandarkar Oriental Research Institute Poona, 1974.
21. Tarka-dīpika Section : 35.
22. (i) Tattva-cintāmaṇi-rahasya, 402.
    (ii) Gaṅgesa's Theory of Truth by Jitendranath Mohanty, Vishvabharati Shantiniketan, 1966 pp. 43-44.
23. (i) TC : 401 (ii) Nyāya-Kosa : p. 64.
24. Adequate explication of the classical definition of Knowledge is given in Theory of knowledge by Chisholm R. M., Prentice Hall India 1977, pp. 102-118.
25. सा च प्रमा चतुर्विधा प्रत्यक्षानुमित्युपमितिशाब्द-भेदात् ।····· प्रमाणमपि चतुर्विधं प्रत्यक्षानुमानोपमानशब्दभेदात् । T.C. p. 538.

11

Gangeśa's Definition of Perceptual Knowledge (Pratyakṣa-Pramā)*

11.1. In the Navya-Nyāya system of Gaṅgeśvara (1300 AD) partyakṣa-pramā (perceptual knowledge) is formulated in relation to pratyakṣa pramāṇa (perception) such that pratyakṣa pramāna[1] (perception is the instrumental cause of pratyaksa-pramā (perceptual knowledge).

Gaṅgeśa critically considers several definitions of pratyakṣa-pramā in order to formulate more adequate definition.

The old school of Nyāya formulates the definition of perceptual knowledge interms of sense-object contact. According to it (D1) perceptual knowledge (pramā) is true cognition (knowledge) produced by the contact of an object with a sense organ. (indriyārtha sanikarṣotpannam jñānamavyabhicāri)[2] This definition implies that perceptual knowledge is a form of true cognition which is conditioned by the stimulation of senses as influenced by their objects. The definition follows from the etymology of the word 'pratyakṣa' which derivatively means the functioning of the sense organs, in relation to its particular

* This paper was read in the 61st Session of Indian Philosophical Congress held at Jadavpur University, Calcutta; October 1986.

object (akṣasya prativiṣayam vrttiḥ pratyakṣam)[3]. Whenever a sense-organ adequately functions in relation to its object, the result is a true cognition of that object.

11.2. The exponent of the modern school of Nyāya, Gaṅgeśa offers criticisms to D1. Firstly, D1 is too wide, for it applies to inference and memory, as forms of knowledge they involve sense object contact. Mind as an internal sense organ functions toward the object known through inference or memory.[4] Secondly, the definition D1 is also too narrow in another sense, for it excludes divine perception which is a direct perception of all the facts.[5] Further there can be species of perception without sense-object contact.

Consequently sense-object contact is not common to all perceptions. Further the definition of perception interms of sense-stimulation begs the question: the nature of sense-stimulation is to be known from the characteristic of perception and we understand what perception is through the meaning of sense-object contact.[6]

11.3. However in the (syncretist) school of Nyāya attempts have been made to defend the older definition of perceptual knowledge (D1). Authors like Udayana,[7] have suggested that the definition of perception given in the Nyaya sūtra interms of sense-object contact applies only, to human perception. Since pramāna sāstra is concerned with the criteria or grounds of knowledge, it, is not primarily concerned with the eternal and unconditioned knowledge of the divine being. However in order to accommodate extra-ordinary (alaukika) perception as well as the divine perception it is necessary to widen the scope of the definition (D1).

11.4. Another definition (D2) without reference to sense-object contact is considered and shown to be inadequate. D2:' 'Perceptual knowledge is that true apprehension produced by sense organ' implies the functions of sense-organ as the characteristic of perceptual knowledge.[8] But this definition is too vide. It is applicable to other forms of pramā including memory knowledge,[9] for mind as a sense-organ functions in every form of pramā.

11.5. Although still another definition (D3) of pratyakṣa as direct aprenension; fomulated by Prābhākaras, does not contain sense object contact as defining property, it is also considered to be inadequate for the following reasons. Perceptual cognition characterised as immediate cognition includes even memory, inference etc. which are considered to be perceptual in the subjective side in relation to the knower (svāṃse jnatrameseca)[10]. Eventhough perceptual knowledge is understood as immediate knowledge, immediacy (sāksātva) in the form universal (jati)[11] is not recognised by Prābhakaras. However every cognition is not reduciable to perceptual knowledge.

11.6. In view of such defects in the avobe definitions Gangeśa formulates the definition of perception as immediate knowledge. And character of immediacy (sakṣātkāritvam) is common to different forms of perceptions. The simpler formula tion of the definition of pratyaksa is as follows :

D: Perceptual knowledge is characterised by immediacy of apprehension.

(Pratyakṣasya sākṣātkāritvam lakṣaṇam)[12]

In this definition immediacy or sākṣātkāritvam is universal (jāti), sakṣātkaromī.[13] (apprehend directly) as anuvyavsāya (after cognition) in perceptual knowledge implies general characteristic of sākṣātkāritvam (immediacy). Another definition of perceptual knowledge given by Gaṅgeśa is as follows :

d: Perceptual knowledge is not brought about by the instrumentality of any antecedent knowledge.

(jñānākaraṇakam jñānamiti tu vayam).[14]

This definition (d)[15] is the negative characterisation of perceptual knowledge which is not derived through the function of any others antecedent knowledge. However the two definitions D1 and d stated above are not mutually exclusive. The definition D logically implies the definition d. because the nature of immediacy of perceptual knowledge, must be understood interms of being directly evident and directly evident as the property of cognition does not presuppose another cognition.

11.7. However the usage of the word 'jñāna' in the definition (d) seems to be ambiguous, for jñāna is either yathārthajñāna (true cognition) or ayathārthajñāna (false cognition). Consequently the definitions d and D are accaisionally applicable to perceptual errors also. For instance in abnormal perceptions such as illusion, hallucination dream and the like there is an element of immediacy or direct awareness without any presupposition of prior cognition.

But this objection is not correct. Contextually the definitions D and d are formulated to characterise pratyakṣapramā (perceptual knowledge) only, because pratyakṣa pramā is caused by pratyakṣa pramāṇa.[16] And pratyakṣa pramā as a species of pramṛ is to be understood as a true congition which corresponds to its fact. It may be asked if a defining property of pramā (knowledge) in general is 'tadvatitatprakārakatva[17] (correspondence of a true cognition with its fact), how are we to demarcate certain species of pramā as pratyakṣapramā ?

The precise answer to this question comes from the definition (D) that the property of immediacy is the unique characteristic of pratyakṣapramā (perceptual knowledge). The definition 'D' is not applicable to pereceptual errors (pratyakṣa-bhrama) which is a species of apramā (error) and apramā (error) is characterised by the property of a congnition which does not belong to its qualificand (viśeṣya) (tadabhāvavati that prakārakānubhavaḥ apramā).

11.8. Whether pratyabhijñā (recognition or reminiscence) is to be considered as perceptual knowledge (pratyakṣa-pramā)? Even though (perceptual) objects are directly given in recognition and perception, there are certain differences between them. Recognition in a wider sense means understanding the nature or character of a thing.[19] Accordingly the recognition of a thing is the knowledge of it as such and such, for example the knowledge of the animal as a cow. Generally recognition in this sense stands for determinate perception (savikalpakapratyakṣa) in which a thing is related to its qualities by, means of predication. But in a narrow sense recognition means knowing a thing which was known before[20] In other words to recongnise means to cognise again which was already cognised before; and it is in this sense, pratyabhijñā is recognition, where there is conscious reference of the past and a present cognition to the object.[21] Eventhough recognition is brought about by sense-impressions of previous experience of an object it canot be memory knowledge. Because pratyabhijñā is not only produced by sensimpression (memory) but also there is the necessity of perception of an object as operating cause in it. But in memory cognition there is absence of the object, recollected.

In pratyabhijñā the novelty of the knowledge consists in the identity of the thing perceived in the present with that one previously seen. The immediate cause of pratyabhijñā is the remembrance of the identity of a thing produced from previous impressions. Hence pratyabhijñā is not produced by sense-impressions alone.

Recognition (pratyabhijñā) brought about by sense-impressions along with previous experience of an object is to be distinguished from perceptual knowledge characterised by immediacy (sākṣātkāritvam) and the absence of previous knowledge as its instrumental cause. If sense-object contact is a necessary condition of pratyabhijña with mamory element in it then it is present in other forms of mediate knowledge like anumiti (inferential knowledge).

The definition (d) implies the absence of prior cognition to perceptual knowledge but pratyabhjñā (recognition) presupposes prior apprehension as a necessary element. Hence the definition d is not applicable to pratyabhijñā. Thus pratyabhijñā (recognition) and perceptual knowledge are different types of knowledge.[22]

11.9. *Structure of perceptual knowledge*:—A knower (pramātṛa) possesses perceptual knowledge (pratyakṣa-pramā) only if pratyakṣa pramā (perceptual instrument) functions towards perceptual object (prameya). Perceptual knowledge is justified true cognition. The justification is said to be direct or immediate.

Since pramā as knowledge is understood as justified true congnition believed in, perceptual pramā is to be analysed into truth, belief and justification conditions. In case of perceptual knowledge justification is direct so that perceptual knowledge claims are self-justified.

Notes and References

1. (i) Gaṅgeśa (1974) *Tattva-Cintāmani* Pratyakṣa-khaṇda with Mathuranatha's *Tattva-Cintāmani-rahasya* Edited by Tarka-vagisa, K. Motilal Banarsidass, New Delhi P-538.
   (ii) Tattva-Cintāmani-rahasya Pp. 538-9.
2. (i) Ganganatha Jha and Sastri, D (Editors, 1925) : *Nvayadarsane Vātnsyānabhṣāyam*, Chaukhambha Sanskrit Series Varanasi. Nyāya Sutra : 1-1.4.
   (ii) *Tattva-cintāmaṇi* P-539
3. (i) *Nyāya-sūtra-bhāsya* 1.1.3.
   (ii) Athalye Y.V. (Editor 1974) : *Tarka-Samgraha* with *Tark-Dīpika* by Annaṃbhaṭṭa. Bhandrakara Oriental Research Institute, Poona, P-211.
4. (i) *Tattva-Cintāmaṇi* : P; 539.
   (ii) Chatterjee S.C. (1939) : *Nyāya Theory of Knowledge* Calcutta University, Calcutta, Pp 137-8.
5. (i) *Tattva-cintamani*, 539-40: Isvara-pratyaksāvyapteh.
   (ii) Visvanatha Nyāya Pañcānana (1972): *Bhāṣā-pariceheda* with *Siddhānta Muktavalī* Pratyakṣa-khanda, edited with notes in Kannada by Bhatta V.G. Balaganapati, Mysore. Siddhānta-muktavalī-52.
   (iii) *Nyāya-theory of Knowledge* (op. ct) P-138.
6. (i) *Tattva-cintāmani* 543 : nacaindriyajanyatvam. . .anyonyāśrayāt.
7. (i) *Nyāya theory of Knowledge* (Pp 137-8.)
   (ii) *Tarka-saṃgraha* : *Athalye's notes*, Pp 212-213.

8. *Indriyajanyam jñānam janya pratyakṣam Tattva-Cintāmaṇi* P-548.
9. smrtyādeh sāksatkārtvāpatteh. *Tattva-cintāmaṇi* P-550.
10. Prabhākarastu sāksaddhih pratyaksam sāksātvanca na jātih niyata vyañjaka-bhāvāt. *Tattva-Cintāmani* P.556-7.
11. Sastri K.S. (1961) *A Primer of Indian Logic*. The Kuppuswami Sastri Research Institute, Madras, P-172.
12. *Tattva-Cintāmaṇi* P-543, Cf. *Nyāya Theory of Knowledge* Pp-138; Vidya' bhusans Introduction to *Tattva-Cintāmaṇi* P. 11.
13. (i) *Tattva-Cintāmani* P-543;
    (ii) Jhalkikar Bhimacharya (1974) *Nyāya-kosah* Bhandarkar Oriental Research Institute, Poona. sakṣātkārah, pratyaksātmaka jñānam, astra sāksātkāratvam, ca saksatkaromi itya nugata pratīsāksiko jāti-viśesah Pp-988-9.
14. *Tattva-Cintāmaṇi* Pp Cf. *Nyāya Theory of Knowledge* P.138, Vidyabhusana's Introduction. P-11.
15. Datta, D.M. (1972) : *The six ways of Knowing* Calcutta University. Calcutta, P-37.
16. *Tattva-cintāmaṇi* P-138
17. *Tattva-cintāmaṇi* P-401.
18. Ibid.
19. *Nyāya Theory of Knowledge* P-224.
20. Uttara visiṣtajñāne pūrva viśiṣtānubhava-saiva viśeṣana-jñānatvena hetutvāt saṃskārasya smraṇetara janakatvāt. *Tattvacintāmani* pp 570-71.
21. (i) Pūrvaparayorvijñāna yoreka viṣaye pratisandhi jñānam pratyabhijñānam. *Nyaya Sutra Bhasya* P-327.
    (ii) *Nyāya Theory of Knowledge* P-225.
22. *Tattva-cintāmaṇi* Pp 566-571.

12

Gaṅgeśa's Concept of Inferential Knowledge (Anumiti)*

12.1. Anumiti (inferential knowledge) is a species of pramā (knowledge) produced by its pramāṇa (instrumental cause) known as anumāna[1] (inference).

Gaṅgeśa's definition of anumiti (inferential) knowledge is as follows :

D : Inferential knowledge is that knowledge generated by (prior) knowledge of the nature of a minor term such as is qualified by a pervasion; the instrumental cause of this is inferense (vyāpti-viśiṣṭa-pakṣa-dharmatā-jñāna-janyam jñānam anumitiḥ tatkaraṇam anumānam).[2] The important component in the definition is pervasion (vyāpti). Since the knowledge of pervasion constitutes the ground or the justification of inferential knowledge (anumiti); it is desirable to understand the nature of pervasion. The question 'how is vyāpti known presupposes what is vyāpti ? 'vyāpti' literally means permeation, which (vyāpti) implies a correlation between fact of which is pervaded (vyāpa) and the other which pervades (vyāpaka).[3] The vyāpaka (pervader) is present in all the places in which the vyāpya

* This paper was read in the 62nd Session of IPC held at University of Kashmir, Srinagar; June 1987.

(pervaded) is present. For instance smoke is pervaded by fire, sinse all smoky objects are also fiery. There are two forms of vyāpti namely asama or viṣama-vyāpti pervasion of unequal extension. A vyāpti between terms of unequal extension such as smoke and fire is asama-vyāpti, because even though smoke is pervaded by fire, fire is not pervaded by smoke as all fiery objects are not smoky. Hence asama-vyāpti is asymmetrical. On the contrary, sama-vyāpti or equipollent concomitance is symmetrical, for vyāpti holds between two terms which are co-existensive. Sama-vyāpti implies either of them from the other. There is a samavyāpti between cause and effect, substance and attribute.

In either form of vyāpti the middle or the mark (linga) must be related to the major (or sādhya). In vyāpti there exists an invariable and unconditional relation (niyata anaupādhika sambandha) of concomitance between the middle and major terms. Gaṅgeśa's definition of vyāpti given in sidhānta lakṣaṇa prakaraṇa is as follows.:

12.2. V: Pervasion is the uniform existence of the middle term in the same locus with the major term such that the major term is not absent in any locus in which the middle term exists.

pratiyogya samanādhikaraṇayat samānādhikaraṇātyantābhāvā pratiyogitāvacchedakāvachhinnam yanna bhavati tena samam tasya sāmānādhikaraṇyaṃ vyāptiḥ.[4]

Gaṅgeśa discusses various definitions of vyāpti and rejects them as inaccurate. The above definition (V) is accepted by him as correct. It covers both the cases of anvaya (affirmative) vyatireka (negative) generalisations. In anvaya-vyāpti the middle term is vyāpya (subject) and the major is vyāpaka (predicate). But in vyatireka-vyāpti, universal negative, proposition, the contradictory of the vyāpya or subject turns out to be the vyāpaka or predicate and the contradictory of the vyāpaka or predicate becomes vyāpya or subject. For example: (a) 'All smoky things are fiery' is an anva-vyapti. And the corresponding (b) vyatireka-vyāpti is 'whatever is not fiery is not smoky.' (a) and (b) are logically equivalent.

12.3. The next question is : How is vyāpti known ? or how are we to ascertain or formulate the universals or generalisations ? We see only particular facts such as the co-existence of smoke and fire in certain places like kitchen but we have not seen all the instances of smoke and fire. Hence the problem of induction concerning the justification of our knowledge claims about true generalisation based on the observation of particular facts. As in the West, in the Indian tradition there is considerable resistance to the knowledge claims about vyāpti (generalisation). Kind of scepticism regarding the legitimacy of vyāpti on the basis of experience is expressed by the Cārvākas (the radical materialists). According to them human knowledge is limited to particulars only. Sense perception is the only source of human knowledge about particular facts and sense-organs do not go beyond observed facts. But in the formation of vyāpti one has to take a jump from observed to unobserved. Hence there is no knowledge of vyāpti or universal propositions.[5] But in the western traditions it has been argued that sense-perception and reason do not give the knowledge of generalisations. The functions of sense-perception is confined to particular facts only. And reason means only deductive reasoning characterised by the relation of implication between the premiss(es) and the conclusion so that conclusion is logically justified by its premiss (es) and it it impossible for the conclusion to be false and the premisses are true. But in inductive pattern of reasoning from particulars to general, it is possible to have false generalisations even though the premisses are true. This kind of strategy lead some radical rationalists to subscribe the view that only deductive reasoning is the means of mediate knowledge, because our knowledge claims of conclusions are logically justified but no such justification is possible in inductive reasoning, hence there is no knowledge of law like statements or generalisations. Generalisations are only in the form of guesses or conjectures.

12.4. The Buddhist thinkers have encountered the Cārvāka contentions in order to show the possibility of the knowledge about general facts. Buddhists have shown that vyāpti or universal proposition is based on the principles of causality and essential identity (tadutpatti and tādātmya).[6] Since cause cannot be separated from its effect, two things are always related to each other. From practical point of view, on account of pragmatic considerations it is necessary to postulate the relation between cause and effect. But the denial of causal relation or the acceptance of effect without its cause is not admissible because such a hypothesis not only involves self-contradiction but makes practical affairs impossible. To this effect Buddhists[7] have suggested the method of pañcakāraṇi in which there are five steps in the determination of causal relation. First, effect is perceived only after its production. Secondly, the perception of cause implies change in the existing order of things. Thirdly there is an immediate succession of an effect. Fourthly cause ceases. Fifthly effect also disappears. The principle of essential identity (tādātmya) implies the relation between two different things that coexist in the same locus (samānādhikaraṇayam). Consequently there is the relation of identity between the genus and the species. For example siṃsupā is identical with a tree for the same object is referred. Thus all siṃṣuspas are trees.

12.5 However the Naiyayikas express their critical views regarding above Buddhists' standpoint. There are many cases of vyāpti neither causal nor based on the principle of identity, namely a universal relation of co-existence between a certain substance and its attributes. According to Nyāya the justification for general propositions is due to the uncontradicted observation of argreement in presence and that of agreement in absence supplemented by tarka or indirect proof.[8] By means of tarka if the contradictory of inferential conclusion is proved to be false then the universal proposition that 'all case of smoke are the cases of fire' is true and hence the validity of universal relation (vyāpti) between smoke and fire.

12.6. Naiyāyikas also suggest some direct means of apprehending pervasion (vyāpti). According to their theory of perception, sāmānya-lakṣaṇa pratyāsatti[9] a species of non-sensuous perception functions as a source of knowledge of vyapti. Because "Induction by simple enumeration" cannot establish conclusively the correctness of vyāpti. However universal propositions like 'all the cases of smoke are the cases fire, cannot be explained by ordinary perception of particular instances because universal cannot be equated with the observed particulars. By means of sāmānyalakṣaṇa perception class-essences are grasped through the ordinary perception of particulars. For instance in perceiving particular cases of smoke we also perceive the universal 'smokeness' inhering in them. Similarly the universal 'fireness' is also perceived through the perception of particular cases of fire.[10] Accordingly the universal proposition 'all smoky objects are fiery' is given by a non-sensuous perception of all smokes as related to fire through the perception smokeness as related to fireness'.

12.7. The Nyāya method of justifying vyāpti on the basis of the perception of class-essences or universals exemplified in particulars seems to be peculiar to modern mind. But Naiyāyikas concept of anumiti reveals the structure of mediate knowledge. And it must consist of certain elements of immediate knowledge as the ground for this mediate knowledge otherwise mediate knowledge as the basis of anumiti may be either circular or it may lead to infinite regress. Thus in order to avoid such difficulties the premisses of inference are to be known directly so that they yield mediate knowledge (anumiti i.e. inferential knowledge).

But it may be objected that the Nyāya view of vyāpti covering all the individual cases of a relation commits inference to the fallacy of petitio principi. Becausc sāmānya-lakṣaṇā pratyāsatti gives the knowledge that all cases of smoke are the cases of fire through the knowledge of the universals 'fireness' and 'smokeness'. Consequently vyāpti, which is in the form of knowledge of the relation between smoke and fire in general, also contains the knowledge of the relation of fire to a particular fact like 'the hill is smoky. To this Gaṅgeśa argues that since inference gives us a new khowledge hence it is neither inconclusive nor a petitio principii.[11] The argument implies that only when the major premise (vyāpti) is combined with the minor, 'there is smoke in the hill' the conclusion that 'there is fire in the hill' can be drawn.

12.8. Another important concept contained in the definition (D) of anumiti is pakṣa (the minor term). As anumiti depends on the knowledge of vyāpti (a relation between the middle and major terms) so it depends on the relation of the middle with the minor term. Pakṣatā is a necessary condition for inferential knowledge. Pakṣa or minor term is an object about which we want to know something. Gaṅgeśa observes that pakṣatā consists in the absence of that condition in which there are the presence of certainty and absence of the will to infer.[12] Accordingly inferential knowledge takes place under the condition that there must be the absence of certainty in respect of the minor term (pakṣa) and the presence of the will to draw the conclusion in order to have inferential knowledge (anumiti).

12.9. According to Gaṅgeśa the kndwledge of vyāpt is the special cause of anumiti (inferential knowlebge) and the knowledge of liṅga-parāmarśa (consideration) is the immediate cause (caramakāraṇa) of anumiti (the conclsion).

Accordingly the inferential knowledge (anumti) is based on the following grounds:

(i) the knowledge of vyāpti (pervasion or the universal relation between the middle and the major terms, e.g., all cases of smoke are the cases of fire; (ii) the knowledge of the minor term (pakṣa) as related to the middle (liṅga), for example the hill is a case of smoke and (iii) the knowledge of middle as correlating the major term in relation to minor term, for example 'the hill is a case of smoke through the pervader of fire'.

Thus anumiti (inferential knowledge) as justified true cognition reveals the following structure. Any knower (pramātṛa) possesses anumiti (inferential knowledge), if and only if (i) the knowledge of pervasion (vyāpti) and (ii) the knowledge of consideration (parāmarṣa) justify inferential knowledge (anumiti). Inferential knowledge is logically and epistemically justified because the conclusion necessarily follows from the premisses.

Notes and References

1. Gaṅgeśa (1974) *Tattva-cintāmaṇi* Pratyakṣa khaṇḍa with *Tattva-cintāmaṇi rahasya.* Edited by K. Tarkavagisha, Motilal Banarsidass, New Delhi, p. 538.
2. Gaṅgeśa (1927) : *Tattva-cintāmaṇi*, Anumāna khaṇda, with *Dīdhiti* and *Gādhādhari.* Edited by Pandit Dundirja Sastri, Chaukhamba Sanskrit Series, Varanasi.
   (i) *Tattva-cintāmaṇi* P. (24). (ii) *Dīdhiti* (p. 25) explains : vyāptiviśiṣṭatva pakṣadharmatvasamānādhikarṇyāvagāhijñānajanyatvamarthaḥ. (iii) Gadhādhar says (p. 26) : vyāptītiviśiṣṭatvasamānadhikaraṇapakṣa dharmatvāvagāhijñānajanyatvamityarthaḥ.
3. (i) Bhimacharya, J. (1974): *Nyāyakośaḥ.* Bhandarkar Oriental Research Institute, Poona, pp. 831-42.
   (ii) Chatterjee, S.C. : (1939) : *Nyāya Theory of Knowledge.* Calcutta University, Calcutta, p. 161.
   (iii) Ingalls, D.H.H. (1951) : *Materials for the study of Navya-Nyāya System of Logic.* Harvard University, Harvard, p. 28.
4. (i) *Tattva-cintāmaṇi* (anumāna-khaṇḍa), p. 391.
   (ii) Dīdhiti (p. 392): Pratiyogyasamānādhikaraṇa yadrūpa visiṣṭasamānādhikaranātyantābhāvapratiyogitānāvacchedakoyodharmastadharmavācchinnenayena kenapi samam samānādhikaranyam tadrūpa viśiṣṭasya adharmavacchinna yāvannirupitāvyaptirityarthaḥ.
   (iii) Bhattacharya, T. (1970) : *The Nature of vyāpti* (According to Navya-Nyāya). Sanskrit College, Calcutta.
   (iv) *Nyāya Theory of Knowledge* (op. cit): 262-64.
5. Gaṅges'a considers Cārvāka's objection to vyāpti and then refutes the objection (i) *Tattva-cintāmaṇi* (Part-II) p.153. (ii) *Dīdhiti*, pp. 133-4.
6. (i) Madhavācharya (1961) *Sarva-darśana-saṃgrah*, Edited and Translated by Cowell and Gough. Chaukhambha Sanskrit Series, Varanasi, p.12.
   (ii) Hiriyanna, M. (1973) : *Outlines of Indian Philosophy*, George Allen and Unwin, London, pp.200-1.

(iii) *Nyāya Theory of Knowledge* (op. cit). p. 266.

7. (i) *Sarva-darśana-saṃgrah* (op. cit) p.13.

   (ii) *Nyāya-Theory of Knowledge* (op. cit), p. 266.

8. *Tattva-cintāmaṇi*, pp.635-62; 675-734.
9. *Tattva-cintāmaṇi* (anumāna-khaṇḍa) p. 771. Vyāptigmāhas-casāmānya-lakṣṇāpratyā-sattya sakala dhūādiviṣayakaḥ...
10. *Tattva-cintāmaṇi*, (anumāna-khaṇda) pp. 808-9.
11. *Nyāya Theory of Knowledge* (op. cit), p.277.
12. *Tattva-cintāmaṇi of Gaṅgeśopādhyāya* with *Prakāśa* of Rucidatta and *Tarka-cūḍāmaṇi* on *Prakśā* of Dharmaraj-adhvarindra (anumāna-khaṇda) (vol. II) (1982), Anumana-khṇḍa Part I. Critically edited by Dr. N.S. Ramanuja Tatacharya, Kendriya Sanskrit Vidyappeetha, Tirupati, p.337; 340.

13

Gaṅgeśa's Parataḥ-Prāmāṇya-Vāda

13.1. Gaṅgeśa in his epoch making work *Tattva-cintāmaṇi* (TC)[1] deals with the prāmāṇya-vāda in two sections namely prāmāṇya-vāda of jñapti-vāda and pramāṇya vāda of utpatti-vāda. Jñapti-vāda implies the justification of true cognition (yathārthānubhava) where the origin or genesis of true cognition is considered in utpatti-vāda. From epistemological point of view jñapti-vāda is more important for explication of prāmāṇya-vāda.

13.2. The word 'prāmāṇya' is derived from pra+mo+lyuṭ. The root 'mā' along with its prefix 'pra' signifies yathārtha-jñāna (true cognition) and the suffix 'lyut' implies the instrumental character such that by virtue of the function of that instrumental cause, pramā or pramiti is obtained (pramīyate anena iti pramāṇam). Accordingly 'prāmāṇya' stands for pramātva (yathārtha·jñānatva) or pramā-karaṇatva (pramāṇatva).[2] Since pramā is caused by pramāṇa (pramā karṇam pramāṇam); pramātva and pramāṇatva are distinct. Pramātva is the generic property (avacchedaka) of four forms of pramā namely pratykṣa, anumiti, upamiti and śābda. And the respective pramāṇas: pratyaksa, anumāna, upamāna and śabda are characterised by, pramā-karaṇatva i.e. pramāṇatva.[3] Thus the word 'prāmāṇya' is ambiguous. But Gaṅgeśvara uses 'pramāṇya' in the sense of pramātva so that the problem of justification of a true cognition is handled with reference to svataḥ-prāmāṇya-vāda and parataḥ-pramāṇya-vāda. The problem of pramāṇya-vāda may be formulated as: If jñāna (cognition) is yathārtha (true) or ayathārtha (false), how are we to acknowledge the truth of a true cognition? Whether true cognition is revealed by virtue of its own structure (i.e. ab initio) or it requires the extrinsic factors for its apprehension. According to stronger version of svataḥ-pramāṇya vāda, a true cognition by itself reveals its true character. And contrary to it prath-pramāṇya-vada implies extrinsic justification of a true cognition.

In the firsst part of jñapti-vāda, Gaṅgeśa presents the opponents' view of svataḥ-prāmāṇya-vāda with special reference to Mīmāṃsā, view. According to Gaṅgeśa the necessity for the deliberation on the topic of pramāṇya-vāda springs from the consideration of the fact that the achievement of something which involves great expense and enormous trouble, presupposes a prior certainty regarding the object.[4]

13.3 Since Svataḥ-prāmāṇya-vāda functions as pūrva-pakṣa of jñāpti-vāda; it is necessary to understand it as it is formulated by Gaṅgeśa. The meaning of the term 'svataḥ' as implied by the statement 'svata evāstu tannirupaṇam[5] (the apprehension of truth be from itself) may be paraphrased as follows. The word 'sva'[6] referes to 'tat' which stands for the apprehension of truth (pramātvāvadhāraṇam). In other words the truth of true coginition is apprehended by the same cognition. For instance if the truth in question belongs to a cognition C_1 then the truth is revealed or apprehended by C_1 itself. This is a stronger version of the Prābhākaras. There are other two versions of svataḥ-pramāṇya-vāda attributed to Kumārila-Bhaṭṭa and Murāri Miśra. According to Bhāṭṭa-school, the truth of C_1 is known svataḥ amounts to saying that the truth of C_1 is apprehended by C_2 which is a species of inferential knowledge. But in Miśra's view C_2 as an introspective awareness (anu-vyava-sāya) captures the truth of C_1. These three views are expressed as forms of svataḥ-pramāṇya-vāda as each of them possess the common or general characteristic of svāśrayagrāhakatva. Accordingly 'svatogrāhyatva' means 'svaviṣaya jñāna-sāmagrijanyatva'. Hence the conditions or the factors responsible for the manifestation of a true cognition also reveal the truth of that cognition. Consequently the truth of a primary cognition C_1 is apprehended either by itself or by anuvyavasāya or inference such that the property of having 'that' as its object and the property of having that as the qualifier (tadvati-tatprakārākatva) are apprehended by the same conditions which also apprehend that cognition.[7]

13.4. Svatḥ-pramāṇya-vādins objection to parataḥ prāmāṇyavāda is in the from of the charge of infinite regress. The force of the objection is that the cognition which ascertains the truth of another cognition must itself be known to be true. If the truth of the cognition C_1 is justified by another cognition C_2, and this C_2 is capable of justifying only if it is also justified by another cognition C_3 which must be known to be true on the basis of C_4 and so on ad-infinitum. And it would not be a way out this situation if it could be said that a cognition used to ascertain the truth of another congnition need not be justified or known to be true in order to stop infinite series of cognition C_1, C_2, C_3. . . . Because if C_2 functions as autonomous cognition to validate or justifyC_1 then same may be said to the primary cognition C_1 itself. That is to say that acceptance of a certain cogntions without being ascertained by another cognition ammounts to svataḥ-prāmāṇya of that cognition.[8]

13.5. Gaṅgeśa formulates an argument to show the incorrectness of the above charge against parataḥ-prāmāṇya-vāda. The argument is based on the distinction between certainty about the truth of the cognition (jñāna-pramāṇya-niścaya) and that of certainty about the object (artha-niścaya).[9] Since the ascertainment of the truth of a cognition is not required for the ascertain ment of the object of that cognition; the Mimāṃsakas' charge is not correct. For instance successful activity need not presup pose a prior ascertainment of the truth of the cognition which leads to that activity. In other words the absence of doubt about the falasity of a cognition leading to successful activity implies the absence of ascertainment of that cognition. Consequently unwavering or fruitful actify requires *arthaniscaya* i.e. *certainty about the object* of primary cognition but not prāmāṇyaniścaya i.e. certainty about the truth of the cognition of that object. For example if there is not doubt about the falsity as in the case of the true cognition of āmalaka (myrabolan) under the palm, there the *primary cognition itself* amounts to certainty about the object, so that fruitful activity follows from that cognition[10] only. However in certain cases due to some reason or the other there may be doubt about the truth of a primary congnition itself and a doubt upsets the certainty about the object of that primary cognition. Consequently doubtful cognition cannot lead to successful activity unless and until thc doubt about that object is replaced by certainty. The cognition C_2 which anppreheds the truth of another cognitlon C_1 and truth of C_2 may, not have been ascertained if there is absence of doubt about that cognition and hence there is absence of doubt about that cognition and hence there is no infinite regress.[11] To this effect Mathurānātha[12] observes that activity based on a certainty need not always be required to ascertain the truth of that certainty ("niścayakāryampratisarvatraniscayaniṣṭha prāmāṇyaniścayānpekṣitatvāt"). Further it has been argued that svataḥ-prāmānya-vāda itself involves infinite regress. According to the Bāṭṭa theory an inferential cognition is the means of apprehending the truth of a certain cognition. But the apprehension of truth presupposes the apprehension of the truth of inferential cognition and the second inference requires another for the same purpose and so on ad infinitum. And Prābhākaras theory also leads to the same difficulty. Because truth of a cognition cannot be established svataḥ and must be established by some kind of argument. Further the truth of such argument has to be again established by another argument. Thus in order to avoid such difficulties it is necessary to admit an initial certainty about an object without ascertaining the truth of certainty.[13]

13.6. Another version of Gaṅgeśa's refutation of svatah-pramāṇya-vāda is as follows :

> If the truth of a cognition is apprehended intrinscically then in the case of a cognition which arises in unfamiliar circumstances there should not be any doubt about that cognition;[14]

but there are doubtful cognitions. The argument implies that in a cognitive situation more often than not an inquiry is conducted regarding the truth-value of a given cognition. Especially in case of unfamiliar cognitions the doubt is to be entertained. But Mīmāṃsakā's view cannot account for doubtful cognitions. Normally doubt presupposes cognition of the substantive (dharma) and remembrance of two different qualifiers. Logically speaking cognition (jñāna) is either true or false. But acknowledgement of truth of a true cognition implies the necessity of certain extrinic factors in order to justify the truth of that cognition.

13.7. Although both the versions of prāmāṇya-vāda subscribe to the same characterisation of truth as the correspondence with fact ('tadvati-tat prakārakatvam') the difference between the two rival theories is due to the difference in their metaphysical standpoints. This difference of stand points emerges from the understanding of the alternatives theories of jñāna as advocated by Nyāya and Mīmāṃsā systems. The concept of jñāna treated in svataḥ theory captures the sense of pramā (yātharthānubhava) having its english equivalent, 'knowledge'. Generally knowledge is defined as a justified true belief.[15] Hence truth constitutes a necessary condition of knowledge so that it becomes analytic consequence of knowledge. Similarly jñāna as pramā or yathārthānubhava necessarily implies truth as a necessary conseuqence of it. Hence it makes some good sense of saying that truth or validity is intrinsic to true cognition (jñāna). Prābhākaras treat every jnāna as a form of yathārthānubhava only and for them a-yathārtha jñāna would be an instance of contradiction.

13.8. But the division of jñāna in to yathārtha and ayathrātha is consistent with parath-prāmāṇya-vāda. Yathārtha jñāna as pramā (knowledge)[16] also implies truth as anecessary consequence. If jñāna is either yathārtha or a yathārtha, then how are we to decide in any particular case whether jñāna is pramā or bhrama (apramā) ? A satisfactory answer to this question is normally expected from parataḥ-prāmāṇya-vāda. Accordingly jñāna is to be acknowledged as yathārtha if it corresponds to fact (tadvati-tatprakārakatva) otherwise it is false. Ascertainment of truth of a true cognition is not an instance of hypothesis but a consequence of the justification of that jñāna (cognition) as pramā by the corresponding pramāṇa.

Notes and References

1. Gaṅgeśa Upādhyāya (1974) : *The Tāttva-Cintāmaṇi* with the commentary of Mathurānātha Tarkavāgīśa. Volume I. Pratyakṣa khaṇda Motilal Banarsidass, New Delhi. Jñaptivāda : Pp. 114-286. Utpatti-vāda: Pp. 307-371.
2. Bhimacharya. Jhalkikar (1978) : *Nyāya-kośa* The Bhandarkar Oriental Research Institute Poona P. 591.
3. (i) *Tattva-Cintāmaṇi* P. 538.
   (ii) Mathurānātha observes that Chaturvidhā anubhava-tvasāksādvyapya-jāticatuśtayavatītyarthah... pratyakṣānumānoti pratyakṣatvānumanatvo pamāṇatva śabdatva-rūpaṇāṃ. Pp. 538-539.
4. Bahuvittavyayasasādhye pravrttiścāvaśyakārtha niśchayādeva. *Tattva-cintāmaṇi* P. 118.
5. *Tattva-cintāmaṇi* P. 121.
6. (i) For the explication of 'svatah', following *Dīdhiti* of Raghunatha in terms of 'svassmāt' or 'svakīyat' See Jitendranath Mohanty (1966) : *Gaṅgeśās Theory of Truth*, Visvabharati Shantiniketan Pp. 90-91.
   (ii) Vijñānasāmagrījanyatve sati
   tadatirikta hetvajanyatvam...
   pramāyāḥ svatastvam.
   jñāna grāhakasāmagryā grāhyam...
   (iti svato grāhyatvam).
   Nyāyakośa Pp. 1048-49.
7. Tadvati tatprakāraka jñānatvam
   tadvati tadvaiśiṣtya jñānatvam vā
   prāmāṇyam vyavasāyeti svenānu
   vyavasāyenānumitya vā

tad grahāt. Tadvisayatvasya tatprakāratvasaya ca jñāna grāhakasāmagrīgrāhyatvāt. *Tattva-Cintāmaṇi* Pp. 181-82.

8. Yadica prāmāṇyam parato jñāyeta...cānavasthā...TC Pp. 182-3. Nanu na grahīta prāmāṇyam jñānam paraprāmāṇya niścaya—rūpam anavasthānāt. *Tattva-Cintāmaṇi* : P. 276.

9. Nanu brūmaḥ jñāna prāmāṇya niścayādevartha niscaya iti *Tattva-Cintāmaṇi* P. 277.

10. Yatrāpramāṇyaśaṅkā nāsti karatalāmalakādi jñāne tatra vyavasāya evārtha niścaya iti tata eva pravrttir niṣkampā. *Tattva-cintāmani* Pp. 277-8.

11. Na caivamanavasthā carma—jñānaprāmāṇyasya-jñāṇābhāvena koṭismaranābhavena viṣayāntara—sañchāreṇa vā prāmāṇyasaṃśayānavasyambhāvāt. *Tattva-Cintāmaṇi* Pp. 278-9.

12. *Tattva-Cintāmaṇi rahasyam* in *Tattva-Cintāmaṇi* Pp. 278-9.

13. Anyathā bhāṭṭamate prāmāṇyasya jñānānumitigrāhyatvenānvasthā syāt. Gurumate ca prāmāṇyasaya svagrāhyatvam na svagrāhyaṃ svarūpa prāmāṇyā bhyām bhahir bhūtatvāt. *Tattva-Cintāmaṇi* P. 279.

14. Siddhāntastu Prāmāṇyasya svato grāhe anabhyāsadaśo—tpanna jñāne tatsamśayo—na syāt. Jñāna grahe prāmāṇya niścayāt aniscaye vā na svataḥ prāmāṇya graḥ. *Tattva cintāmaṇi* P. 184.

15. The traditional definition of knowledge as justified true belief has the following structure :

    S knows that p=Df. S believes/accepts that p; that p is true and S has ground (s) to accept that p

    (where S=a knowing subject; p=a true proposition)

    An interesting analysis of the concept of knowledge is given in Chisholm R. M. (1977) : *Theory of knowledge* Prentice Hall, India; Pp. 102-4.

16. The structural similarly between the concepts of pramā and knowledge has been investigated in the thesis (published) by Ingalalli, R.I. (1982) : *Śabda-pramāṇa, An Epistemological Analysis.* Sri Satguru Publications Indian Books Centre, New Delhi; Pp. 8-58.

14

Postulational Knowledge*
(Arthapatti-Pramā)*

141. The word 'arthāpatti', which is derived from the sanskrit words 'artha' (fact) and 'āpatti' (kalpana) i.e. supposition) is generally rendered as postulation.[1] Arthāpatti stands for a seyerate pramāṇa (i.e. means of knowledge) according to Advaitins and Mīmāṃsakās. However, Indian thinkers are not unanimous regarding the nature and status of postulation. Traditionally the problem of postulation is expressed as whether our knowledge claims are justified by means of arthāpatti (postulatlon) and whether it is an independent pramāṇa.

14.2. Mīmāṃskās and Advaitins give different answers regarding the nature of arthāpatti. According to the Bhāṭṭā school of Pūrvamimāṃsā, arthāpatti is a source of knowledge (pramāṇa) in which a true cognition comes to be apprehended by way of resolving a conflict or contradiction between known (true) cognitions. And accordingly arthāpatti is defined as the postulation of a true cognition, when something is otherwise unintelligible and postulation of which will make it intelligible[2]; whenever there is a clash between two conitions, the need of a

* This paper was read in the 54th Session of Indian Philosophical Congress held at Madras University, Madras; December 1979.

third cognition arises in order to resolve the conflict (or clash). The example of postulation commonly used is as follows. If we know that Devadatta is alive and do not find him in his house, we conculude that he is somewhere else. The two true cognitions : (i) Devadatta is alive and (ii) he is absent from home, clash with each other, and this kind of conflict cannot be resolved unless it is presumed that Devadatta is outside. The postlation of his being outside explains his being alive and yet not being in his house.' Of course, the conflict, or contradiction is not real but only apparent, when there is a real contradiction between two cognitions, there cannot be any reconciliation as one of the cognitions must be false. But in arthāpatti both the cognitions are true, though at first they appear to be conflicting However, it would be a clear case of contradiction or conflict if it is said that 'a living Devadatta is absent every where.' But the above definition of postulation as a means of resolving conflict (or making intelligible what appears to be unintelligible) is too wide. For instance, we also use perception as a means of resolving apparent conflect, as when we are puzzled by seeing an apparently bent pencil, which is partly immersed is water we resolve the conflict with reference to the laws of refraction, that is by saying that a straight pencil appears bent when part of it is immersed in water. We may explain it rightly or wrongly in other ways too.

14.3. Prabhākaras differ from Bāṭṭās regarding the nature and function of postulation. According to Salikanātha, the follower of Prabhākara, postulation involves an element of doubt about the truth of the two apparently confiicting cognitions.[3] For example, Devadatta was known to be alive; since he is not found at home there can be doubt about his being alive. It is this doubt about his being alive, which makes known to us his being outside. Nārāyaṇa, the author of Mānameyodaya (a mannual of the Bhāṭṭā school) refutes this view of Prabhākaras by stating that there cannot be an apprehension of Devadatta's being outside from a doubt about his being alive, because, when there is a doubt about his being dead to, his being outside cannot be a legitimate postulation.[4]

The above view is different from that of Bhāṭṭā school. According to Mānameyodaya, the fact of Devadatta not being in the house is explained by the postulation of his being outside, and that doubt has no place in the structure of arthāpatti. It appears that Prābhākaras' view of postulation is odd or pramaṇas yield knowledge and doubt is not a characteristic of a pramāṇa (source of knowledge).

14.4. According to Vedāntaparibhāṣā,[5] postulation is the assumption of a cognition that explains what is to be explained. In arthāpatti the two true cognitions constitute the instrumental cause which yield another true cognition. For example, the cogitions that Devadatta is fat, and that he does not eat during day constitute the instrumental cause and thus cannot be accounted for unless it is assumed that he eats at night. The fatness of the person is to be explaihed and the assumption of eating at night explains it.

Authors like Banerjee[6] interpret the Advaitic view of postulation as the framing of an explanatory hypothesis instead of as a source of true cognition (pramāṇa). On Banerjee's view the situation that a person who desists from eating during day time is still stout (pīna), calls for an explanation. And sort of explanation is to be found in the hypothesis that the person concerned eats at night. Banerjee[7] gives the following reasons in support of his view: "Postulation cannot be said to be a way of knowing (pramāṇa) unless the verb 'to know' is used in the widest sense and indeed postulation is a sort of guessing or supposing and hence not the same as a means of knowing. Thus postulation is placed among the methods of scientific investigation which are intended to explore the region of facts with a view to explaining whatever lies unexplained within it."

Although the above view is sensible on the whole it is not faithful to the texts. I wish to argue that postulation as conceived by Advaitins and Mīaṃsakās is not merely supposition or guess but it is a pramāṇa (a means of knowledge). If we give an appropriate contextual meaning to the word 'kalpayāmi' (I postulate), it would not mean mere guess or hypothesis, for 'kalpayāmi' is species of true cognition.[8] But Banerjee understads 'kalpana' in its ordinary meaning. Banerjee[9] is also inconsistent as he wishes (i) to consider postulation as an as an instrumental cause (karaṇa) and (ii) to account for the conjectural nature of postulation as being akin to hypothesis. According to (i) postulation is a source of knowledge i.e. it yieldes true cognition. And (ii) has the sense of hypothesis. In an inductive reasoning hypothesis is framed and then accepted as legitimate on the basis of confirmation i.e. a given hypothesis would be legitimate (or highly probable) if there are good number of confirming instances say evidences and the possibility of confutation by contrary instances is kept at minium. However, it is desirable to point out some of the differences between hypothesis and postulation (arthāpatti).

Although hypothesis is a guess work, it can be enlightened guess work. A hypothesis is employed to explain the facts, if it were true, something that one believes.[10] According to the theory of hypothesis, a certain proposition is asserted because we may not know that it is true but because it is required as an explanation for the given (observed) phenomemon under consideration. In order to account for some observed happenings one has to formulate a hypothesis, such that if the hypothesis is true things will happen.[11] But it is not so in case of postulation as postulation inivolves a deductive technique i.e. conclusion necessarlly follows from the given premises. And since the form of arthāpatti is valid and as a matter of fact constituent cognitions are all true; hence it is an instance of sound inference. A hypothesis is only a preliminary stage of scientific procedure, and would have little reliance placed on it by any observer until various steps had been taken. Hypothesis will be confuted if there are contrary instances. But since postulation is deductive in nature; its premisses entail its conclusion. In postulation if given premisses are true then its conclusion, is necessarily true. Although it is possible that true conclusion is implied by false premisses, such possibility was not considered in the Indian tradition.

14.5. All the above three views are idadequate as they stand. However the Bhāṭṭās view seems the most promising to the three and it may be modified as : Postulation is a means of resolving an apparent conflict between two true cognitions by a third true cognition which is non-perceptual. And in this regard, postulation may be compared with Quine's[12] view of veridical or truth telling paradox.

According to Quine a paradox is that which at first sounds absured but that has an argument to sustain it. There are three kinds of paradoxes viz., veridical (valid) falsidical (false) and an antinomy.[13] An example for veridical paradox is that a certain person has reached the age of 21 after passing only five birth days. Several circumstances conspire to make this possible. Age is reckoned in elapsed time whereas a birthday has to match the date of birth; and February 29 comes less frequently than once a year. In other words, the sense of paradox arises if something clashes with normal or plain way of thinking. Thus the two propositions (i) A certain person has passed 21 years and (ii) he has passed only 5 birthdays, apparantly clash each other. And such a paradox would be resolved by stating another proposition that his date of birth is February 29, which as a matter of fact is implied by (i) and (ii). Thus the above paradox is a veridical one if we take its proposition not as something about the person but as the truth in general that a man can be 4n years old on his nth birthday. And a veridical paradox contains a surprise which quickly dissipates itself as we ponder over the proof. Thus in traditional example the presence of Devadatta somewhere in the world cannot conflict with his absence in the house; and when it is not so set aside his absence in the house cannot fail to be a ground for his presence outside the house. In other words consider the following propositions : (i) Devadatta is alive (ii) Devadatta is absent from home (iii) Devadatta is somewere else i.e. outside (iv) Devadatta is present at home (v) Devadatta is missing. It is to be noted that (ii) is really inconsistent with (iv) whereas (i) and (ii) apparantely clash with each other which constitute the nature of postulation. There are several points of similarity between the veridical paradox and postulation. These are (1) both are the sources of true cognitions only, and (2) both are (formally) valid inferences (3) and element of surprise is packed in both veridical paradox and postulation. There are also significant points of differences between the two viz., (1) in case of veridical paradox it is possible that true and false propositions together yield true proposition whereas postulation yields true proposition from true propositions only. (2) Postulation is capable of being expressed in the form of disjunctive syllogism having disjunctive major premiss but it is not so in case of verdical paradox as for instance the pervasion "whoever is 4n years old on his nth birthday must have born on February 29" is not disjunctive proposition as it stands.

14.6. The next problem is whether arthāpatti is an independent pramāṇa (source of knowledge) or reducible to inference also throws some light on the nature of arthāpatti. Trditionally Advaitins and Mīāṃsakās give the following reasons for regarding arthāpatti as an independent pramāṇa: (i) Postulation arises from a need to reconcile two conflicting data. Or postulation is characterised by its unique instrumental cause i.e. having its disjunctive type of universal cognition.[14] (ii) 'I postulate' and 'I infer' are two different intuitions. In other words, introspection does not support the view that postulation is inference. (iii) postulation can only be reduced, if at all, to universally contrapositive inference which is not an inference proper for them.

Regarding (i) postulation is not the only pramāṇa (source of knowledge) to reconcile two conflicting data it may arise in case of other pramāṇas as well. And disjunctive cognition my also be an element of disjunctive syllogism. In case of (ii) the difference is only verbal as pointed by Naiyayikas[15] (iii) The question to be considered here is this : Is arthāpatti reducible to kevalavyatireki inference (contrapositive inference)? If so what is its reduction? Or what is the form of argument of arthāpatti?

Advaitins, and Bhaṭṭās hold the view that arthāpatti is reducible to kevalavyatireki inference (contrapositive inference).[16] Advaitins and Mīmāṃsakās argue in order to claim the independence of arthāpatti that kevalavyatireki contrapositive inference is not inference proper because only anvaya vyateriki (positive-contrapositive) inference is the inference. Authors like Athalye[17] also think that postulation is reducible to kevalavyatireki inference (contrapositive infeence).

However, reduction of postulation is not given in the texts like Vedāntaparibhāśā, and Mānameyodaya. According to

Vedāntaparibhāśā,[18] if we try to reduce arthāpatti to the infer ence, we shall have for its major premise not a proposition expressinga universal concommittance between the middel term and major term (anvaya vyāpti positive i.e. pervasion), but a proposition expressing a universal relation between the absence of the major term and the absence of the middle term (vyatireki-vyāpti). And vyatirekivyāpti cannot lead to an inference. Thus kevalavyatireki inference (contrapositive inference) is that which consists of kevalavytireki vyāpti (universally contra-positive pervasion) as its main element. And kevalavyatireki vyāpti (contrapositive pervasion) is characterised as that vyāpti (pervasion) which has negative instances only and there are no positive instances. Consider the following paradigm case of kevalavyatireki inference i.e. contrapositive inference [19].

Al : 1. Earth differs from other things.
2. Because it has smell.
3. Whatever does not differ from other things (than earth) has no smell e.g. water.
4. This is not like it.
∴ 5. This is not like it.

3 of Al, is kevalavyatireki (contrapositive pervasion) because it does nct have any agreeing or positive instance other than the earth which is the part of the formulation of 3. The smell as quality is the property of earth only. But the following is a reduction of postulation to its corresponding vyatireki inference which does not involve kevalavytiaki vyapti (contrapositive pervasion).[20]

A2 : 1. A man who does not eat at night while fasting by day is not fat;
2. Devadatta who fasts at day is fat;
∴ 3. He is not a man who does not eat at night i.e., he eats at night.

The vyāpti (pervasion) in the above argument my be paraphrased as whoever eats neither by day nor by night is non-fat, which is also in negative inform. But it cannot be viewed as kevalavyatireki inference (universally contrapositive pervasion) as it implies positive pervasion (anvayavyāpti) i.e. whoever is fat must eat either by day or by night. Both negative pervasion and its positive pervasion have confirming instances. 'Fat persons like Devadatta who fast by day' is a confirming instance for positive pervasion. And a lean person who never eats confirms negative pervasion. Authors like Potter[21] also think that postulation involves law like statement. Therefore, above vyatirekivyāpti cannot be viewed as kevalavyatirekivyāpti (contrapositive pervasion). Need of kevalavyatirakivyapti arises if there are negative instance only. In the paradigm case there is no corresponding legitimate positive pervasion because earth is the only positive instance which is already the subject of an inference and cannot be utilised as confirming instance for positive pervasion without begging the question. To sum up: vyatirekivyāpti involved in A2 cannot be called kevalavyatireki (contrapositive inference) since there are positive instances to confirm its corresponding positive pervasion say 'whoever is fat must eat (by day or night)' whereas in the case of Al, its vyatireki vpāpti my be expressed in its corresponding positive pervasion say 'whatever has smell differs from other things which is unacceplable' as there are no agreeing instances (other then earth).

Nevertheless, arthāpatti is inference of the anvayavyatireki type as is held by authors like Viśvahāth and Vācaspati. Visvanath[22] gives the following formulation of reasoning involved in postulation which consists of anvayavyāpti (positive pervasion) :

(a) Where being alive is known to be pervaded by being either outside or at home, when either in being proved being outside shines fourth in conclusion, since being at home is contradicted.

Viśvanātha's saying of (a) amounts to the following formulation of postulation i.e. Devadatta is alive and not at home; therefore he must be outside.

A3 : 1. Whoever is alive must be either at home or outside ;

2. Devadatta is alive and is not at home;

∴ 3. He must be outside.

Above argument may be symblolised as follows:[23]

1. $(x)(Ax \rightarrow (Hx \vee OX))$
2. $Ad.\neg Hd$

∴ 3. Od

(b) According to Sāṇkhya Tattva-kaumudhi[24] reduction is as follows: when a finite object is not present in one place, it is present in another place, and also that when a finite object is present in one place, it is not present in another place. When therefore, we find that the living Caitra is not in the house we deduce the conclusion that he must be somewhere outside the house. Vācaspati's expression of (b) may be formulated as:

A4 : 1. Whoever is alive and absent from home must be outside;

2. Chaitra is alive and is absent from home;

∴ 3. He must be outside.

The form of the above argument, is as follows :

1. $(x)((Ax.\neg Hx) \rightarrow Ox)$
2. $Ac.\neg Hc$

∴ 3. Oc

It is to be noted that,

$(x)(Ax \rightarrow (Hx \vee Ox)$ is logically equivalent to
$(v)(Ax.\sim Hx) \rightarrow Ox)$.

Similary their contrapositive formulations are also logically equivalent:

$(x)(\sim(Hx \vee Ox) \rightarrow \sim Ax) \equiv$
$(x)(\sim Ox \rightarrow \sim (Ax. \sim Hx)$

Thus postulation is a case of anvayavyatireki anumāna (positive-contrapositive inference) as there are positive and negative instances to confirm the vyāpti i.e. anvaya-vyatireki vyāpti.

Notes and References

MM Mānameyodaya, of Narayana. Edited and translated by Raja K. and S.S. Sastry (1975). Adyar Library and Research Centre, Madras.

VP Vedānta Paribhāśā Dharma Raj, Edited and translated by Swami Madhavananda (1972). Advaita Ashrma, Calcutta.

TS Tarka Samgraha, Annambhatta. Edited and translated with notes by Y.V. Athalye and M.R. Bodas (1974). Bhandarkar Oriental Research Institute, Poona.

BP Bhāśāpariccheda, of Viśvanāth. Edited and translated by Swāmi Mādhavānanda (1977). Advaita Asharama, Calcutta.

SM Nyāya-Siddhānta-Muktāvalī, of Viśvanātha. Edited with notes in Kannada by G. Visnumurty Bhatta (1972). M.V. Balaganapathi, Mysore.

ST Sāṅkhyā-Tattva-Kaumudhi of Vācaspati Misra. Edited and translated by MM. Ganganatha Jha (1965). Oriental Book Agency, Poona.

1. Datta, D.M. (1972): *The Six ways of knowing*. University of Calcutta, Calcutta, pp.238.
2. MM., p. 120.
3. Ibid. p. 129. Sālikanātha's view is presented by the author of MM and then rejected.
4. Ibid. p. 130.
5. VP., p. 117.
6. Banerjee. N.V. (1974): *The Spirit of Indian Philosophy*. Arnold Heinemann. New Delhi, p. 92.
7. Ibid. pp. 92-93.

   It is to be noted the word arthāpatti is used both as a pramāṇa and as the retult of that pramāṇa i.e. pramā. In order to avoid this ambiguity I specify its usage wherever necessary.
8. (i) MM. p. 120-121.
   (ii) VP. p. 73.
9. Banerjee, N.V. (1974). p. 88.

10. Quine, W.V. and J.S. Ullian (1971): *The Web of Belief*. Random House, New York, p. 43.
11. Woozley, A.D. (1967) : *Theory of knowledge*, Hutchinson university Library, London.
12. Quine W.V. (1976) : *The ways of paradox and other essays. Harvard University, Harvard*, pp. 3.
13. Ibid. pp. 3 and 5. Three kinds of paradoxes are as follows :

    (i) A veridical paradox contains surprise which dissipates as soon as the proof is pondered and thus it is a source of truth.

    (ii) A falsidical paradox also contains surprie but its falsity is seen when its intrinsic fallacy is detected, thus it is a mis-proof.

    (iii) An antinomy gives rise to crises in thought i.e. it yields a self contradiction by accepted ways of reasoning.
14. Datta, D.M. (1972) : p. 245.
15. BP., p. 144.
16. (i) MM., p. 57.
    (ii) VP., p. 123-124.
17. TS. pp. 350.
18. VP., p. 122.
19. (i) TS., Section 48.
    (ii) VP., p. 123.
20. Chatterjee, S.C. (1939): *The Nyāya Theory of Knowledge*. University of Calcutta, Culcutta.
21. Potter, K.H. (1977) : *The Encyclopaedia of Indian Philosophies Vol.* II. Motilal Banarsidass, New Delhi, p. 178.
22. SM., Verse 144.
23. Mullatti, L.C. (1977) : *The Navya Nyāya Theory of Inference*. Karnatak University, Dharwad, pp. 120.
24. ST., p., 31.

15

The Advaita Conception of Knowledge*

15.1. Advaita philosophy is well known for its rationalistic outlook by virtue of rigorous logical arguments employed in the system. The main aim of the system is to inquire into the nature of Ātman (self) within the frame work of *jñāna-mārga*—the path of knowledge. But, what is jñāna ? The specific object of this paper is to answer the question concerning the nature of jñāna and then to focus on the analysis of the notion of Self-knowledge (Ātma-jñāna) in terms of the contemporary conceptual frame-work.

The word jñāna[1] comes from the root *jña* (to know). Etymologically the word 'jñāna' captures the sense of knowledge. The term 'jñāna' in its wider sense stands for knowledge in general, whether it is empirical knowledge (*aparā-vidyā*) or self-knowledge (*parā vidyā*). But in its narrower sense 'jñāna' normally designates *parā-vidyā* or self-knowledge. In the contemporary epistemology, the concept of knowledge is defined as justfied true belief. In other words three conditions truth, belief and justification—constitute necessary and sufficient conditions for knowledge.[2] Consequently, to know a certein proposition 'P' means to believe in the truth of that proposition 'P', with adequate grounds for so believing.' "P' is known but it is false",

* Reprinted, with the permission, from the publisher *Vedānta kesari*, 1984, Vol. LXXXI, No. 10 pp. 376-80. Vedānta kesari office Madras.

is a contradiction. But "a proposition 'P' is known and 'P' is true" is trivial, because knowledge implies truth as its defining property. Now in the Advaita system, jñāna is used in the sense of knowledge. That is to say that jñāna as '*pramā*' implies '*yathārthānubhava*'. As far as the consistent use of jñāna as knowledge is concerned, the usage of *ayathārthajñāna* seems to be a contradiction. Hence Advaita thinkers use *ajñāna* (false belief) as the negation of *jñāna* (knowledge).

In Advaita system especially in Śamkara's system, knowledge (*jñāna*) in its narrower sense stands for pure awareness i.e. self-knowledge. But Śamkara has to accommodate the knowledge of the manifold reality upto a certain level without eliminating its truth. Accordingly for Śamkara, '*jñāna*' is not just any belief or casual appehension, but it should be backed up with *pramāṇa* (source of knowledge) for justifiction. He characterises *jñāna* (knowledge) as follows :

'Jñāna (knowledge) is derived from the *pramāṇas* which have for their objects things as they are. It is not optional in the case of knowledge either to do, or not to do, or to do it otherwise; it solely depends on things, neither upon injunction nor upon the individual'.[3]

Śamkara implies that jñāna is an impersonal entity in the sense that it is objective in character, in the manner in which scientific knowlege is characterised by universality, objectivity and impersonality. The above definition eliminates Mīmāmsaka's characterisation of jñāna as an activity of the Self. In his thoroughgoing critical analysis of human knowledge and man's cognitive mechanism, Śamkara says that the ultimate reality is non-dual Atman, but all determinate knowledge presupposes the modification of the basic consciousness or pure awareness through the mental mode (*antaḥkaraṇa-vṛtti*) corresponding to its object. Whenever the basic consciousness takes various forms through mental modes corresponding to different objects, we have modal consciousness (*vṛtti-caitanya*) in the form of determinate knowledge (*vṛtti-jñāna*). Determinate knowledge presupposes (1) *pramātṛ caitanya* (a knowing subject or the cognitive consciousness characterised by the internal organ); (2) *pramāṇa*-caitanya (the faculty of knowledge determined by the modification of the internal organ); and (3) *viṣaya-caitanya* (the pure awareness determined by the object known). Though mental mode or internal organ is said to reveal the objects, it is the Ātman that reflects in it.[4]

Jñāna or knowledge in general is to be undertood as a blend of both : a *vṛtti* of the internal organ and *sākṣin*, the basic consciousness. The *vṛtti* element is contingent in jñāna but the element of basic awareness is eternal.[5] Accroding to Śamkara, the notion of knowledge implies an objective content i.e., its reference to extrinsic reality and subjective element. Knowledge presupposes an object, and absence of object implies absence of knowledge also. If truth of knowledge is characterised by reference to real object then the denial of such knowledge would be self-contradictory.

Both mediate and immediate knowledge are *vṛttis* of the internal organ in which *sākṣin* is immanent. Immediate knowledge is not necessarily born of sense-perception. For instance, without sense-object relation the empirical self is immediately known. Although the word *pratyakṣa* literally means 'presented to sense', in its wider sense it stands for direct i.e., 'non-mediate'. A given piece of knowlege is immediate (non-mediate) if and only if the *prameya* (knowable object) existing in a certain time is the object of direct awareness. Further, a certain sort of intimate relation between the subject and the object must exist. Normally *vṛtti* is the means of such relation which projects towards external objects. The process involved in immediate knowledge may be described thus : Whenever there is contact with sense object the *antaḥkaraṇa*, goes out towards it like a light and assumes the 'from' of that object. Movement of *antaḥkaravṇavṛtti* presupposes an object as a necessary conditions of knowledge. Perceptual knowledge arises if *vṛtti* coincides with the object. In case of mediate knowledge an object is not directly given to sense-organ or mind. An indirectly given object is apprehended through something directly given where there exists a legitimate relationship between the two. For example, mediate knowledge of fire in the yonder mountain is based on immediate knowledge of smoke and the legitimate relationship between smoke and fire.

Thus according to Advaita, a mental *vṛtti* refers to an object (*visaya*). There is no such thing as knowledge of knowledge, since knowledge is self-luminous (*svaprakāśaka*). Validity or truth of knowledge is intrinsic to knowledge.[6] As said above, 'knowledge' by virtue of its definition is justified true cognition. Truth is a necessary condition of knowledge. Although knowleledge reveals its own truth or validity, such self-evident character of knowledge is to be scrutinised in order to free it from psychological prejudices and flaws. In order to acknowledge or to certify knowledge (*jñāna*) empirical tests like practical efficiency (*samvādipravṛtti*) and coherence (*samvāda*) are often employed. Śaṃkara's definition of knowledge as seen above impies the correspondence between cognitive belief and its object. Empirically, correspondence constitutes the nature of truth. The principle of non-contradiction (*abādha*) as a test of truth is often used by Śamkara. A cognition is true if it is not contradicted by another cognition. This definition of knowledge also emphasizes the systematic character or harmonious nature of truth. When a straight stick appears bent in the water, its crookedness is as real to the eye as its straightness to touch, because either phenomenon is explained away by the laws of optical science. To this effect Śaṃkara makes use of logical techniques to certify truth and acknowledge by way of removing obstructing factors. Dr. S. Radhakrishnan observes : "Logical rules are working tools, serving as negative checks by which we break down our prejudices."[7]

15.2. Strictly speaking, Śaṃkara's theory of truth is structured in realism. This realistic attitude at empirical level refutes the subjective idealism of Buddhists. Śaṃkara does not believe that the perception of physical objects like a chair or a table is the perception of a mental state. He admits objects outside our knowledge. Variety of objects determines variety of knowledge. In this context it is interesing to note down Śaṃkara's refutation of Buddhist idealist's argument that there is no objective reference in knowledge or jñāna, Śaṃkara argues that simultaneous occurrence of things and ideas does not mean the identity of the two. If cognitions do not refer to corresponding objects and are devoid of any content then the cognitions about the absence of things are also empty. And hence there is no difference between affirmative and negative cognitions, which is a controdiction. Cognitions of waking state should not be compared with those of dream state. Dream experience is subjective and private and even to the same person dream experiences are not uniform. But objects of waking knowledge are enduring. A person in his dream travels great distances, but cannot wake up at the place to which he has travelled in his dream. Basically, waking experience affects us practically so that we infer the falsity of dream congnitions. However, non-existing things cannot be perceived. We are always conscious of something. There should not be a confusion between an object depending on mind and an object as a part of mind. It is absurd to say that peceptual consciounsness takes on the form of the thing cognised so that we are never conscious of a thing, but a form belonging to our consciousness. The existence of objects is a pre-requisite for the consciousness to take any form. If external objects are non-entities or if there is nothing external, then there could not have been an illusion of externality. It is impossible to imagine or superimpose an idea of snake in the rope if there is no real snake at all. Therefore, external objects exist as the pre-requisite for our knowledge of the external reality of objects.[8]

15.3. Veda (*śruti*) is the source for self-knowledge. However, lower knowledge (*aprā-vidyā*) is not illusory or it is not absolutely untrue. *Aparā-vidyā* is obtained from the standpoint of empirical consciousness.[9] Relativity and probability of empirical knowledge is due to our cognitive frame-work based on space, time and causality. Modern scientific theory of knowledge holds somewhat similar view that no empirical knowledge implies absolute truth. Empirical knowledge is subject to revision and modification. Of course, for a given time, a fairly well established scientific theory is to be respected and followed unless and until a better or more comprehensive theory is formulated. Inadequacy of empirial knowledge is due to its distinctions and relativity, whereas Absolute Truth is devoid of relations. Due to the relative characteristic of empirical knowledge it is not possible to know the exact nature of things (*vastusvarūpam*). Swami Vivekananda expresses the inadequacy of empirical knowledge in the following words : "...supposing we represent the external world by 'X', what we really know is 'X' plus mind and this mind element is so great that it has covered the whole of that 'X' which has remained unknown and unknowable throughout...What we know of it is as moulded, formed, fashioned by our own mind. So with the internal world.[10]

15.4. Śaṃkara points out certain similarities between human empirical knowledge and knowledge possessed by animals. "Just as the animals, when, for instance, a sound strikes theirears, in case the perception of sound is disagreeable to them, move away from it, and in case it is agreeable, move towards it—as, when they see a man with a stick raised before them, thinking he will strike me', they try to escape, and when they see one with a handful of fresh grass, approach him—so men also whose knowledge is more developed, when they perceive strong men of terrible aspect, with drawn swords in their hands, turn away from them and turn towards the contrary".[11] Another (imitation of empirical knowledge is its inability to eliminate deep-rooted human ignorance in the from of absence of self-knowledge. And self-knowledge (*ātma-jñāna*) alone is able to remove ignorance (*avidyā*). Empirical knowledge being a from of lower knowledge is at thought-level, whereas self-knowledge is structured in intelligence which is basic consiciousness.

15.5. Śaṃkara characterises self-knowledge in various ways. Self-knowledge is obtained in the form of intuitional consciousness, *anubhava*, where the distinctions of subject and object are absent.[12] A consequence of such ineffable experience is that it transforms life and yields the certainty of a divine presence. Śamkara's opinion is that this kind of *anubhava* is open to all, but only a few attain to it. And he has no sympathy with the view that self-knowledge is the outcome of mystical revelation and that Ātma-jñāna is revealed to a few chosen souls in moments of illumination through mystical voices and doubtful dreams. However self-knowledge is unattainable to a person lacking strength—*na ayam ātmā balahīnena labhyaḥ* Therefore a seeker of self-knowledge must possess physical and mental vigour and a keen understanding as a preliminary requisite.[13]

A clue to self-knowledge is derived from the contents of of situations where empirical knowledge implies belief. And at empirical level, human cognitive mechanism is structured in the truth-falsity web of consciousness. Futher, every one is aware of cognitive process pertaining to truth, falsity, doubt etc. And every one is conscious of the existence of his own physical and mental state and it is not possible to deny self-awareness.[14] Further all sources of knowledge (*pramāṇas*) presuppose self-experince (awareness), and such experience is its own proof (*svataḥsiddha*). No proof is necessary for the fundamental postulation of self-awareness. But a negative proof is that the denial of self-awareness leads to contradictions in life. Therefore self-awareness is to be taken as a basic fact of human life. Śaṃkara observes:. . ."each function and faculty, the gross body and the vital breath, the senses and the internal organ, the empirical 'me' appear only on the basis of and in relation to the Ātman. They all serve an end beyond themselves and depend on some deeper ground of of existence. Ātman cannot be doubted for it is the essential nature of him who denies it."[15] Ātman is identified with intelligence which is its exclusive nature of defining property. Analogically, as the sun shines even when there is nothing for it to shine on, so the Ātman has consciousness even when there is no, object.[16]

15.6. A methodological difficulty to be encountered in the path of self-knowledge is that it is not possible to know the self in the manner in which an object is known through senseperception or reasoning. Secondly, although self-knowledge carries highest degree of certitude. it has only a low degree of conceptual intelligibility or clearness which requires an interpretation. Śaṃkara's suggestion is to investigate the truth following the principle of non-contradiction. Normally self-knowledge is derived from Vedic testimony or Sruti (scriptural testimony). Of course, Śruti is not to be considered as an authority on empirical facts. Śaṃkara says that a hundred texts (Śruti) cannot make fire cold.[17] Reasoning (*tarka*) acts as an auxiliary to scriptural testimony. Reason is to be used as a critical weapon against untested assumption. To this effect Swami Vivekannada says: "The Vedanta recognises the reasoning power of man a good deal, although it says there is something higher than intellect; but the road lies through intellect".[18]

Traditionlly certain logical techniquess have been developed to have a glimpse of self-knolwedge. For instance, Arundhati-Nyāya is emloyed to point out the source of self-knowledge. In order to show a man the fine star Arundhati, one refers to a more brilliant and bigger star nearer to it upon which he is asked to fix his eyes first and then it is very easy to direct his sight to Arundhati. Similarly in order to know the self, an aspirant of self-knowledge is directed towards the upaniṣads.[19]

15.7. Śaṃkara makes use of analogical reasoning to describe the nature of Ātman.[20] Analogical reasoning is framed in such a way that non-material Ātman is compared with non-spiritual stuff of a physical entity or an empirical fact. On the basis of the known character of an empirical fact, he inferes a prallel property about the Ātman. Consider the following argument : As a lighted lamp does not need another lamp to mainfest its light so, Ātman, being consciousness, does not need another instrument of consciousness to illumine itself. The argument implies that whatever is self-luminous or self-conscious is capable of illuminating by itself. The Ātman being self conscious is conscious of itself and its consciousness does not require another conscious entity. Self-consciousness of Ātman not only apprehends itself but also makes us aware of non-conscious things. Ātman illuminates the mind, the sense-organs and so on.

Though appeal to reason and scirpture is a necessary condition to obtain self-knowledge, it is not sufficient for the acquisition of self-knowledge. Ultimately appeal to one's own experience *svānubhava* is the final arbiter for self-knowledge. Since Ātman is basically *jñānasvarūpa* (of the form of knowledge), to know the Ātman means to be the Ātman.

Notes and References

1. Jñāna is synonymous with *pramā*. *Pramā karaṇam pramāṇam.* See *Vedāntaparibhāsā of Dharmaraja.* Edited and translated by Swami Madhavananda, Advaita Ashrama, Calcutta. 1972. p.4.
2. (*i*) *Theory of Knowledge* by Chisholm R.M. Prentice Hall, New Delhi, 1977.pp. 104.
   (*ii*) *Web of Belief* by Quine W.V. and Willan J.S.; Random House, New York. 1970, p. 6.
3. *Śamkara's bhāsya on Brahma Sutras*: 1:1:4.
4. *Śamkara's bhāsya on Taittiriya-Upanisad*, ii-1.
5. *Outlines of Indian philosophy* by Prof. Hiriyanna M. George Allen and Udwin Ltd. India, New, Delhi. 1973. p. 344.
6. *Vedānta-paribāsa*. p. 146 (opp. cit)
7. *Indian Philosophy* (Vol. II) by Dr. S. Radhakrishnan. Blackie & Sons, Bombay. p. 502.
8. *Indian Philosophy* (Vol. I by Dr. S. Radhakrishnan, Blackie & Sons, Bombay. 1977. pp. 633-4.
9. *The System of Vedanta* by Deussen P. Oriental pubishers, Delhi. 1972. p. 100.
10. (*i*) *Lectures from Colombo to Almora* by Swami Vivekananda. Advaita Ashram, Calcutta. 1978. p. 329. See also.
    (*ii*) *Vedanta-Philosophy* (At the Harvard University, a lecture and discussion) by Swami Vivekadanda Udbodhan Office, Calcutta. 1972 p. 50.
11. Paśvādibhiscaviśeat-*Śamkara's bhāsya on Brahma Sutraś* introduction. See *The System of Vedanta*, p. 57 (opp. cit) Indian Philosophy (Vol. II) p. 503 (opp. cit)
12. *Śaṃkara's bhāsya on Bṛahma Sūtras* (opp. cit) 1.1.2; ii. 1.4.
13. *Method of Knowledge* by Swami Satprakashananda, Advaita Ashrama, Calcutta. 1974. pp. 264.
14. Śamkara' bhāṣya on *Bṛahma Sūtras* : 1.1.1.
15. Ibid; ii. 3.7

16. Ibid; ii.3,18
17. Ibid; iii.2.21
18. *Vedanta Philosophy* p. 45 (opp. cit.)
19. *Lectures from Colombo to Almora* : p. 316.
20. *Ātmabodha of Śamkaracārya.* Translated by Swami Nikhilananda, Sri Ramakrishna Math, Madras. 1967. p. 187.

16

The Advaita Doctrine of Mahāvākya*

16.1. A cardinal tenet of the Advaita system is that scriptural testimony (*śruti*) is the only source of Self-knowledge (*ātmajñāna*). Other sources of knowledge (*pramāṇas*) like percption and reason normally function only in the world of empirical objects. Traditionally, testimony denotes the Vedas having four subdivisions, namely *saṃhitā*, *brāhmaṇa*, *āraṇyaka* and *upaniṣads*.[1] However, in the Advaita tradition only the Upaniṣads, which constitute the *jñāna kāṇḍa* (knowledge portion) are regarded as the genuine source of Self-knowledge. Swami Vivekananda says : 'The jñāna kāṇḍa of the Vedas comprises the Upaniṣads and is known by the name of Vedānta, the pinnacle of the Śruti, as it is called.'[2] Among the Upaniṣads specific importance has been accorded to four[3] as they contain the *mahāvākyas* or great dictums in the form of cardinal formulas of Advaita Vedānta. The *Aitareya Upaniṣad* (3-1-3) of the *Ṛg-Veda* contains *prajñānam brāhma* (Consciousness is Reality), the *Cāndogya Upaniṣad* (6-8-7) of the *Sāma-Veda* has *tat tvam asi* (That thou art), the *Bṛhadāraṇyaka Upaniṣad* 1-4-10) of the *Yajur-Veda* has *aham brahmāsmi* (I am Reality); the

* Reprinted, with the permission, from the publisher *Prabuddha Bharata*, 1985. Vol. 90, pp. 55-61. Advaita Ashram, Calcutta.

fourth *mahāvākya*, *ayamātmā brahma* (This Self is Reality) belongs to the *Māṇḍukya Upaniṣad* (2) of the *Atharva-Veda*. Thus we find that each Veda has its own specific *mahāvākya*.

The object of this paper is to inquire into the logical status of the four *mahāvākyas*. Of the several *vākyas* (sentences) contained in the Upaniṣads, the four *vākyas* mentioned above are qualified as *mahāvākyas*—literally, great sentences or great dictums. Since scriptural testimony (*śruti*) is the only source of Self-knowledge and the cardinal sentences of the Upaniṣads are in the form of the four *mahāvākyas*, the question arises as to whether each *mahāvākya* is necessary for Self-knowledge but not sufficient, or all the four *mahāvākyas* together constitute the necessary and sufficient conditions to yield Self-knowledge.

16.2. *Prajñānam brahma*

The first *mahāvākya prajñānam brahma* ('consciousness is Brahman') occurs in the *Aitareya Upaniṣad* (3-1-3). The context in which this *mahāvākya is* formulated implies a scheme or matrix for the manifold world containing the domains of the gods, the five elements etc. The seer of this Upaniṣad seems to have had in mind the idea of *prajñā* or consciousness as the basis of the manifold universe when he stated: 'The universe has consciousness as its eye (*prajñā-netro lokaḥ*)'. According to Śaṃkarācārya's interpretion also *prajñāna* is the underlying reality of the world.[4] But in the the formula 'prajñānam=Brahma', the notion of 'Brahman' is ambiguous. Since Reality or Brahman has two aspects, namely, Saguṇa (determinate) and Nirguṇa (indeterminate), it is necessary to decide in which sense it is to be taken. Contextually, the *mahāvākya* implies Saguṇa Brahman. Since the central concept of *mahāvākyas* is 'Brahman', it is desirable to consider certain techniques involved in the definitions of Brahman.

The Advaita system gives two types of definition about Brahman, namely Svarūpa lakṣaṇa (essential definition) and taṭastha Lakṣaṇa (accidental definition).[5] This kind of distnction in definition is peculiar to the Advaita system but, as a matter of fact, the definitions have universal application. That is to say all things in the universe can be defined in terms of svarūpa lakṣaṇa and taṭaṭastha lakṣaṇa. Normally, definitions are the means to precise understanding of the concepts in a given system of knowledge. The soundness of any system of knowledge is also measured in terms of the precise formulation of its definitions. That is why Aristotle said: 'Definition is the beginning and end of all knowledge'. This statement implies that adequate definitions are an essential ingredient in a system of knowledge. Traditional Indian thinkers have fully realized the importance of the art of defining the terms.

By means of a definition it is convenient to specify the exact nature of a thing under consideration by differentiating it from the rest of the things. For example the term 'cow' is defined as an animal with a dewlap (*sāsnā*). The defining property of the animal 'cow' is *sāsnā* which is a specific characteristic of a cow only. Since the defining characteristic is an essential property or part of the nature of the animal defined, the definition is an instance of svarūpa-lakṣaṇa. Taṭasthalakṣaṇa is also a means to distiguish a particular thing from other things, but it does not reflect the essential nature of a thing. For instance, a house in a certain village is distinguished from other houses by referring to some kind of a tree, say a mango tree by the side of that house, and no other house possesses that characteristic of having a mango tree. The fundamental difference between the two types of definitions is now clear. Only the svarūpa-lakṣaṇa gives us an idea about the essential characteristic of a thing defined.

Now it is quite interesting to consider the application of these definitions the nature of Brahman. But there is a difficulty to be encountered in the formulation of an adequate definition of Brahman; it is generally expressed in the from of the following argument. The argument is against the feasibility of a definition about Brahman. Since nirguṇa Brahman is altogether without attributes, there is nothing outside the sole reality of Brahman and it has no characteristics by means of which it may be defined, consequently no svarūpalakṣaṇa is possible. However to a certain extent the said difficulty may be overcome by appealing to the principle of human knowledge :

jñānantu pramāṇajanyam pramā ṇañca yathābhūtavastuviṣayam (knowledge is born of the pramāṇas, it relates to the things as they are.)[6] And for the purpose of communication of the knowledge of Brahman, a definition of Brahman is indispensable without which no *jijñāsā* or inquiry is possible. Accordingly, Advaita has devised the technique to formulate the definitions about Brahman in terms of its svarūpa-lakṣaṇa and taṭasthalakṣaṇa.

The formulation of taṭastha-lakṣaṇa for Brahman is derived from the belief that the manifold universe as an effect owes its existence to God. Consequently the term, Brahman is defined as the cause of the world. This definition distinguishes Brahman from other entities like prạrti, atoms etc. Śaṃkarācārya in his commentry on the *Vedānta Sūtra* regards *janmādyasya yataḥ* (sūtra 1.1.2) ('Brahman from which are derived the brith etc. of this universe'), as an instance of taṭastha-lakṣaṇa. In that context he refers to the instruction of Varuṇa to his son Bhṛgu: 'Seek to know that from which all these beings take birth, that by which live after beings born, that towards which they proceed and into which merge; that is Brahman.'[7]

It is fairly clear that Taṭastha-lakṣaṇa only marks off Brahman from certain other entities and does not characterize the actual nature of Brahman. The formulation of Svarūpa-lakṣaṇa refers to certain essenential characteristics like knowledge (*jñāna*) and bliss (*ānanda*) without which Brahman as a spiritual Reality cannot be conceived. This kind of definition occurs in *Taittirīya Upanisad* (2-1-1), where Brahman is defined as 'Truth, Knowledge and Infinity is Brahman'.

In the light of the above considerations, *prajñānam brahma* is to be taken as a statement implying the essential characteristic of Brahman in terms of *prajñānam.* It may be objected that if Brahman is the sole spiritual stuff and is the locus of consciousness, then consciousness is the property or quality of that stuff. This argument is advanced by Nyāya thinkers, according to whom consciousness is an accidental property of the individual self (*jīva*) or cosmic Self (*Īśvara*).[8] Saṁkarācārya refutes this argument by saying that a substance is identical with its essential property (*dravyātmakatāguṇasya*).[9]

16.3 *Tattvamasi*

We now turn to the second *mahāvākya*, '*tat tvam asi*.' The importance of this *mahāvākya* is tow-fold. Firstly in the process of communicating spirtual knowledge a competent teacher imparts that knowledge throught this *mahāvākya*. Secondly, this *mahāvākya* has been discussed in greater length than the other mahāvākyas. The component words in it are *tat tvam* and *asi;* the respective literal meanings are 'that' (Īśvara or sagunṇa Brahman or God), 'thou' (individual self or jīva) and 'art' (indicates the existential import of the mahāvākya). Thus the literal meaning of the mahāvākya is as flows :

Tattvamasi (That thou art) = the individual self is God.

But it is obvious that such a literal sense of the mahāvākya does not yield the desired truth because God and individual soul blelong to different categories. There are several points of difference between the two entities; omniscience, omnipresence and omnipotence are the characteristics of God only and they are absent in an individual. An empirical paradigm like 'This is that Devadatta' (*so'yam devadatta*) is formulated to bring out the exact sense of *tattvamasi.*[10] In the paradigm 'This is that Devadatta', there are two mutually incompatibe propertises associated with Devadatta : 'this or the present Devadatta' qualified by present attributes such as his fatness, tallness, maturity etc, differs from 'that Devadatta' observed in the past who was lean, short and immature. In view of such incompatible properties. the proposition 'this is that Devadatta' appears to be false. Or the proposition is paradoxical. But in spite of its paradoxical nature, the principle of personal identity helps to identify the present Devadatta to be the same as the past Devadatta. According to the principle of personal identification, 'a person observed at present is the same person observed in the past if there is the continuity of unchangeable consciousness'. By virtue of continuous awarness, an apparently paradoxical statement turns out to be true. But how are we to understand 'tattvamasi' after the model *so'yam devadatta* ? An answer to this question requires the analysis of the Advaita Theory of Meaning.

The meaning of an expression may be either literal (direct) meaning (*śakyārtha*) or metaphorical, i.e. implied meaning (*laksyārtha*).[11] Since the literal meanings of *tat* and *tvam* lead to a paradoxical sense of mahāvākyas, it is necessary to go by their implied meanings in order to establishe the non-dual truth of *tattvamasi.* But the implied meaning—*lakṣyārtha*—is itself of three types : *jahallakṣaṇā* (exclusive meaning), *ajahallaksaṅā* (inclusive mening) and *jahad-ajahallaksaṇā* (inclusive-exclusive meaning. In *jahallakṣaṇā* the primary menaning of an expression is to be completely given up, and only its implied meaning leads to the truth. For example : *gaṅgāyām ghoṣaḥ,* literally means 'There is a hamlet on the Ganges'. This meaning is evidently wrong for, as everyone knows, villages cannot exist on a stream of water. But the metaphorical sense of the sentence leads to the true sense, namely 'There is a hamlet on the *bank* of the Ganges.' In the case of *ajahallakṣaṇā* (inclusive sense), part of the direct meaning is retained and interpreted. For instance, *śoṇo dhāvati* which literally means 'red is running.' Here the dircet senses of 'red' and 'running' are retained and the implied meaning of red as 'red horse' is conceived so that the true sentence of the sentence is brought out as 'the red horse is running'. Otherwise 'red is running' would be a false expression. In *jahad-ajahallakṣaṇā* only incomptibale attributes are eliminated to establish consistency so that the sentence turns out to be true. For eample, the sentence *so'yam devadatta* becomes a true statement if Devadatta seen in the past without accidental properties such as leanness, shortness etc. is the same as the present Devadatta devoid of present attributes like fatness, tallness etc. It is this jahad-ajahallakṣaṇā that is applied in the explication of *tattvamasi.* According to this technique of interpretation, *tattvamasi* becomes a true sentence because the underlying basic consciousness of jīva (individual self) is qualitatively identical with that of Īṣvara (God). Contextually in *Chāndogya Upaniṣad* (6-8-7) *tattvamasi śvetaketo* implies that the pure consciousness of Śvetaketu is qualitatively identical with the eternal consciousness of God (Īṣvara).

'Tattvamasi' is an *upadeśa-mahāvākya* because it presupposes a competent teacher who imparts Self-knowledge through the mahāvākya to his disciple. While instructing a disciple he teaches the identity of the disciple with the ultimate Reality, i.e. Brahman. Hence this mahāvākya is called *akhaṇdārthabodhaka vākya*.

16.4. *Aham brahmāsmi*

The spiritual instruction communicated to the disciple through 'Tattvamasi' mahāvākya triggers *svānubhava* up i.e. Self-knowledge, in the qualified disciple. Such a disciple expresses his *anubhūti* (experience) through the mahāvākya *aham brahmāsmi* (I am Brahman). The true meaning of *aham brahmāsmi* also is to be conceived after the semantic model set up for *tattvamasi*. That is to say, the proposition *aham brahmāsmi* becomes true if according to jahad-ajahallakṣaṇā; we capture the sense of identy by virtue of the common denominator, the pure consciousness.

16.5. *Ayamātmā brahma*

The fourth *mahāvākya, aymātmā brahma* seems to be not so much different from *aham brahmāsmi*. The concept of Ātman, from the logical poiet of view, is not conceptually different from *ātma-jñāna* or knowldege of the Self. For *jñāna* is the very essence of the Atman; that is to say, the Atman is *jñānasvarūpa*. For further conviction about the nature of the *ātman* certain guide-lines have been given. The guide-lines provide á clue to the rediscovery of one's own self (Ātman). A possible guideline emerges from the domain of experience, and in the background of these experiences we contruct and reconstructs thoughts on the basis of the principle of consistency. The principle of consis tency states that our thoughts or ideas are harmonious if our experience is non-contradictory (*abādhita*). We normally employ the sources or means of knowledge such as perception and reason to get appropriate acquaintance with facts or states of affairs. But sometimes our perceptions and inferences go wrong. Therefore we make use of our critical faculty (*vimarśa śakti* or *viveka*) to sort out knowledge from error. According to Advaita logic, the postulation or hypothesis about the existence of self is indispensable. The indispensability or necessity of the self implies a certain module of awareness as the ground for manifold contingent experiences. When an experiencer of subject possess the natural ability to report his stereotypes of cognitive and conative experiences, he intuitively feels quite certain about the background awareness without which patches of experiences cannot be accommodated in a unified system of human beliefs. Thus the functions of sense organs and intellect presuppose an intelligence known as the self which is different from them.[12]

The logical investigation of the nature of Ātman is found in the *Māṇḍūkya Upaniṣad* (1-12). The Ātman has three successive mutually exclusive states : waking, dreaming and sleeping. But the Ātman is also always characterized by the fourth major state of awareness which is common to the other three states. Therefore, the fourth major state of awareness is not successively the fourth state but is simultaneous with the three successive states of waking, dreaming and sleeping. The quantum of happiness or bliss enjoyed in each successive state is directly proportional to the degree of self-identification. The Upaniṣad (verse 7) states that when in deep sleep we are lifted above all desires, we taste the nature of absolute bliss, as in that state of dreamless sleep a man's a mind is cut off from its modifica tions and brought to zero state. Consequently, the Ātman is peaceful, and all blissful.

But the semantic structure of the fourth Mahāvākya *ayamātmā brahma* is such that we directly understand the identity of Atman and Brahman, for they are synonymous and do not imply contradictory attributes. Consequently there is no need to apply the technique of *jahad-ajahallakṣaṇā.*

16.6. *Interrelationship of the four Mahāvāksas*

Of the four Mahāvakyas *prajṇānam brahma* gives the svarūpa-laksana, essential characteristic, of Brahman; hence it is in the form of a definition. Similarly the fourth Mahāvākya *ayamātmā brahma* gives a synonymous definition of Brahman.

In a system of knowledge definitions are necessary but not sufficient. In Advaita system communication of Self-knowledge and intuitive cxperience of that knowledge are also necessary. The Mahāvākya *tattvamasi* serves to transmit knowledge from the teacher to the student. The resulting experience in the disciple is reported through the Mahāvākya *aham brahmāsmi.* Thus each mahāvākya is important and necessary, but all the four Mahāvākyas together constitute necessary and sufficient conditions for self-knowledge.

16.7. The function of the mahāvākyas in human knowledge and culture is unique. They integrate man's subjective experience and objective knowledge into a whole thereby giving meaning to life and enabling man to orient himself to reality.[13] By effecting the fusion of outwardly different but inwardly similar dimensions of reality, the mahāvākyas remove the apparent philosophical and existential contradictions of life. Regarding this Prof. Hiriyanna observes: 'The enunciation of this doctrine marked the most important advance in the whole history of Indian thought. It introduced almost a revolution in the point of view from which speculation has proceeded till then'.[14] The significant change of perspective on the reality introduced by these great sayings is analogous to the transformation of the view about venus. Two persons A and B hold mutually exclusive views about the planet Venus. venus is an eastern star for A, and a western star for B. But the discovery that the eastern star is itself the western star leads to a transformation of the two views held by A and B.

16.8. Swami Vivekananda, the fore most among the modern exponents of Vadanta, emphasized the need for re-interpreting our ancient text in order to make them relevant to human life. He said :

"A broader and more generous conception of life is before us; and although at first we had been deluded a little and wanted to narrow things down, we are finding today that these generous impulses which are at work, these broader conceptions of life, are the logical interpretation of what is in our ancient books. They are the carrying out to the rigorously logical effect, of the primary conceptions of our ancestors. To become broad, to go out, to anmalgamate, to universalise, is the end of our aims."[15]

The logical implications of this view are: (1) a more comprehensive and rigorous form of unified framework for human knowledge is necessary to accommodate variety of human views; (2) a unified theory of human knowledge gives scope for the development of each branch of knowledge in a consistent manner satisfying a criterion of universality that 'knowledge is useful if it solves personal and impersonal problems'.

The pragmatic outlook implied in the docitrine of mahāvākya becomes clearer when applied at the leval of interpersonal affairs in order to understand the nature of true human relations.

Notes and References

1. Cf Swami Satprakashananda *Methods of Knowledge* (Calcutta: Advita. Ashrama 1974) Pp 309-10. The author gives a systematic and authentic classified list of the Vidic Texts. According to the classification there are five Samhitās, eighteen Brāhmaṇas, four Āraṇyakās and sixteen Upaniṣads in Vedic literature.
2. *Complete Works of Swami Vivekananda*: (Calcutta: Advaita Ashrama. 1973) 5:456.
3. Cf *Pañcadasī* of Sri Vidyāraṇya Swāmi : edited by Swami Swahananda (Madras: Sri Ramakrishna Math, 1975) Pp. 122-5.
4. *Eight Upanisads*: Volume 2 with the commontary of Śaṃkarācārya. Translated by Swami Gambhirananda (Calcutta: Advaita Ashrama, 1978) P. 73.
5. *Vedānta Paribhāśā* of Dharmarāja Adhvarīndra, edited and translated by Swami Madhavananda (Calcutta : Advaita Ashrama, 1972) Pp. 151-4.

   Prof. M. Hiriyana, *Indian Philosophical Studies* Vol. 1 & 2 (Mysore : Kavyalaya Publishers. 1957) p. 103.

6. *Brahmasūtra-bhāṣya of Śrī Śaṃkarācārya*, 1-1-4.
7. *Taittrīya Upanisad* III-i
8. *Tarkasamgraha* of Annambhatta. Edited by Y.V. Athalye and M.R. Bodas (Poona : Bhandarkar Oriental Research. 1974) verse 17.
9. *Brahmasntra-bhāṣya of Śrī Śaṃkarācārya*, 1-1-4.
10. *Vedānta Paribhāṣā* Pp. 99-101.
11. Ibid Pp. 93-94
12. *Brahmasūtra-bhāṣya* of *Śrī Śaṃkarācāryay*, 2-3-7: 1-3-12.
13. Cf. Professor M. Hiriyanna: *Outlines of Indian Philosophy* London : George Allen and Unwin, (1956) p. 57.
14. Ibid p. 58.
15. *Complete Works* (1973) 3:271.

17

Role of Reason in Advaita System*

17.1 THE ADVITA SYSTEM belongs to the jñānamārga (path of knowledge). Knowledge in its two principle ramifications of lower-knowledge (*aparā-vidya*) and higher knowledge *parā-vidyā*) is analysed in the Advaita system. The system of Advaita is a complex structure of scriptual knowledge and empirical knowledge.[1] In the course of rational inquiry (*jijñāsā*) it makes use of empirical models and metaphors to maintain its intallectual rigour. Swami Vivekanand says: 'Vedānta recognizes the reasoning powers of man a good deal, although it says there is something higher than intellect; but the road lies through the intellect.'[2] So reason is necessary but not sufficient. What is the role of reason during an inquiry into truthda ? Is reason capable of revealing that truth ? If truth is revealed by some other faculty (say, *anubhūti*, or revelation) does reason have any function in it ? Answers to these questions require an understanding of the structure and function of reason (*tarka*).

17.2. The types of reasoning generally recognized in Advaita tradition are: (*i*) Syllogistic inference (*anumāna*) (*ii*) Comparison (*upamāna*) and (*iii*) dialectic.

* Reprinted, with the permission, from the publisher *Vedānta Kesari*, 1987, Vol. 74, No. 8; Pp. 333-36. The Vedānta Kesari Office, Madras.

(i) INFERENCE (*anumāna*): The term *anumāna* literally means 'knowing after'. *Anumāna* is the method by which mediate knowledge (*anumiti*) is derived from the knowledge of an unchanging relation between the perceived things (*Vyāpti-jñāna*).

Śri Śaṃkara makes use of a five-membered to syllogism establish the phenomenal character of the world. The syllogism formulated in *Māṇḍūkya-kārikā-bhāṣya* (4.4)[3] is as follows:

(a1) *Pratiñā* (Proposition): The objects of the waking state are phenomenal.

Hetu (Reason): Because they are perceptible.

Udāharaṇa (Illustration): Whatever is perceptible is phenomenal, such as dream objects.

Upanaya (Application): So is an object of the waking state.

Nigamana (Conclusion): Therefore the objects of the waking state are phenomenal.

The structure of this inference is similar to the pattern of five-membered syllogisms formulated by Gautam and other Naiyāyikas.

From the point of view of modern logic, the argument (a1) is valid because it satisfies the criterion of validity that 'no false conclusion follows from the true premises.' The argument (a1) could be expressed in the from of Western syllogistic infernce as follows:

Major Premise : All the ojects of the waking state are perceptible.

Minor Premise : All perceptible objects are phenomenal.

Conclusion : Therefore all the objects of the waking state are phenomenal.

The significant difference between Indian and Western syllogisms is the presence of an example in Indian syllogism.

Śaṃkara has used *anvaya-vyatireka tarka*[1] in the *Upadeśa-Sāhasri*. During an inquiry into 'Who am I?', the *mahāvākāya* 'that thou art' is arrived at as the conclusion. This is based on the process of rejecting the mind, senses, and the body as not being the Self. Using this negative mode of reasoning, Sureśvara in his *Naiṣkarmya Siddhi* developed *anvayavyatireka-tarka* in which conclusion is drawn from affirmative and negative statements. Following examples represent *anvaya-vyatireka tarka*:

(a2) 1. Whatever is not self-luminous is material ; for example, physical body.

2. The *ātman* is self-luminous.

3. Therefore, the *ātman* is not material.

(a3) 1. Whatever is an object of cognition cannot be the *ātman*.

2. The body, sense-organs, mind, intellect are objects of cognition.

3. Therefore, they cannot be the *ātman*.

(ii) COMPARISON (*upamāna*): *Upamāna* is a process of reasoning from similar cases to establish probable conclusions. The structure of analogical reasoning by comparison is characterized by certain points of resemblance between two objects without considering their essential differences. Some of the interesting illustrations from Śaṃkara's *Ātma-bodha* are considered below :

(a4) As fire is the direct cause of cooking, so knowledge is the direct cause of liberation, and no other discipline is the direct cause of liberation.[5]

In this argument knowledge is compared with fire. The comparison is drawn on the basis of causal mechanism involved in fire and cooking and knowledge and liberation. Thus the conclusion that knowledge is the direct cause of liberation is justified. To take another example :

(a5) As the moon appears to be moving when the clouds move in the sky, so also the *ātman* appears to be active, when in reality the senses are active.[6]

In this analogy, the *ātman* is compared with moon. Though the *ātman* and the moon belong to different orders of reality, apparent activity or motion is common to both. When the clouds move in quick succession, it appears as if the moon is moving. Similarly, the movements of the sense-organs give the impression that the *ātman* is moving.

It is important understand the subtle differece between (a4) and (a5). The former is a positive analogy to establish the truth of an affirmative conclusion that 'Knowledge is the direct cause of liberation.' But (a5) is a negative analogy to show the falsity of hypothesis that the *ātman* is active. In reality, the *ātman* is the *sākṣi-caitanya* or the witness-consciousness.

(iii) DIALECTIC : This is the most important type of reasoning frequently used in the Advaita system. Dialectic is a form of critical reasoning in which the opponents' views are first systematically formulated and then logically refuted to establish one's own doctrine. It involves chain of arguments as pros and cons. A skilled dialectician somtimes creates interesting objections or considers effective counter-arguments to refute the opponents' arguments. Following is an example of dialectic from Śri Śaṃkara's commentary on the *Vedānta Sūtras*.

(a6) Śaṃkara's refutation of Buddhist's Vijñānavāda (*Brahma-Sūtra-Bhāṣya* 2.2.28)

S.1. *Vedāntin* : It cannot be asserted that external things do not exist, because they are perceived and, as a matter of fact, such things as a pot, a cloth etc. are perceived along with each act of cognition.

S.2. *Vijñnavādin* : I don't say that I do not perceive any object, but I hold that I do not perceive any thing part from the perception.

S.3. *Vedāntin* : But something other than the perception has to be admitted because it is perceived. Nobody says: 'Viṣṇumitra appears like the son of a barren woman.' In order to accept the truth of perception, it is necessary to accept a thing as it actually reveals itself externally and not *as though appearing outside*.

S.4. *Vijñānavādin*: Since no object can possibly exist it only *appears* as though it is outside.

S.5. *Vedāntin*: This argument is not correct, because the possiblity or impossibility of the existence of a thing is determined by the applicability or non-applicability of the means of knowledge to it. And what is known through any one of the means of knowledge, such as direct perception etc., is possible, and what cannot be known through any one of that means of knowledge is impossible. In the case under discussion, the external things are known individually by the means of knowledge. Therefore, external things exist.

17.3. The above dialectic as a series of arguments (S. 1 to S. 5) reveals the progressive development of reasoning. The Vedāntin convincingly refutes the arguments of the *Vijñānavādin*.

An important function of reason is to serve as a criterion for the validity of scriptures. A correct interpretation of the basic text requires fullest use of reason. Gauḍapāda in his *Kārikā* (3.23) explicitly states that scripture (*Śruti*) must be treated valid if it is compatible with reason (*yukti-yukta*), and not otherwise. If the primary sense of a text is unintelligible then the text is to be understood through the secondary implication or a figurative meaning (*Kārikā*: 3.14). Reason as a criterion takes for granted consistency in the system of knowledge (*Śruti*). In a consistent system every proposition exhibits the logical relationship of coherence in such a way that it is impossible to accommodate in it two mutually conflicting statements. A statement and its negation can be accommodated only in an inconsistent system. And such a system cannot be the source of knowledge. Therefore, *upapatti* or intelltgibility in the light of reasoning functions as an important criterion of purportful scripture.[7]

Śri Śaṃkara admits the role of reason to investigate truth. He himself adopts the principle of non-contradiction in criticizing rival systems. He holds that Śruti (scriptural testimony) is superior and does not depend on reason. At the same time, he does not allow Śruti to contradict reason and perception. In the domain of emprical reality, empirical means of knowledge are autonomous and valid. Even if a hundred texts say that fire is cold, we cannot accept it. Śaṃkara says: 'Knowledge arises from its valid means and it conforms to its object *just as it is*.

It can neither be produced by a hundred injunctions nor debarred by a hundred prohibitions.'[8]

17.4 Reason and Śruti are independent, yet interaction betweeen them is possible. The function of reason is controlled by Śruti, and reason, therefore, has a subordinate role. Prof. Hiriyanna has made an interesting observation: 'As regards the claim of rationalists that such truths can be reached through reason, it is pointed out that there is a case of reasoning when once the revealed truth is there. They do not know because they reason; rather, they reason because they know.'[9] So reason by itelf is incapable of revaling scriptural truths. At best, it my help to reach plausible conclusions.

Śri Śaṃkara recognizes the importance of reason in testing scriptual statements and tries to confirm scriptural statements by logical arguments. He uses reason as a critical weapon against untested assumptions.[10]

He recommends reasoning (*tarka*) as an auxiliary to intuition (*anubhava*).[11] He upholds the view of *Bṛhadāraṇyaka Uyaniṣad* that hearing (*śravaṇa*) should be followed by reflection (*manana*) and self-enquiry (*nididhyāsana*). Logical reflection is important. It should, however, conform to the conceptual framework of the Upaniṣads.

In the ultimate analysis, the quest for truth should culminate in *anubhūti*, a direct understanding of the self (*ātmajñāna*).

Notes and References

1. Śaṃkara admits that lower knowledge is a step to higher wisdom. See.
   (i) *Śaṃkara's Bhāṣya on Brahma-sūtra* 2.1. 2.1.14 Translated by Swami Gambhirananda (1972), Advaita Ashrama, Calcutta, p. 330.
   (ii) Radhakrishana. S. (1977): *Indian Philosophy*, Vol. I George Allen and Unwin, Madras, Pp. 518-520.

2. Swami Vivekananda (1972): *Vedanta Philosophy* (At the Harward University, a lecture and discussion) Udbodhan Office, Calcutt, p. 50.
3. Śamkara's *bhāsya* on Māṇdūkya-Kārikā in *The Māṇḍukyopaniṣad* with Gauḍapāda's-Kārika and Śaṃkara's Commenary. Translated and annotated by Swami Nikhilananda (1974) Sri Ramakrishna Ashrama, Mysore, pp. 88-89.
4. Sachchidananda Murty K. (1974) : *Reason and Revelation in Advaita Vedānta,* Motilal Banarsidass, New Delhi. pp. 152-3.
5. *Self-knowledge* (*Ātma-Bodha*) of Sri Śaṃkaracharya. Edited and translated by Swami Nikhilananda (1967). Sri Ramakrishana Math, Madras. pp. 150-1.
6. *Self-knowledge* (op.cit), pp. 176-77.
7. Mahadevan T.M.P. (1976); *The Philosophy of Advaita,* Arnold Heineman, New Delhi pp. 57-58.
8. *Śaṃkara's Brahma-sūtra-bhāṣya* (op.cit) 3.2.31 pp. 622-3.
9. Hiriyanna M. (1974): *Outlines of Indian Philosophy,* George Allen and Unwin, India, p. 182.
10. *Brahma-Sūtra Bhāṣya* (op.cit) 2.1.11, pp. 321-3.
11. *Brahma-Sūtra Bhāṣya* (op.cit) 2.1.6, p. 314.

18

Darśana as a Source of Knowledge

18.1. In Indian tradition darśana[1] functions as a system of knowledge of reality. A system is a set of ideas or concepts which are interrelated so as to serve as an adequate explanation of reality. Etymologically, the term 'darśana' is derived from the root 'dṛś' which means 'to see' or 'observe'. Seeing, may be either perceptual observation (cākṣusa-pratyakṣam) or conceptual knowledge or intuitional experience (anubhūti).[2] But it may be asked whether darśana is merely set of dogmas and opinions; is it a system of critical inquiry ? The aim of this paper is to consider this question in order to investigate the structure and function of darśana interms of modern ideas.

18.2. Generally darśana stands for critical expositions, logical inquiry or insight of soul. When darśana is understood as a system of knowledge (jñāna sādhanam śāstram) it implies critical inquiry. Not only etymological significance of darśana but also in the long tradition of darśanas begining from Vaiśesika darśana (Atomic system) of Kanāda there is considerable justification of usage of the 'darśana' as a matrix for rational deliberations. To this effect authors like Radhakrishnan (1977 48) observe that darśana does not merely designate set of intutive beliefs but indicates a system of thought acquired by intuitive experience justified by logical argument.

18.3. There are different types of darśana; each system is unique in its structure uniqueness of a particular darśana is due to its conceptual autonomy. But in virtue of the fact that divergent forms of darśanas converge under the class of darśana, it must be a class characteristic or a general characteristic shared by every form of darśana. This common characteristic is in the form of critical inquiry.

18.4. Darśana in order to be a system of knowledge should conform to certain criteria. Following are the criteria : since a system of knowledge is in the form of a set of sentences or statements, the sentences which constitute the system must be formally adequate. The criterion of formal adequacy implies the internal consistency in the system; hence the absence of self-contradiction. Of the contradictory sentences only one of them must be true. A false sentence should be removed as it does not fit in the coherent body of true sentences. The primary function of language of darsana is to formulate and convey information about the facts or reality. If the sentences are about thc world we live in, the principal unit designed to convey information is the declarative sentence as bearer of truth value. Through direct investigations of the subject matter, concerned sentences are acknowledged as true of false. However if such an investigation is either inconvenient or impractical due to certain practical difficulties, we have to find out an indirect but accurate method of determining the truth of falsity of a given sentence S by comparing it with certain other sentences say P_1, P_2. . .Pn, whose truth is already known. Turth of P_1, P_2 etc, is known directly if they are self-evident in character. Axioms or postulates and definition of a system are normally treated as self-evidently true sentences. Or even if some of the sentences are known to be true as they are the consequences of othe true sentences, ultimately our knowing must be direct or self-evident in order to encounter infinite regress. Given a set of true sentences (P_1, P_2. . .Pn) within a system, following the rules of valid inference, if S is deduced from P_1, P_2. . .Pn then S must be true.

The series of steps leading from P_1,. . . Pn to S is called a deduction. S is said to be deducible from P_1, . .Pn. Sūtras or aphorisms of a darśana function as axioms and rules. For instance in Pāṇini-darśana exhibits the characteristics of a deductive system.

18.5. The notion of deducibility is very closely related to the notion of consistency. Because for a given set S and sentence P, it can be shown that S yields P and $\neg P$ if S is inconsistent. In other words if S is consistent then P is deducible but $\neg P$ cannot be deduced. Thus formal adequacy is a necessary condition. But formally adequate system must be able to explain the facts of the world, so that explanation of a phenomenon makes certain difference with reference to what is the case and what is not the the case. Along with the explications of the technical concepts utilised in the system, interpretations of experience also constitutes the part of the system.

Adequacy of conceptual scheme of a system is also determined by the kind of logic used in the system. That is to say that the laws of non-contradictions (abādhita niyama) and identity (tādatmya niyama) should be observed in the system. And the kind of language used in a system is comprehensive enough to accomodate subject-predicate and relational types of sentences so that the system of language serves as an efficient instrument for the expression of thoughts in relation to reality. While handling the words in a system the distinction between use and mention is also significant. Words like 'pot' and 'cloth' are used while the corresponding objects pot and cloth are mentioned. Such a distinction avoids the possible conceptual confusion in the system of discourse. The referential terms within the system nomally function as the subject of a sentence but not the predicate in the sentence. Consequently the usage of referential terms implies ontological commitment.

18.6. A sytem in order to explain the facts of the world normally involves certain models in that direction. A model may be physicalistic or phenomenalistic. The entities to be explained are either spatio-temporally extended or events occuring in spatio-temporal point. Physicalistic model is based on the choice that the postulates refer to physical entities where as phenomenalistic model presupposes phenomenal entities.

Although the distinction among physicalistically oriented and phenomenalistically oriented systems is much discussed, certain systems like Nyāya-Vaiśesika accommodates both the models. Of course precise general distinction cannot be drawn betwen the two models. In either case the basic units are 'observable' or 'pereceptible' individuals.

18.7. But the choice of one model rather than other type depends upon the conceptual scheme of the system. According to phenomenal model there is the underlying presupposition that nothing beyond the phenomenal needs consideration in order to explain the facts. We have an instance of such a theory in the system of Early Buddhism characterised by kṣaṇikavāda (momentariness). But what is the basis of choice for phenomenalistic model ? If is usually argued that everything that can be known at all must be explicable interms phenomena because the phenomenal by its very nature implies the content of immediate experience. According to this argument our knowledge claims about the facts are justified through the immediate experience of phenomena. Such a phenomenal system is constituted by phenomenal reduction of the predicate terms defined. The definitions of terms are formulated in such a way that they indicate the testable and pragmatic significance of the terms.

18.8. The physicalistic model differs from the above view because experimentation and pragmatic test operate not exclusively with phenomena but with actual things of the world. Accordingly there is the justification of our beliefs about the presupposition of the existence of extra-phenomenal entities say physcal objects. However physicalist partly agrees with phenomenalist that our beliefs about the physical things is derived from the immediate experience of the things.

18.9. In most of the darśanas like Nyāya-vaiśesika and Sāmkhya-yoga there is the blending of both physical and phenomenal perspectives. A darśana as system is expected to deal with the areas of epistemology metaphysics or ontology, logic, and ethics. Let me consider the Nyāy-vaiśe sika darśana. The Nyāya-vaiśeṣika list of categories accommodates epistemological and logical topics. Most vigorous efforts have been made for the construction of a substantialist or the realist ontology. This ontology is compared to Platonic ontology because it admits repeatable properties and the world is conceived as the totality of individuals as spatio-temporal events related to timeless things. However Nyāya-vaiśesika adopted their own empiricist view of causality. Epistemological topics such as criteria of truth, techniques of distinguishing true belief from error are thoroughly discussed. In the Nyāya theory of inference the criterion of consistency is thoroughly observed. Reasoning in Nyāya-vaiśesika is closest to common-sense. And methodology of Nyāya is followed by almost all other darśanas. Prof T.R.V. Murti observes that "we are all Naiyāyikas first and continue to be so unless by a special effort we free ourselves from the empirical habits of our mind".

18.10. Naiyāyikas are not only empirical as most Indian theorists but they are also at the same time the most imagina tive of systematic thinkers. They have developed the theory universals, of relations, and of absenecs.[3]

18.11. In Indian tradition Nyāya-darśana is rightly claimed as the basis of all the branches of learning (pradīpaḥ sarva vidyānām). The study of Nyāya darśana is almost indispensable to the other darśanas. An indispensability of the study in other darśanas is exhibited through the criticisms of Nyāya using Nyāya methodology itself. Every darśana focusses on the discussions of the theory of values in the areas of ethics and aesthetics, because they are concerned with the theory of release or perfection in relation to material and ethical values.

18.12. Darśana as a system of knowledge functions maily in two ways. Firstly each darśana reflects on the content of human experience in order to conceptualise that experience so that certain criteria are formulated. The cognitive criteria such as the criteria of truth, and knowledge determine the structure of a darśana. That is to say darśanas provide theoretical frame work for practical relisation of the values; secondly at the level of application darśanas furnish necessary guidelines for enriching practical life. Thus darśanas as systems of knowledge function at theoretical and practical levels of human life so that realistion of reality is an instance of enlightened experience.[4]

Notes and References

1. The Sanskrit word darśana is derived from the root dṛṣ which literally means to see. However 'darśana' in its wider sense stands for any form of systematic knowledge; in its narrower sense 'darśana' means 'Tattvajñāna sādhanam sāstram' (=Darsana as Philosophy is the source of philosophical knowledge (tattvajnānam)). See
   (i) *Indian Philosophy* (Vol. I) by Dr. S. Radhakrishnan, 1977, Pp. 43-4. Blackie and sons, Bombay.
   (ii) *Nyāya-Kośaḥ* by Bhimacarya Jalkikar, 1978, Pp. 349-50. B.O.R.I. Poona.
2. *Indian Philosophy* (Vol. I) P. 43. (cited above)
3. *Encyclopedia of India ı Philosophies* (Vol. II) Edited by K. H. Potter 1977, Pp. 38-40. Motilal Banarsidas, Delhi.
4. *Outlinus of Indian Philosophy* by M. Hiriyanna. 1973, p. 182. George Allen and Unwin, London.

19

Structure of Scientific Knowledge

19.1 Scientific knowledge as species of human knowledge is constituted by a set of true propositions systematically related to each other. We claim to have scientific knowledge only when the known propsitions are organised in a systematic way to display their interrelations. Since scientific knowledge is formulated in the propositions, some propositions can be deduced from or proved on the basis of other propositions.[1] Consequently the relationship among the propsitions of a science is deducibility. For example Kepler's laws of planetary motion are derivable from Newton's more general laws of gravition and motion [2] The ideal of human knowledge is characterised as a deductive system and hence science is a system in which a minimum number of propositions are sufficient to deduce the remaining propositions of the system.

19.2 Since classical definition of knowledge as justified true belief[3] implies the truth, belief and justification to constitute necessary and sufficient conditions, consequently scientific knowledge is characterised as follows:

> S knows that scientific proposition p if and only if S believes (accepts) that p, that p is true and S is justified in believing that p.

Accordingly scientific knowledge implies the following analytic consequences:

(i) If S knows that p then S believes that p,

(ii) If S knows that p then p is true, and ;

(iii) If S knows that p then p is justified.

19.3 But there is some kind of resistance to the classical view of knowledge including scientific knowledge. Authors like Popper[4] argue for the untenability of scientific knowledge as justified true belief. Popper (1975 : 107-150) a champion of objective knowledge criticises subjective components like belief in the above definition. Objective knowledge is characterised by logical content of scientifics theories, conjectures or guesses.[5] Theory of subjective knowledge is made explicit by Descartes. According to him 'knowing' is an activity and presupposes the existence of a knowing subject. Subjective knowledge is a kind of belief or opinion which is a special state of the mind. And in order that a kind of belief (a state of mind) should amount to an item of knowledge, the believer should possess sufficient reasons for his knowledge claim to be true and certain. Subjective knowledge is a kind of disposition to be characterised as biological theory of knowledge, because an organism becomes conscious in the form of a belief (disposition).

Objective knowledge of natural sciences is essentially conjectural or hypothetical in character and there are no sufficient reasons holding the hypotheses to be true. However, Popper (1975 : 75) acknowledges an element of justification in demonstrable knowledge which comprises the propositions of formal logic and arithmatic.

19.4. Traditional epistemology implies knowledge of thought in a subjective sense as "I know", or "I am thinking." And such subjective knowledge claim refers to Popper's second world of mental states (or consciousness). But scientific knowledge belongs to the third world of objective theories and objective arguments. Knowledge in the objective sense is totally impersonal or independent of anybody's claim to know, and consequently it is independent of person's belief or disposition to assent or to assert. Thus knowledge in the objective sense means knowledge without a knowing subject (a knower). It is be noted that objective sense of knowledge is similar to Frege's objective sense of thought. Frege says: "I understand by a thought not the subjective act of thinking but its objective content."[6] Popper (1975 : 110-2) illustrates the distinction between subjective knowledge and objective knowledge by means of the following examples :

Subjective Example :

(1) 'I know that Fermat's last theorem has not been proved but I believe it will be proved one day.'

(2) 'From the entry 'knowledge' in *The Oxford English Dictionary* : Knowledge is a 'state of being aware or informed.'

Objective examples :

(1) 'Taking into account of the present state of mathematical knowledge, it seems possible that Fermat's last theorem may be undecidable.'

(2) 'From the entry 'knowledge' in *The Oxford English Dictionary* : Knowledge is a 'branch of learning; a science; an art.'

First two examples involve reference to a knowing subject whereas the other two examples of objective knowledge do not contain any reference to a subjective conditions such as belief or awareness.

Knowledge in the subjective sense is irrelevant to scientific knowledge. Because only objective knowledge comprises the study of third world of scientific theorses. The objectivity of scientific statements lies in the fact that they can be inter-subjectively tested but never fully justifiable or verifiable. Testability of scientific knowledge implies falsifiability.

19.5. Popper's (1960:41)[7] empirical test in a negative sense implies that it must be possible for empirical scientific system to be refuted by experience. Popper thinks that there is an asymmetry between varifiability and falsifiability. An alleged asymmetry emerges from the understanding of the logical form of universal statements. Acording to verificationists universal propositions are established on the basis of singular propositions such that singular propositions or observation propositions confirm those universal propositions, but according to Popper universal statements are never derivable from singular or observation statements through the relation of confirmation. But his falsifiability criterion is implied by deductive testability.

Popper's (1960 : 76) techinque of falsification of the system through the modus of tollens classical logic is as follows :

Let t be a system of statement constituting a theory and p is a true conclusion of the system. The deductive relationship i.e. derivability of p from t is symbolised as '$t \rightarrow p$'. In a valid deductive relation no false conclusion can be drawn from true prmises (a theory); but a false theory may (validly) imply true or false conclusion. Suppose p is false-($\bar{p}$) and given the relation of deducibility, $t \rightarrow p$, it is posible to infer t so that it is justified. Thus falsifying inference takes the following form :

1. $t \rightarrow p$
2. $\bar{p}$

$\therefore$ 3. $\bar{t}$ or $((t \rightarrow p).\ \bar{p}) \rightarrow \bar{t}$

19.6. Proper is aware of certain objections to his falsifiability theory. It seems somewhat odd to suggest that science as a source of positive information should be characterised as satisfying a negative requirement of falsifiability. Popper replies that the falsfiability theory does not save untenable systems but on the contray it helps to choose the one which by comparison the fittest. It is interesting to note that a falsified scientific theory suggests a new alternative theory as the out come of the negation of falsified theory.

19.7 Popper's proposal appears to be revolutionary. His radical alternative to classical or traditional concept of knowledge implies his view of knowledge as a process of conjectures and refutation. Consequently he rejects the problem of epistemic foundations as process of justification. For Popper (1975:115) objective knowledge may be true or false. But as seen above (S.2) truth is a necessary condition of the classical conception of knowledge. And consequently the expression 'true knowledge' is redundant and 'false knowledge' is contradiction.

19.8. Recently authors like Pandit (1983:33) (fn. 3 : ii) have shown certain inconsistency in Popper's objectivistic epistemology. There is inconsistency between (i) Popper's rejection of traditional definition of knowledge and formulation of objective knowledge without a knowing subject, and (ii) his postulation of relatively independent worlds: material world (W1), mental worlds (W2) and scientific world of objective structures of scientific theories (W3). Poppers (1975 : 255-6) allows the worlds W1, W2 and W3 to interact but he denies the possibllity of the corresponding interactions between subjective and objective elements in epistemology. Popper (1975 : 156) says : "Moreover, it seems to me to support not only the thesis that a subjective mental world of personal experiences exist. . . but also the thesis that it is one of the main functions of second world to grasp the objects of the third world."

19.9. It seems to me that there is also an inconsistency between the view that objective epistemology without a knowing subject and the third world (W3) as a man made product. According to Popper (1975 : 159) it is possible to accept the reality or the autonomy of the third world, and at the same time he admits that the third world originates as a product of human mental activity. Popper would have postulated the objective reality of W3 similar to that of Plato's theory of Ideas in order to save his theory of objective knowledge from inconsistency. In modern times authors like Frege and Church have postulated mind independent objective propositions.

I think classical definition of knowledge as justified true belief is the blending of objective and subjective elements. Truth condition, fot instance, is exclusively objective element where as belief condition is subjective component.

19.10. Quine's view of scientific knowledge differs from Popper's notion of scientific knowledge as the process of conjectures and refutations. The difference between two view points hinges on the difference in the goals of science. According to Quine the business of science is the pursuit of truth. Scientific activity is selective in order to understand the world.

Empirical truth attaches to statements by virtue of the nature of the world. In other words a statement is true when it correrponds to reality so that it mirrors the world. Quine (1962:xi)[8] says: A fundamental way of deciding whether a statement is true is by comparing it, in some sense or other, with the world—or, which is the nearest we can come, by comparing it with our experience of the world." In contradistinction with Popper's falsifiability of scientific theory Quine advocates confirmation of scientific statements on the basis of observations. The scientific pronouncements about sub-atomic particles are known to us as part of a systematic conceptual structure related to human experience. Quine also allows the possibility of confutation (falsification) of scientific theory. A theory is to be changed when the predictions turn out false. And scientific systems are subject to revision when revisions are called for by unexpected experiences (Quine, 1962 : xiii).

19.11. According to Quine epistemology is just a branch of biology (Quine 1975 :213 Smart 1975: 7).[9] Because Quine views man biologically and experiences are just events that go on in specimens of homo sapiens and also in other animals. Human brain is a processor of information which comes as a result of the irradication of the animal's sensory surfaces. The information coming to our receptors is processed by our brains to give rise to knowledge.

Quine's epistemology seems to be another radical alternative to classical epistemology. But unlike Popper's radical alternative Quine's view is more empirically combined with subjectivism which Popper opposes in the interest of his objective knowledge of third world of scientific theories.

19.2. Quine is critical about scientific knowledge; he views science as a set of sentences properly related. His critical view is expressed through an intersting analogy that science is like a boat which we must rebuild plank by plank while staying afloat in it (Quine 1960 : 3). In this regard Quine seems to be in agreement with Popper (Smart 1975 : 7). But it seems to me that Popper's proposal is more radical and stronger than that of Quine's view of scientific theory. Because there is asymmetry between Popper's falsifiability and Quine's confirmability of scientific theories. Quine's way of testing scientific knowledge is through the processes of induction and deduction whereas Popper's method of testability is exclusively deductive.

19.13. Since Quine treats epistemology a branch of biology two important questions arise: (i) whether the subject matter of biology is the same as the subject matter of epistemology; (ii) how does the aim of epistemology differ from that of biology ? Subject matter of epistemology is more comprensive than that of biology or any others science. The focus of epistemological inquiry is about the knowledge claims in general whereas biological science has narrower scope. The aim of epistemology is the rational justification of our knowledge claims but on the contrary most of the biological theories are in the form of conjectures. Quine's argument is essentially genetic in character. Authors like Pandit (1983 : 37) think that epistemology aims at an analysis and criticism of the antecedently available methodological frame works of empirical sciences. And secondly it aims at exploring the possibility of better alternatives to these frameworks. Thus epistemological enterprise is concerned with the inquiries into nature and growth of human knowledge.[10]

19.14. The three characterisations of scientific knowledge expressed above are the classical or tradition epistemological which views scientific knowledge as justified true belief, Popper's objective epistemology implies that scientific knowledge is process of conjectures (and refutations) and Quinean naturalistic epistemology as a branch of biology, treats knowledge claims in science as the consequences of primitive sensory mechanisms. I think scientific knowledge is to be understood in terms of truth and justification in the light of the criticisms offered above. Empirical truth is contingent in nature, the denial of an empirical propositions does not lead to contradictions. For a given time and circumstances most of the scientific theories are accepted as vaild or justified otherwise the field of science becomes unstable. Justification in science implies acceptance of a scientific theory on the basis of consistency and positive evidences in the absence of negative evidence. Evolution of scientific knowledge is also consistent with justification of scientific truths. The structure of scientific knowledge reveals the truth component in the form of true empirical propositions and the justification of empirical truth by means of observation and logic.

Scientific knowledge as a Species of pramā (knowledge) is normally caused by pramāṇas of (sources of knowledge) like Observation (perception) and reasoning (anumāna). In Indian context scientific knowledge as from of lower knowledge is considered to be useful for attaining higher knowledge (spiritual wisdom).

Notes and References

1. All the prositions of sciences need not be proved by deducing them from others. To avoid infinite regress and circularity certain self-evident or self-justifying propositions as the premisses are to be accepted so that non-self-evident scientific propositions are deduced from them See—

   (i) Copi I.M. (1973) : *Symbolic Logic,* Macmillan Publishing Co., New York, p. 153.

   (ii) Quine, W. V. and J. S. Ullian (1970): *Web of Belief,* Random House, New York, Chapter 3.

2. Newton's theory is a from of scientific knowledge. This theory explained precisely not only movements of all stars in their courses, but also precisely the movements of bodies on earth. See—
   (i) Popper, K. R. (1975) : *Objective Knowledge.* The Clarendon Press, Oxford, p. 211.
   (ii) Copi (op. cit). p.1ç2.

3. Traditionally an inquiry about the nature of human knowledge begins from Plato. Since Plato's time epistemo logical questions are about the nature of knowledge, its justification, its foundations in relationship with belief. See—
   (i) Chisholm. R.M. (1977) : *Theory of knowledge,* Prentice Hall India. p.5, Chapter Six.
   (ii) Pandit G.L. (1983): *The Structure and growth of Scientific Knowledge.* D. Reidel Publishing Co., Holland, pp. 17, 22.
   (iii) Lehrer, K (1974) : *Knowledge.* The Clarendon Press, Oxford, Chapter 3.
   (iv) Armstrong, D.M. (1973): *Belief, Truth and Knowledge.* Cambridge University Press, Cambridge, pp. 137-149.

4. (i) Popper (op. ctd.): pp. 107-150.
   (ii) See Pandit (op. citd.) 29-35. The author treats Popperian epistemology as radical alternative to traditional epistemology.

5. Popper (op. citd.) pp. 73.
6. Cited in Popper, p. 109l.
7. Popper, K.R. (1960): *The Logic of Scientific Discovery* Hutchinson of London.
8. Quine, W.V. (1962) : *Methods of Logic.* Routledge and Kegan Paul, London.

9. (i) Smart J.J.C. (1975): "Quine's Philosophy of Science" in *Words and Objections*, edited by Davidson, D and J. Hintikka. D. Reidel Publishing Co., Holland, pp. 3-13.

(ii) Quine W.V. (1975): 'Replies to Smart' in *Words and Objections*, pp.292-4.

(iii) Quine. W.V. (1960) : *Word and Object*. MIT Press, Cambridge Mass. pp. 120-3.

10. Pandit, G.L. (op. cited.): p.37.

20

Structure of Apriori Knowledge and Gödel's Proof

20.1. The classical definition of knowledge as justified true belief[1] is also applicable to apriori knowledge. Accordingly apriori knowledge implies truth, belief and justification. In other words truth, belief and justification constitute necessary and sufficient conditions for apriori knowledge. Apriori knowledge implies necessary truths; logic, arithmatic and geometry are the main sources of necessary truths. In the long tradition beginning from Plato truths of reason as necessary truths constitute the nucleus of genuine knowledge. And for centuries deductive reasoning as a proof technique or procedure employed in mathematics was a paradigm of human thinking. And it was firmly believed that in an axiomatic system of apriori truths every non-axiomatic truth in that system can be deduced as a theorem in conformity with the accepted rules of reasoning. But Kurt Gödel's[2] famous paper published in 1931 attacked the central doctrine of the foundations of mathematics. According to that astomishing discovey of proof even in arithmatic there are ture propositions in the form of theorems which cannot be proved with the accepted rigorous methods of reasoning. To this effect John Von Newman said: "Kurt Gödel's achievement in modern logic is singular and monumental-indeed it is more than a monument it is a landmark which will remain visible for in space and time". Prof. Quine (1962 : 247-86) observes : "Gödel's discovery came as a shock to prenconceptions . . . One of the few things more surprising than the incompletability of elementary number theory, is the fact such incompletability can actualy have become known to us."[2]

20.2. Kurt Gödel (1931) in his famous paper entitled "On Formally Undecidable Propositions of *Principia Mathematica* And Related systems" confined to the most comprensive formal system of *Principia Mathematica* and the axiom system for set theory. All the methods of proof used in mathematics have been finalised in theses systems. Hoping that formulised systems are characterised by a few axioms and rules of inference such that these axioms and rules of inference are sufficient to decide all mathematical propositions. But Gödel (1931 : 38) argued that, this is not the case because in both the systems mentioned there are relatively simple problems in the theory of ordinary number which cannot be decided from the axioms. To this effect Quine (1981 : 124) says: Since we can express number theory in set theory, it follows that there is no hope of a complete system of a set theory.

20.3. Since Gödel's (1931) theorem belongs to meta-mathematics, the name given by Hilbert to the study of proof in mathematicsand logic; it is desirable to have some brief account of thestate of meta-mathematics in 1930. Logic entered its modern crenaissance since the publication of *Begriffsschrift* by Gottlb Frege (1879). Subsequently *Principii Mathematica* (1910-13) was an important step for formalization. It had exhibited the important parts of mathematics such as arithmetic as a deductive system. A deductive system is characterised by limited number of axioms such that each theorem in the system follows logically from the axioms in conformity with limited number of rules of inference. The formulas used to express the axioms and theorems of a given deductive system facilitate the derivation of sequence of formulas from other formulas and consequently such a (deductive) system of formulas is called a *calculus*.

Hilbert originated meta-mathematics or proof theory.[3] His proposal called for formalisation of suitable portion of classical mathematics so that it should be embodied in a formal system. A formal system consists of all the formal techniques of constructing formulas to express mathematical propositions and principles of logic to be used in proving theorems mechanically. Consistency of a formal system implies that no two configurations or formulas should exist in the system to constitute proof of a formula A and of its negation ¬A. In Hilbert's programme of the formalisation, mathematics was believed to be complete. Accordingly each closed formula of the formal system should be provable or refutable in it.

20.4. Gödel's paper (1931) established the view that in a formal system obtained by the combination of Peono's axioms[4] with the logic of *Principii Mathematica* (*PM*) the desired completeness for the system of arithmatic is lacking.[5]

Gödel's proof of the undecidability of some arithmatical propositions is in the formal system P. Gōdel (1931 : 41) says :

> 'P is essentially the system obtained by superimposing on the Peonòs axioms the logic of *PM* (numbers as individuals, relation of successor as undefined basic concept)[6]

Gödel's novel meta-methematical method is characterised by arithmatization according to which natural numbers are attached to signs, to the series of signs (formula) and the series of series of signs (proof-schemata) of a formal system. (Braithwaite 1962 : 7). Gödel (1931 : 45) provides a co-ordinating rule according to which different Gōdel numbers are assigned to each element in his formal system P.

20. 5 Gödel's (1931:57) proof for the unprovability theorem for the system P is based on his proposition VI,[7] which may be paraphrased as follows:

'If the formal system P satisfies a certain condition of consistency, then there is at least one formula Ap (P) such that, neither AP (P) nor ¬ AP (P) is provable within P'.

What kind of reasoning has been used by Gödel in the proof of unprovability theorem? Gōdel (1931 : 40) says that his reasoning is analogous to pattern of reasoning in Richard's paradox[8] or liar's paradox[9] and any epistemological paradox can like wise be used for undecidability proof. Gödel implies that reasoning involving self-referring proposition constitutes the nucleus of Godel's proof. However the paradoxes like Richards' and liar's as they stand are not veridical paradoxes. But Godel's proof is an instance of veridical paradox (Quine : 1976 : 16-18). [10]

Let me formulate Gödel's reasoning in his theorem following Kleene (1976 : 765-6). Let us consider the formula Ag (V), where 'V' is a particular variable of a certain formula and g is the Gödel number of such a formula so that resulting formula is Ag (V).

Now consider another formula $\forall x \sim A$ (v, x) ("for all x, not A (v, x)) having one free variable v whose Gödeal number is P so that (i) it is the formula AP (V). Next consider the formula AP (p) as $\forall x \sim A$ (p, x) (ii). Since we know that p is the Gödel number of a formula AP (v) where x is free variable, so for each x, A (p, x) is equivalent to "x is the Gödel number of proof of AP (P)". Hence AP (P) i.e. $\forall x \sim A$ (x) (i) implies that for every x, x is not Gödel number of a proof of Ap (P). In other words Ap (p) means "I am unprovable".

The sentence "I am unprovable" appears to be paradoxical due to self-reference. But it is unlike the falsidical paradox "I am false". Because the sentence 'I am false', if it is true, then by what it says is false; and if it false then it is true This kind of paradox is solved by the introduction of a distinction between object language and meta-language. Gödel's sentence "I am unprobabie" is not paradoxical. Because there is the difference between 'true' and 'provable' and there is no apriori reason that every true sentence must be provable. Thus the sentence AP (P) as "I am unprovable" is simply unprovable and true (Kleene 1976 : 765; Findlay 1942 : 262-65), Hijenoort 1967 : 352).

Suppose Ap (P) is provable. If Ap (P) is provable then what it says is false. And there is contradiction to the assumption that only true sentences are provable. Hence the proposition Ap (P) is provable does not hold good. So Ap (P) is unprovable. And under the same assumption $\sim$Ap (P) is also unprovably, since it implies falsehood and only true sentence are provable.

Thus Ap (P) is formally undecidable in the system i.e. it is neither provable nor refutable. The proof four undecidability of Ap (P) presupposes an assumption that system is consistent. Suppose Ap (P) were provable, then there would be proof of it having Gödel number x, so that for this x, A (p, x) would be true and provable. Consequently $\exists$ x. A (p, x) and $\sim\forall$x $\sim$A (p, x) i.e.$\sim$Ap (P) are provable. Thus both Ap (P) and$\sim$Ap (P) would be provable, and hence the system turns out to be inconsistent. Thus if the system is consistent Ap (P) is not provable.[11]

And in order to establish that$\sim$Ap (p) is unprovable Gödel (1931:57)[12] used the stronger assumption of 'w-consistency'. w consistency implies simple consistency and simple consistency implies the unprovability of Ap (P). Consequently no natural number (0, 1, 2 etc) is the Gödel number of a proof of Ap (p); thus A (P, 0) A (P, 1)...are false hence$\sim$,A (P, 0),$\sim$A (P, 1) are provable. Consequently$\sim$,Ap (P) i.e.$\sim\forall\sim$,A (p, x) is provable and in that case the system would be w inconsistent. Thus if the system is w-consistent them$\sim$Ap (P) is not provable.

We have obtained a well-formed formula Ap (P) of the system P such that neither Ap (P) nor $\neg$Ap (P) is provable in system P and hence the system P is incomplete. Incidently undecidable true proposition Ap (P) is arithmatical and implies absence of decision procedure for the system of arithmatic. Since the underlying logic adequate for number theory is predicate calculus of first order (i.e. quantification theory) and there is no decision procedure for quantification theory and hence elementary number theory also lacks decision procedure. A decision procedure is a mechanical procedure leading to an answer in every case, valid or invalid, for instance logic of truth functions (propositional logic). Quine (1964:191-246) says that a mechanical procedure for proving validity is only a part of decision procedure for it reports only valid cases; the other half would be the method of disproof so that the two parts together constitute decision procedure. Thus decision procedure answers the quest of a proof or disproof. Though quantification theory lacks decision procedure, it possesses complete proof procedure, because in it there is a complete procedure for proving validity so that every valid (true) formula can be decided or proved. But elementary number theory backed up by quantification theory lacks completeness as demonstrated by Gödel.

20.6. However the elementary number system is consistent and consistency is one of the virtues of formal deductive systems. Whether consistency of the system can be proved ? Gödel in his second theorem offers the proof for unprovability of consistency for number theory. The corresponding proposition XI[13] simplified may be stated as follows :

If the formal system P is 'consistent', its consistency is unprovable within P. (Braithwate 1962:24). In order to prove this theorem Gödel uses the result of the proof of his unprovability theorem according to which, if P is consistent then the formula Ap (P) is undecidable. Ap, (P) is self-referring proposition. Some important consequences of theorem 1 are expressed as :

(1) There is no well formed formula Ap (P) such that both Ap (p) an¬Ap (P) are provable, or

(2) There is at least one well-formed formula A that is not provable.

Gödel (1962:70) says that he has given the sketch of the proof in theorem 2, and he intended to present it in detail which he never published (Braithwaite 1962 : 24). However Brathwaite (1962:25) following Rosser reconstructs Gödel's outline of the proof for theorem 2. Accordingly 't' is a particular formula which is provable in P say as one of the axioms of P. If~t is also provable, P is' inconsistent; if P is inconsistent, every well formed formula is provable' in P. So the consistency of P is logically equivalent to the unprovability of 't' and the inconsistency of P to the provability of 't'.

Suppose the well formed formula (AP) (P) states that 'P' is consistent, formula Ap (P) is not provable, it expresses, in P, part 1 of theorem 1. The proof of the theorem 1, part 1 can be formalised in P consequently Ap (P) is provable in P. If C were provable (by the rule of detachment) Ap (p) is provable which contradicts part 1 of theorem 1. Therefore if P is consistent, its consistency is not provable in P.

Implication of the second theoem is that non-contradictorness of the system P cannot be dedemonstrated, using only the logical machinary in contained that system. Suppose we have managed to prove with the means offered only by the system of arthmatic that the system P is not contradictory, the proof begs the question. Because for a proof in P to be valid we must know that the system is noncontradictory. But in that case what is to be proved is just the very non-contradictoriness of the system.

Suppose the consistency of P is proved by means of the another system say Q. The proof for P would effectively attain its object. If there is prior proof of consistency for Q which in turn presupposes proof for R and so on.

20.7. There seems to be inconsistency between Gödel's theorem of incompletability and his realism (Barker 1969:4). Gódel's realism implies the postulation of existence of mathematical objects. Gӧdel (1944-220) says ;

"Classes and concepts may, however, also be conceived as real objects, namely classes as pecularities of things or as structures consisting of a plurality of things and concepts as the properties and relations of things existing independently of our definitions and constructions···" It seems to me that the assumption of such objects is quite as legitimate as the assumption of physical bodies and there is quite as much reason to believe in their existence". Gödel appears to hold Platonic realism which takes the view that mathematics only discovers its object but does not create or invent them.[14]

The theorem of incopletability gives the impression that we cannot suppose that we are studying an objectively real, mind-independent subject matter belonging to Popper's 3rd world of objective facts[15] if we understand that no formal theory about that objsctive reality can be both complete and consistent.

And it is generally believed that any account of real objects must in principle provide some sort of description in terms of consistency and completeness.

However there is no real inconsistency and themorem of incompletability is compatable with Gödel's realism. Incompletability theorm does not imply subjectivism in the description of reality but rather indicates an essential limitation in the human power of symbolism in the fuller characterisation of system of objects. However the realist continues to believe in the existence of numbers and classes as real entities, though he knows that there is no list of consistent axioms formulated to describe the completeness of the system.[16] (Barker 1969:5).

To this effect Gödel (1947:272) says :

"...the acceptance of criterion of truth...is the fact that continued appeals to mathematical intution...this follows from the fact that for every axiomatic system there are infinitely many undecidable propositions...Besides mathematical intution another criterion of the truth of mathematical axioms, namely their faithfullness...as application of the criterion in computation".

20.8. The results of Gödel's theorems imply limitations to the powers of discrete state of machines (Turing 1950 : 444). The limitations on machines is precisely expressed interms of unprovability in the system (Slezake 1982:42). According to Gödel's theorems in any logical system, statements can be formulated which can neith be proved nor disproved within the system unless the system itself is inconsistent. Authors like Church, Kleen and Turing refer to machines like digital computer of an infinite-capacity. The limitation of such a machine means that there are certain operations that such machine can not perform. If the machine is rigged up to answer the questions either it gives wrong answers or donot give any answer. Turing says (1950:445): "When the machine described bears a certain comparatively simple relation to the machine which is under interpretation it can be shown that the answer is either wrong or not forthcoming. . .it proves disability of machines."

Gödel's result also implies that the notion of truth in case of undecidable propositions belings to metalinguistic (metamathematical) proof. Gödel (1931:41) says "...the proposition which is undecidable in the system PM yet turns out to be decided by metamathematical considerations. Consequently Hilbert's formalist programme was unrealizable since provability in a given system cannot be identified with mathematical truth."

Since the notion of truth is semantic and it is characterised by the relation of statements to the facts, the statements in the present context are jutified in the metalanguage.

20.9. Epistemological status of undecidable proposition implies that our knowledge claim about undecidable proposition is not justified within the system but justfication is provided abextra i.e. in metalinguistic system or meta mathematical system. But there is a difficulty to be encountered in the metalinguistic justification. An undecidable true proposition is justified by means of metalinguistic statements but the statements which function as justifying statements also need justification by means of other statements possibly belonging to meta-meta-language and so on add infinitum, so that infinite hierarchy of metasystems are to be allowed. However this may not be the case if meta-linguistic statements are self-justifying by virtue of being intuitively true statements or that meta-linguistic system offers informal proof. Thus the truth of the undecidable proposition is to be known by meta-linguistic proof in the meta-language. The spirit of exfrinsic justification used in such contexts probably captures the sense of the theory of extrinsic justification (parataḥ-prāmāṇya-vāda) formulated in Navya nyāya system. There are also significant differences between the two theories of cognitive justification.

Notes

1. According to classical conception of knowledge, three conditions are required in order to know a proposition (p). First, the proporition must be true; second, the knowing subject (s) must believe or accept it and third, the subject must have good or legitimate grounds to accept that proposition. Accordingly the classical definition of knowledge may be exprerssed as follow:

   S knows that p is true=Df. p is true, S believes p and p is justified by S.

   For the explication of this definition see Chisholom (1977:102-118); Lehrer (1974, Chapter 3); Armstrong (1973 137-149).
2. See Meltzer (1962: 37-72) for English translation of Gödel's theorem originally published in German as "Uber formal unentscheidbare sätze der principia mathematica and verwandter system I", in Monatsheffe fiūr Mathematik and Pysik Vol. 38 (1931), Pp. 173-198.

   My references are to Meltzer's translation.
3. Heizenoort (1967-349): Parwitz (1974:63-64) Kleene (1974: 763); Agazzi (1974:23) Braithwarte (1962: 2-3); Nagel and Newman (1959; 26-30).
4. Peano's aximoms are formulated by means of the three undefined terms: 'number', 'zero', and 'immediate success or of ; There are five axioms:

   (i) Zero is a number. (ii) The immediate successor of a number is a number (iii) Zero is not the immediate successor of a number. (iv) No two numbers have the same immediate successor. (v) 'Any property belonging to zero, and also to the immediare successor of every, number that has the property, belongs to all numbers'.

   5th axiom implies the principle of mathematical induction. (Nagel and Newman 1959:163; Rundle 1967:556).
5. Gödel (1931:41-42); Kleene (1974:763); Braithwaite (1962: 13).
6. For exact description of the formal system P, Gödel (1931:42) specifies the basic signs as follows:

I Constants: '⁻' (not), 'V' (or), 'II' (for all), 'O' (nought), 'f' (the successor ( ); '(r)' Bracket).

II Variables of first type for individuals i.e. natural numbers including O): 'x_1,' 'y_1' 'z_1' . . . . variables of second type (for clase of individuals) 'x_2,' 'y_2,' 'z_2'. . . and so on.

7. Gödel (1931:57) formulates proposition VI as :

"To every w-consistent recursive class a of formulas those correspond recursive class signs 'r' such that neither V Gen, r nor Neg (V Gen, r) belogs to Flg (e) (Where V is the free variable of r)".

According to Gödel Gen=Generalisation. Neg=Negation; Flg=set of consequences. (See Meltzer 1962:33-4).

Braithwiate (1962:18) has given simplified version of proportion VI in the following way. "If the formal system P satisfies a certain condition of 'consistency' then there is at least one recursive class sign r (V) in in P such that neither V Gen r (V) nor Neg (V Gen r (V)) is provable within P".

I have paraphrased Braithwaite's simplified verson of proposition U1 using Keene's (1974:765-6) symbols.

8. Richard's Paradox is devised by J. Richard in 1905. In that paradox, the expresson 'Richardian' is associated with a certain number 'n' so that the sentence 'n' is is Richardian is constructed'.

Richard Paradox implies 'n' is Richardian if, and only if, 'n' is not Richardian. In Gödel's reasoning, undecidable formula is also associated with a certain number to get the statement.

The formula is not demonstrable. Gödel also showed that a certain proposition is demonstrable if and only if its negation is demonstrable.

See Stoll (1976:446-7); Nagel and Newman (1959:85-6) Heijenoort (1967:352-3).

9. Liars paradox otherwise called the paradox of Epimenides runs as 'I am lying'. By dropping personal réference one

can directly express the sentence 'This centence is false" which means that' the senteuce is true if and only if it is false'. See Quine (1976:8-9); Heijenoort (1967:352).

10. Quine (1976:9) draws the distinction between veridical and falsidical paradox by saying that an element of surprise present in veridical paradox disappears quickly as its proof is made explicit where as a falsidical paradox also packs up a surprise but it is turned out be false.
11. Kleene 1974:765; Heijenoort 1967:352, Stoll 1976:449; Quine 1958:246.
12. Gödel (1931:57) says: 'every w-consistent system is naturally consistent. The converse, however is not the case'. The relation between consistency and w-consistency is similar to the relationship between consistency and validity. Thus in either case consisteny does not imply validity or W-consistency. Quine (1962:28) illustrates that a certian schema like 'pq' is consistent (i.e.) true under a particular interpretation that when 'p' is true, and 'q' is false. But 'pq' is invalid because there are other interpretation 'p' and 'q' so that 'pq' turns out to be false.
13. Gödel's (1931:70) formulation of the proposition XI is given as:
    If c be given recursive, consistent class of formulae, then the propsitional formula which states that c is consistent is not c-provable; in particular, the consistency of P is unprovable in P, it being assumed that P is consistent (if not of course every statement is provable) see Heijenoort (1967:353).
14. Gödel's argument implies that no final description can be given regarding the precise logical structure of valid mathematical demonstration. Under such circumstance the possibility of comprehensive logical proof and Gödel's belief in a thoroughgoing "realism" of the ancient Plantonic type constitute the problem for investagation. See Negel and Newman 1959:99-100; Heijenoort 1967:355.
15. Popper (1974:106-111) postulates three worlds; Firstty the world of physical objects, secondly the world of states of consciousness (or mental states) and thrdly, the world of objective contents of thought. The third world resembles

closely, the universe of Frege's objective contents of thought. Hence the third is world is the automonous source of impersonal truths in the from of theories.

16. Gödel's results bear on the question whether computing machine may be the substitute for humen intelligence. The man made machines have a fiixed set of directives built into them the directives correspond to the fixed rules of axiomatic system. The answers supplied by the machine are based on or controlled by the fixed directives. But Gödel's incompleteness theorem implies functional incompleteness of calculating machines.

Gödel's results bear on computer engineering. The business of programming is of analysing and paraphrasing a problem so that its solution is sought by a computer in appropriate steps. Authors like Quine (1976:38-39) observe that between logical theory and machine computation there are fundamental connections. The basic notions of proof theory like Gödel's theorem converge with those of the theory of machine computing.

References

1. Agazzi, E. (1974): 'The rise of the Foundational Research in Mathematics'. *Synthese* Vol. 27, PP 7-26.
2. Armstrong D.M. (1973): *Belief, Truth and Knowldge* D Cambridge University Press.
3. Barker, S.F. (1969) : 'Realism and Philosophy of Mathematics'. *Symposium papers Commemorating 60th Birth day-of Kurt Godel.* Editors: Buloff, J.J. & others Heidelberg.
4. Braithwaite, R.B. (1962): 'Introduction' in *Kurt Godel On Formally undecidable propositions of principia Mathematica and Related systems.* Translated by Meltzer B. Oliver & Boyd London.
5. Chisholm, R.M. (1977)*Theory of Knowledge*, Prentice Hall, India.

6. Findlay T. (1942): 'Goedelian Sentences: A non-numerical approach' *Mind*, Vol. 4, 1942; Pp 259-265.
7. Gödel, K (1931): "On Formally Undecidable propositions of Principia Mathematica And Related Systems" inculuded in Meltzer B. See Below.
8. Gödel, K. (1944): 'Russell's Mathematical Logic' in *Philosophy of Mathematics* Editors : Benaceraf P and Putnam H. Prentice Hall, N.J. Pp 211-232.
9. Gödel, K. (1947): "*What is Cantor's Continuum Problem* ?" *Philosophy of Mathematics.* Editors Benacerraf P and Putnam H. Prentice Hall N.J. Pp 258-273.
10. Heizenoort J.V. (1967) : 'Gödel's Theorem' *Encyclopedia of Philosophy* Editor: Edwerds, Paul Macmillan Publishing Co. Inc. & The Free Press, Newyork Vol. 3 Pp 348-357.
11. Kleene, S.C. (1976): 'The work of Kurt Godel' *The Journal of Symbolic Logic.* Editors : Alon 30 Church.
12. Lehrer, K. (1974) : *Knowledge* Charendon Press, Oxford.
13. Meltzer, B. (1962): *Kurt Godel* On Formally Undecidable propositions of Principla Mathematica and Related systems English translation. Introduction by Braithwaite R.B. Oliver & Boyd London.
14. Nagel E and Newman J.R. (1959) : *Godel's Proof*; *Routledge cnd Kegan Paul,* London.
15. Parwitz, D. (1974) : 'On the idea of a General Proof Theory' *Synthese* 27, Pp 63-77.
16. Popper, K.R. (1974): *Objective Knowledge*. The Clarendon Press, Oxford.
17. Quine W.V.O. (1951) : *Mathematical Logic.* Harward University press, Cambridge, Mass.
18. Quine W.V.O. (1962) : *Methods of Logic.* Routledge & Kegan Paul, London.
19. Quine, W.V.O. (1976) : *The ways of Paradoxgnpand other essays.* Harvard University Press, Cambrige Massa-Chusetts.
20. Quine, W.V.O. (1981) : *Elementary Logic*. Harward University Press, Cambridge Mass.

21. Rundle, B. 1967 : 'History of Logic'. *Encyclopedia of Philosophy* Edited by Edwards P. Macmillan Publshing Co. Inc & The Free Press, New York. Vol. 4 Pp 554-566.
22. Slezak, P (1982) : 'Gödels' Theorem and the mind. The *British Journal for the Philosophy of science* Vol. 33 Pp. 41-52.
23. Stoll, R.R. (1976), *Set Theory and Logic*. Eurasia Publishing House, New Delhi.
24. Turing A. M. (1950) : 'Computing machinary and Inteligence'. *Mind* Vol. LIX. Pp. 433-460.

Index

Adhārādheyabhāva 106
Advaita System 1, 4, 5, 17-26, 37-43, 80-86, 91-97, 164-190
Adjuncthood 70-71
Akaṣapāda Gautama 35
Alston W.P. 80
Ajahallakṣaṇā 81, 90-91
Annambhṭṭa 1, 18, 110-11
Anumāna 137, 185-186
Anumiti 8, 137-42
Anuyogi 71, 106
Anvaya-vyatireki anumāna 186-87
Apramā 104, 126
Aristotle 21, 176
Aristotaleans Logical theory 24
Aristotalean Syllogism, 12
Arthāpati 9, 10, 153-63
Asādhāraṇa-dharma 1, 18-19
Asambhava 19
Ativyāpti 18
Atmānubhuti 12
Avyāpti 18

Banerjee N.V. 155
Bhāṭṭas 154, 158

Cartesian Product 4, 70
Cognition 3, 99
Connotation 2
Consciousness 174-175
Criteria of truth 96-97

Darśana 12, 192-197
Definite description 51
Definition 1-2, 17-26
Dharmarāja 80, 83, 86

Epistemology 1, 14, 204
Epistemological argument 49-50
Epistemic structure 106
Essence 52

Frege 49, 51, 213
Factual Structure 112
Frege 47, 5I, 202

Gaṅgeṣa 6-9, 57, 61, 100-118, 120-9, 144
Gaurishankara 91
Gödel 13, 208-21

Hiriyanna M. 182, 190

Ideas; theory of 202, 214
Indian Epistemology 1, 14
Indian Syllogism 186
Inferential Knowledge 8
Ingalalli R.I, 198, 152
Ingalls H.D.H. 77
Iśvara (God) 42, 179
Jahadajallakṣaṇā 41, 42, 83, 179
Jahallakṣaṇā, 40, 81, 179
Jāti 31, 37-39
Jāti-viśiṣta-vyakti-vāda 34, 46
Kāiaṇatā-Sambandha 75
Knowledge 1, 6-7, 12, 91, 93, 120-127, 135, 149, 164-171, 192
Kevalavyatireki 1, 20
Kripkes 5, 49-50

Laksaṇa 26
Laksaṇā 38-41, 80-85, 179-80
Liar's paradox, 210
Logic 205
Logical Structure 105-106

Mahābāya 31,.35
Mahāvākya 174-83
Matilal B.K. 1, 52, 53, 61, 72

Meaning
—Advaita theory of 37-43
Metaphor 80, 86
Meta-system 14
Mīmāmsakā 149, 153
Miśra 146
Modal argument 49
Modal semantics, 49
Mullatti, L.C. 163
Mohanty J.N. ; 63, 115

Navya-nyāya 46-87, 99-152
Navya-nyāya-semantics 46
Nilakaṇṭha 18
Nyayā-bhaṣya 1, 17, 35

Ordered pair 3, 4, 66
Ostensive definition 23-4

Pāṇini 2, 31-35
Panṇinis system: 31-35
Patañjali 31-35
Parataḥ-prāmāṇya-vāda, 8, 146-9, 216
Plato 39, 214
Popper K.R. 13, 206, 215
Postulation 9-10, 153-61
Potter K.H., 197
Prabhakara 8, 146
Prakāratā 3, 56-67
Pramā 6-7, 120-27
Pratyabhijñā 7, 133-34
Pramāṇa 100, 120, 126, 145
Pratiyogi, 71
Prāmāṇyam 45-50
Pratyakṣa pramā 7, 130-135
Proper names 49

Qualificand 56, 105-6
Qualifier 56, 105-6
Quine W.V. 13, 68, 78, 156-7, 203-4, 209, 212

Radhakrishnan, S. 64, 85, 97, 197
Reason 12, 186-90
Reference 3, 49
—theory of direct 49
Rigid designator49-50
Relation 3, 66-76

Śabda 100, 127
Scientific Knowledge 198-205
Sakyārtha 46, 48
Samaniyatatvam 19
Samanadhikaranya 90
Sambhandha, 3, 66-76
Smakara 5, 10, 91, 96, 175, 186
Saṇsargatā 56
Sceience 92
Saṃayoga 204
Sarvadarśana-samgrah 35, 45
Satyam 5-6, 90-96
Semantical argument 50
Siddhānta muktavalī 87
Sense 46-52
Sruti 174, 190
Svarupa sambanandha 59
Svataḥ-prāmāṇya-vāda 78, 145-50

Tādātmya sambhandha 76
Tarka-dipika 27, 110
Tarski, A 112-16
Taṭastha-lakṣṇa 21, 176
Tattva-cintamani 63, 99-151
Thales 50
Truth 5-6, 90-96
Truth-value 99
Turing A.M. 215, 222

Udayanacarya 1
Universal 2, 37
Upamāna 129
Upamiti 12

Vācaspati 161
Vācyārtha 46, 58
Vajapyāyana 2, 32
Vedānta-sāra 90
Veda 174, 168
Viṣayatā 3, 55-63
Viśeṣyatā 56
Viśvanātha 117
Vivekananda, Swami 174, 182
Vṛtti-niyāmaka-Sambandha 72
Vyakti vāda 33
Vyādi 2, 32
Vyāpti 8, 137-8
Vyāvartaka-dharma 18, 22

Yathārtha-jñāna 102, 120, 165